Philosophy
of
Sexuality

Philosophy
of
Sexuality

Don E. Marietta, Jr.

M.E. Sharpe
Armonk, New York
London, England

Library of Congress Cataloging-in-Publication Data

Marietta, Don E.
Philosophy of sexuality / Don E. Marietta, Jr.
p.   cm.
Includes bibliographical references and index.
ISBN 1-56324-933-2 (hardcover : alk. paper). —
ISBN 1-56324-934-0 (pbk. : alk. paper)
1. Sex.
2. Sex—Philosophy.
3. Sexual ethics.
I. Title.
HQ21.M454   1996
306.7—dc20
96-16110
CIP

Printed in the United States of America

The paper used in this publication meets the minimum requirements of the
American National Standard for Information Sciences—
Permanence of Paper for Printed Library Materials,
ANSI Z 39.48-1984.

BM (c) 10   9   8   7   6   5   4   3   2   1
BM (p) 10   9   8   7   6   5   4   3   2   1

To Robert, Jay, Don, Vicki, Lisa, Gordon, Rosanne,
Veronica, Teresa, and Gregory

∼ *Contents* ∼

Philosophy
of
Sexuality

~ *Introduction* ~

The term *sexuality* is used in the title of this book in preference to *sex* because it includes more than *sex*. It is not meant as a euphemism, but as a word that suggests a comprehensive aspect of life that is important throughout life. Social and psychological elements are as important as the biological in understanding what it is to be a male or female human being. Sexual acts and relationships are important parts of sexuality, but they have their richest meanings and bring their greatest rewards in terms of contexts far wider than the bedroom. This book does not minimize the importance or the joy of physical sex, but it seeks to understand it in the context of life in its totality.

I see as the major parts of a philosophy of sexuality the nature of sexuality and sexual ethics. Following a historical survey of the limited philosophical work on sexuality before this century, two chapters consider specifically the nature of sexuality. Chapter 2 stresses the need to understand sexuality in its social and psychological aspects, not just as a biological phenomenon. Not all psychological and social interpretations of sexuality are adequate, however; some are one-sided and incomplete. Difficulties in some social and psychological interpretations of sexuality are explored, along with recognition of what can be learned from these images of sexuality. Seeing sex in terms of manipulation, for example, does not do justice to all that sexuality can be in a person's life, but recognition of the element of manipulation in sex is part of a comprehensive view of sex. The concept of sexual relationships as a kind of communication is insightful, but the limitations of this image of sex are recognized. Although seeing sexuality as simply a bodily function, or an appetite such as hunger and thirst, is rejected as an adequate picture, denying the importance of body is also rejected. Sexuality cannot be transformed into something sweet and ethereal, as a modern version of courtly love or as something like religious ecstacy. It is important to recognize and understand the role of the body in sexual relations, and in this chapter a balance of bodily and social components of good sex is discussed.

Chapter 3 focuses on the question of whether sex has a purpose. Problems with the concept of sex itself having a purpose, as opposed to the various purposes that people have for sexual behaviors, are examined. Failure to see the difference between the several functions that sex can have and the notion of sex's having a purpose causes confusion. Some of the purposes that people have for sex can be hurtful, whereas a variety of others can contribute to the well-being of the sex partners. The natural law concept of sex's having a purpose and its bearing on the practice of birth control is examined and contrasted with basing decisions about birth control on human interests.

Some of the other chapters, especially chapter 9, on pornography, bring out beliefs about and attitudes toward sexuality. Discussions of pornography indicate differing concepts of what sex is and its importance in human life. Concepts of female sexuality figure in negative, and even positive, views about pornography, along with beliefs about male sexuality, which some writers see as inherently violent toward women. The issue of abortion (chapter 8) involves beliefs about sexuality, including the belief that reproduction is the primary purpose of sex. Beliefs about love, marriage, the family, and parenthood (chapters 13 to 15) are closely related to beliefs about sexuality. Homosexuality (chapter 7) is the sexual orientation of a large number of women and men. That most people are heterosexual does not diminish the importance of homosexuality, both because of the moral issues raised by the way homosexual people are treated and the light it throws on the nature of sexuality.

What we see, then, is that moral issues involving sexuality cannot be dealt with apart from considerations of the nature of human sexuality, and this should come as no surprise to us. The basic question of philosophy of sexuality is the nature of human sexuality, or perhaps we should say, the natures of sexuality. We should not assume that sexuality is the same for all people. Perhaps making this assumption was one reason why earlier philosophical views of sexuality seem abstract and distanced from life.

Chapter 10, which deals with the question of differences between the sexes, should not be read as assuming that all males are alike and all females alike. Similarities and differences between sexuality as females experience it and as males experience it remain a matter of dispute. This discussion is not helped by failure to take seriously the possibility that females may differ from other females and males from other males.

Feminism is a very important matter in philosophy of sexuality. The chapter on feminism (chapter 4) is doubly important since feminism should be seen both as an approach to sexuality and as a social and political matter that raises a number of moral issues. The areas of agreement within the various approaches to feminism, as well as the areas of disagreement, illuminate a number of questions about the nature of sexuality. The chapter on feminism is put early in the book since the matters discussed have bearing on most of the issues treated in later chapters. I believe we must turn to feminism, of some type or types, if we are to integrate sexuality successfully into our personal lives and our society. Someday, when we have solved the problems that feminism has made clearer to us, we can go beyond feminism to a broader humanism. I once thought we could go directly to humanism, with its concern for all people and its goal of justice and personal fulfillment for all people. Now I see the personal, social, economic, even medical problems of gender to be crucial and critical, so that they must have an intense focus of our attention and commitment before we can go beyond them. One day, I hope, we can afford to be "color blind" and indifferent to gender differences in a society in which justice and equality are realities of every person's life.

The nature of sexuality is the central topic of philosophy of sexuality, but many areas of moral concern arise because of the importance of sexuality. To treat all of these would make an uncomfortably large book, so the focus will be on a few issues, such as abortion, pornography, gender equality, treatment of homosexuals, and the semantics of talk about women and sex. These topics are treated in separate chapters because they are controversial. Sexual assault is very important and is almost universally condemned. It is treated in the chapter on pornography, which examines the claims that pornography is a form of sexual assault and that pornography leads to sexual assault.

Moral issues, then, cannot be separated from discusssions of the nature of sexuality. The moral issues cannot be understood adequately without this discussion, and the nature of sexuality takes sharper focus in relation to social and moral problems associated with it. As we discuss the nature of sexuality and see that many moral issues must be faced, this is what we should expect. Sexuality is centrally important in our lives, and what is this important inevitably impacts on the way we live those lives. This is the subject of the book: what our sexuality is and how we are to live with it.

It might be noticed that on some controversial issues I do not state my personal opinion. One reason for this is that the book follows the method of my classroom teaching. I want my students to examine the main views on a topic in order to improve their ability to read critically and evaluate claims and points of view. Getting the students to accept my opinions is not important, since they will face many new questions and probably will change their minds about a number of things as new information becomes available. I might change my mind about some things also. Of course, a book is not a classroom, but I see no reason to state and argue for my point of view on unsettled issues on which I might change my mind. In fact, I do not see this as a book that argues for a point of view. Such books have their value, but I want this book to help people who have not been attending closely to issues related to sexuality to enter the discussion for themselves. One purpose of the book is to make readily available to the reader material that might be difficult to find outside a university library.

This book is written by a philosopher who doesn't feel competent to write at length on matters of psychology, physiology, or social science. Topics not dealt with in this book and specialized works on topics treated only in a general way here can be found in books referred to and in books and articles in the sciences. I hope the reader will make up for any deficiency in this book by following up topics of interest in other books and articles. The author does not expect to answer all questions but hopes that the book will answer some questions and help the reader ask the right questions of other authors.

~ 1 ~

Philosophers on Sexuality

Ancient Philosophy

A positive and constructive philosophy of sexuality is largely a product of the twentieth century. Very few philosophers said anything at all about sexuality until this century. Most of what was said only reflected commonly held notions about family life and the roles of males and females. Some philosophers looked upon sex as a necessary evil or even as an evil to be avoided as much as possible. Actual misogyny was not given voice very often, but condescension toward women was common, almost universal, and Saint Paul, Thomas Aquinas, and some other theologians came close to being contemptuous of women.

Plato made a significant contribution to the psychology of love in seeing that all love is erotic—that is, that it grows from a need and seeks to fulfill that lack. What he thought that love was seeking, immortality and intellectual growth, is not so obviously correct. The striking thing about Plato's view of love is that he did not value love for its own sake. Love was valued as a means to something else. Sex was seen as a bodily matter, which limited its importance. Plato relegated the body to a low level of significance. It was one of the worldly objects that was subject to change and eventual destruction, which made it less important than the intelligible forms that never change and are the only things about which there can be real knowledge. He did not realize that sex is in large part mental, so sex shared the low estate of body. It was not a fit subject for philosophical contemplation. Plato plainly stated that sex was for reproduction only[1] and that couples

7

childless after ten years of marriage should be separated.[2] Any pleasure taken in sex was detrimental to mental development. Plato held
that the purpose of life was to tend the soul, and this was done through
intellectual growth, consisting of continually turning one's thought
from sensible things to intellectual things and from particular things to
general truths. Relations of love and friendship should lead to intellectual growth, not to physical enjoyment.[3]

Plato used the concept of an ideal republic as his image of what a
just soul would be like. The important aspect of this healthy soul is that
the rational part of it would rule the appetites and the ambitious part of
human nature. His political image of the rational ruling part of the soul
was a group of educated rulers whom he called guardians. Surpris-
ingly, he said that very intelligent women could be educated to perform the role of guardians.[4] Unfortunately, this equality of males and
females was limited to an imaginary city. His proposed laws for an
actual city show that Plato was no champion of women's liberation. In
the *Laws,* a dialogue about the best law codes for a city, Plato was not
an innovator in matters of sex and family life. He advocated athletics
and military training for women, but he was heeding precedents of
what had been done or was being done in some cities of the Greek
world. He advocated a different education for boys and girls and different work for men and women.[5] It is clear that Plato considered
women inferior to men.[6] His suggestion of holding women and children in common was restricted by too many rules to be seen as libertinism, but the notion of women's being possessions of the men is
compatible with common customs of the time, which made women
little more than chattel property.[7]

Aristotle considered the family a sort of government in which the
man is the ruler of wife, children, and slaves. Only men have a developed deliberative faculty and the highest kinds of virtue. Women are
capable of reason, but they have no need for it, and in children reason
is undeveloped. Slaves are incapable of reason. Aristotle held that the
husband is superior to the wife and should rule in accordance with his
superior virtue. He considered marriage a sort of friendship that is for
"utility and pleasure" as well as for reproduction.[8] Aristotle's views on
sex and the roles of man and women were made parts of Christian
belief by Thomas Aquinas in the Middle Ages, which made these ideas
influential up to the present time.

Some of the Sophists, such as Alcidemus and Antiphon, held that slavery, social distinctions, and customs that relegate women to a lower estate than that of men have no basis in nature and therefore were morally wrong. Other Sophists, such as Callicles and Meno, did not share this progressive vision, however, and Plato and Aristotle scorned the Sophists, who were not Athenians and taught for money. The prestige of Plato and Aristotle overshadowed the visiting teachers, as bright as some of them were. Frankly, the Sophists were a threat to conservative Athens, and they did not make appreciable social change.

After the death of Alexander the Great came the Hellenistic age, a time of great advances in learning and commerce, beautiful planned cities, and the spread of Greek culture into most of the Mediterranean world. Many people were forced to leave their native towns, familiar social arrangements were lost, and many became slaves or joined the urban poor, especially during the Roman period. The lot of people who had been displaced from their old sources of security and meaning in life was difficult, and philosophies, as well as religions, sought to provide them with ways to cope with this life and have hope in an afterlife. The philosophies were religious quests for salvation with strong philosophical underpinnings from earlier Greek philosophies. Philosophers tended to ignore bodily matters in favor of matters of the intellect. Even the Epicureans, who are commonly thought to have advocated the pursuit of pleasure, actually thought of pleasure as the avoidance of pain. The best state of mind a person can achieve, they held, is one of calm serenity. They did not consider sex a source of pleasure or happiness. They sought a serenity that is achieved through knowledge that there is nothing to fear, since there is no life after death, a view they borrowed from Democritus, and the gods, who are just clusters of atoms as are humans, cannot do people any harm. It is interesting to note that this freedom from fear of gods did not lead people to joyful and fearless sexual license.

The Cynics and their more sophisticated intellectual heirs the Stoics had an equally modest concept of happiness. Their escape from pain lay in avoiding concern about matters beyond a person's control. They believed that the world was governed by a world mind that would make everything work out well in the end, and in the meantime everything that happened did so of necessity. Happiness was not to be found in sexuality. Marriage and family were social duties and not to be avoided, but they were just part of the life that is to be endured. This disregard of sexuality was not a matter of placing a high value on the spiritual and disvaluing the material. The Epicureans and Stoics were materialists; mental life was itself material, but only in thought was escape from suffering to be found.

In his guidebook on achieving happiness, Epictetus explains that happiness is found in paying little attention to the body and instead concentrating on intellectual growth. "If you happen to turn your attention to externals, for the pleasure of anyone, be assured that you have ruined your scheme of life. . . . Provide things relating to the body no further than absolute need requires." "As in walking you take care not to tread upon a nail, or turn your foot, so likewise take care not to hurt the ruling faculty of your mind." "It is a work of want of intellect to spend much time in things relating to the body."[9]

The highest development of intellectual religious paganism was undoubtedly the philosophy of Plotinus, whose philosophy deemed the inscrutable One and the Divine Intellect and World Soul, with which it forms a divine trinity, the only true reality.[10] Of things in the world, the human soul, which is part of the World Soul, is the only thing real. The human soul, having fallen into association with a body, must not let its concern for intellectual matters become distracted by bodily appetites. The soul's salvation lies in eventual reunion with the divine reality from which it came, and this is accomplished through highly disciplined intellectual growth.[11]

The influence of Plotinus upon the developing Judaism and Christianity was great indeed. Only through the Neoplatonists, as his followers were known, were the ideas of Plato available to the late Roman and medieval world. A complete translation of Plato's dialogues into a Western language was first made by Marcilio Ficino in the fifteenth century.

Of course, only the learned few were likely to know much of the works of Plotinus and his successors, but gnosticism provided crude popular versions of a view of the world as evil, with sex as the ultimate aspect of the evil of material things. Gnosticism was a heretical movement in Judaism, in Christianity, and in paganism. Judaism and Christianity made a valiant effort to overcome the influence of gnosticism, but they were both influenced by the world-despising attitude of the heresy in spite of all they could do.

In fairness, we should recognize that the negative attitudes toward sexuality that appeared in Christianity and Judaism were not products of the ancient Hebrew culture. The Hebrew scriptures show a much more wholesome view of sex than that for which Christianity and Judaism have often been blamed. The primary source of the view that sex is wicked was in certain strains of Greek philosophy that flourished in the Roman period. Perhaps it was inevitable that the religions that became dominant in the medieval period would be affected by a negative view of sex.

The Medieval Period

In the medieval period, most of the philosophy was done by theologians, and the influence of the religions did not lead to positive notions of sexuality. Augustine, who was the most influential Christian theologian of the Middle Ages, and who is still accepted as a major doctrinal authority, taught that the body is corrupted by original sin. He expressed great shame for the sexual activity of his youth. He held that all love should be love for God and that lust is evil; the wise person would prefer (were it possible) that procreation be achieved without sexual lust. Sex was only for procreation, of course, and even legitimate conjugal intercourse is attended by shame, which he said is indicated by the secrecy in which intercourse is practiced.[12]

Thomas Aquinas, who finally achieved an authority second only to that of Augustine, promulgated eight truths,[13] some of which seem wrong-headed to many Christian believers as well as to humanistic people today, but their influence upon Christian thinking and the social practices of Western societies is undeniable. First, Thomas taught as Christian doctrine that seminal discharge defines the essence of sexual intercourse. This sees sexual intercourse only from a male perspective, and a very limited male perspective at that. Thomas's second teaching is that procreation is the only morally right function of sexual intercourse; emission of semen in a way that prevents conception is un-natural and immoral. The Roman Catholic Church insists that intercourse be open to conception and rejects the use of the biological, chemical, and physical barriers that are commonly employed as contraceptives. Even by Roman Catholic standards, however, Thomas's second truth is not completely adequate. Modern Catholic doctrine does not limit the function of sexual intercourse to procreation but rather sees it as a union that enriches the relationship between husband and wife, as well as being a means of conception. Thomas's third truth, that procreation naturally completes itself in the generation of an adult, can be taken as an obvious biological fact, but Thomas undoubtedly meant by *natural* what is morally right according to natural law. His fourth teaching, that those who engage in sexual intercourse should provide what is necessary for the rearing of any child created, is accepted by most people as a simple matter of personal responsibility. The fifth truth makes a claim with which most people agree, that the family is the best place for rearing children, but some people do not believe it is true. It is certainly something that we should be able to discuss rationally and upon which more research can be done.

Thomas's sixth and seventh truths must be an embarrassment to those who feel a need to defend his teaching; most of my students see these truths as a joke. Thomas said that females are inferior to males and that the male is the female's governor in marriage. Thomas's eighth truth is that divorce is improper. Some people who agree with his disapproval of divorce might have trouble with his argument. Thomas rests his rejection of divorce on his sixth and seventh truths, so his eighth truth has little to say regarding contemporary discussions of divorce.

Perhaps the most surprising thing about the thinking of philosophers in ancient and medieval times is that they seem to have had little comprehension of the degree to which sexuality involves the mental and emotional aspects of life. Within a dualistic conception of the human person, sex was associated with the body and was of importance to the mind positively only in its role in producing new generations of minds and negatively in the damaging effect it had upon human attention to the important matters of intellectual growth and the leading of a pure moral life.

The Renaissance did not produce a joyful and wholesome view of sexuality. It further developed the cult of courtly love, which placed the woman, or more accurately a few favored women, on the pedestal that few women find a comfortable place to be. Dante's attitude toward Beatrice and that of some of the Tuscan poets held the untouchable woman in high honor, but she was not pictured as having a full life, and certainly not as competing with men in the social world or the marketplace.

Marcilio Ficino, head of the Platonic Academy of Florence, developed the concept of Platonic love, holding that every love should be love of God and further the contemplation whereby the soul ascends toward the holy beatitude that is its natural desire. This concept of love does not promote greater appreciation of sex.

Savonarola, the monk who dominated Florence for a time, did nothing to raise the social standing of women, and he made war against all pleasures of the flesh.

The popular notion of the Renaissance as a time of sexual liberation probably grows out of the stories of Boccaccio and reports of the behavior of dissolute clergy, but this was not a time of growth in understanding of sexuality or liberation of women.

The Modern Period before the Twentieth Century

The modern period did not bring much radical change in the way sexuality was treated. Even though a wide array of views of sexuality can be found among modern philosophers before the twentieth century, most philosophers ignored sexuality. They seem to have considered other things much more important. Those who did write about sexuality usually reflect the commonly held opinions about marriage, family life, and sexual behavior. Expression of new, progressive, or radical views was limited to a handful of thinkers. The mainstream of philosophers tended to affirm theoretically the equality of men and women, but they did not call for practices that express and promote equality.

In chapter 6 of *Second Treatise of Government,* John Locke objected to the term *paternal power* and wrote of *parental power,* holding that mothers and fathers share the rights and duties of parenthood. In chapter 7, he referred to the family as "the first society." Marriage is a compact; its chief end is procreation, but it also brings "mutual support and assistance" to the couple, and unlike the sexual unions of most species, it lasts beyond the period of child raising. Even though husband and wife are united in a common concern, they will occasionally have "different understandings" and "different wills." When disagreements arise, the man "as the abler and stronger" is the ruler. The man's rule is limited, however, and in many cases, the woman has "a liberty to separate from him."[14]

In *Lectures on Ethics,* Immanuel Kant departed from the traditional view that sex is only for procreation. Kant believed that outside of marriage, sex degrades human nature and a person is used as an "[o]bject of appetite." A person is not desired as a person but is used as a thing. In monogamous marriage, on the other hand, the two persons "grant each other equal reciprocal rights" in a union of human beings that involves the whole person. Marriage is the only morally right use of sex. In a monogamous marriage, a person is not being used as a sex object. So far as I know, this is the first published explanation of how a person can be used as a sex object. Kant's concept of marriage would now be considered traditional, but he was one of the few philosophers who wrote about the nature of sexuality, he recognized that people engage in sexual activity for the pleasure of it, and the relationship he advocates seems to be one of mutuality and equality.[15]

In *Science of Right* (first published in 1795), Johann Gottlieb Fichte held that the two sexes are equally free and endowed with reason, but he still held back from recognizing a full political role for women or sexual equality for women. He held that a woman will not usually desire to exercise her rights. Politically, women will exercise their rights through their husbands. Practically, this would mean either that each family had a shared political will or that women are apolitical and can trust their husbands to vote for what is good for them. It took more than a century for the law to progress beyond this approach in the United States, and I remember hearing people who accepted Fichte's notion of women and political life.

Fichte accepted uncritically the view supported by the authority of Aristotle and Thomas that the male is active in procreation and the female inactive. He thought that this placed a woman in a contradictory position in which she, a free rational agent, chooses a passive role in sex, the passive female role in procreation. What the woman does, Fichte claimed, is to choose to satisfy the male for the sake of love. The man, he said, should not try to satisfy the woman. Fichte held that women love naturally, whereas men have to learn to love. It is interesting to see how durable some of these ideas are. Many people still think that women cannot, or should not, enjoy sex and that the man has no responsibility for considering the enjoyment of the woman in intercourse. Some feminists argue that men are not capable of loving.

Fichte did depart significantly from the classical and medieval view of sex as justified only for procreation. He held that marriage is an end in itself; procreation is not its value.[16]

In his early writings (1844), Arthur Schopenhauer said that in sex, nature manipulates the person for the sake of procreation, nature's purpose. Sex, he said, is objectively procreative but subjectively hedonic. People think they are engaging in sex for pleasure, but what is really happening is that nature is using them to produce new members of the species. In the next chapter, I will comment on this view of the nature of sexuality.[17]

Libertinism was the most radical departure from traditional views of sexuality. Libertinism, which held that people should be free to engage in sexual activity of all types simply for the pleasure to be gotten from it, was usually antifeminist and sometimes clearly misogynistic. Marquis de Sade held that women, by nature, belong to all men. Women cannot justifiably refuse one man on the grounds of loving another. Men have a right to compel the submission of women.[18] De Sade is not considered a philosopher, but in his later writings, Arthur Schopenhauer claimed that women are the second, inferior sex. He referred to women as "that undersized, narrow-shouldered, broad-hipped, and short-legged race" and "grown-up children," who never achieved anything of permanent value. He complained of their moral deficiency and held that they are not fit objects of veneration or respect. He argued that they should not be free to dispose of inherited property or to receive the guardianship of their children. He held that monogamy is wrong; it does not provide for every woman, and it falsely treats women as equals of men.[19]

Friedrich Nietzsche also gave voice to a misogynistic concept of women. He thought of women as a second sex whose genius for adornment shows that they have an instinct for the secondary role. Man, the barren animal, is the proper ruler, the maker of culture and politics, whereas the woman who has scholarly inclinations has something wrong with her sexually.[20] Nietzsche scorned the literary achievements of women, calling Madame Roland, Madame de Staël, and George Sand "three comical women," who were counterarguments against feminine emancipation and autonomy. Women should not be independent, he said, but restrained and dominated by the fear of men. Men have treated women as birds, "as something delicate, fragile, wild, strange, sweet, and animating—but as something also which must be cooped up to prevent it flying away." Wisdom calls for treating a woman "as a possession, as confinable property, as a being predestined for service."[21] The old woman who said to Zarathustra, "Thou goest to women? Do not forget thy whip!" expressed clearly Nietzsche's derogation of women.[22]

In sharp contrast to the misogynistic libertarians stand the feminists. There were strong feminist sentiments in France before the Revolution. Condorcet (1743–1794) held that males who were struggling for equality should recognize that women should have the same rights as men.

Marie Gouze published a "Declaration of the Rights of Women" in 1791, calling for education and property rights. After the French Revolution, feminist sentiment was put down. Gouze was beheaded, and liberty and equality were limited to fraternity. In the nineteenth century, there was a resurgence of feminism in France, led by social theorists such as Charles Fourier and Saint-Simon.

In England, Mary Wollstonecraft and Mary Shelly were the leading eighteenth-century feminists and promoters of the rights of women. In the United States, there was a strong women's rights movement, led mostly by abolitionists.

In his essay, "The Subjection of Women" (1869), John Stuart Mill argued that we do not know the nature of the sexes apart from social influences because we have never known them apart from the effects of education and custom. He advocated opening all jobs and positions to members of both sexes, allowing ability to determine what people would do. He held that not using fully the talents of women was hindering the development of humanity. He declared the subjugation of women to be morally wrong and unreasonable, a carryover from a time when the physical strength of males gave them power. There is no evidence that men have superior rationality.[23]

Early in the twentieth century, Karl Marx and Friedrich Engels advocated the social equality of women, to be undergirded by full economic equality. Engels's critical assessment of the family life of the propertied classes pointed to the underlying economic causes of the sexual double standard, marriages of convenience, and the unhappiness of women. He advocated revolutionary economic change that would take the tools of production (factories, ships and railroads, mines, and so on) out of the hands of private persons. After the revolution, women should be employed in industry, housekeeping and child care should be provided by the society, and people of both sexes would be free to have relationships based on "sex love," not on economic need.

Contemporary Thinkers

In the period between the world wars, more philosophical attention was paid to the nature of sexuality itself. Existentialist and phenomenological philosophers especially considered the significance of being embodied and the nature of sexual desire. Once these issues were raised as philosophical subjects, attention to them continued. Still, many philosophers have not recognized that sexuality is a matter of philosophical concern, but many philosophers have engaged various aspects of sexuality. With the growth of feminist literature, there has been a wealth of literature on family life, sex roles, sexual relations, issues in social ethics, and other aspects of sexuality. Philosophy of sexuality has become a new, important, and recognized part of the philosophical discipline.

~ 2 ~

What Is Sexuality?

An important aspect of the philosophy of sexuality is dealing with the nature of human sexuality. What is sexuality? A number of answers to that question have been stated or suggested. I do not intend to explore all that might have been said on the subject, but I will cast the net broadly to bring to our attention a wide variety of views. I do not intend to find and support a favorite definition. I will be critical of some notions of sexuality, usually because of their incompleteness, but will find important insights in a number of views. Looking carefully at various ways of understanding sexuality should help us contemplate the nature of sexuality and work toward the richest understanding we can achieve.

Reductionistic Biological Explanations

Some views of sexuality that have been well accepted should have been examined much more critically. Some ways of understanding sexuality have been adopted because they were thought to be scientific. What this means is that they have emphasized aspects of sexuality that can be explained biologically while ignoring more difficult social and psychological aspects. Explaining all aspects of sexual behavior in terms of evolutionary biology or explaining love in terms of the secretions of glands would be examples of such theories. We do not need to deny the evolutionary development of human sexuality to see that cultural developments and even personal patterns of growth have also affected our sexuality. We do not need to deny that certain ductless glands play a role in making other people attractive to us to see that our preference for certain individuals over others is also affected by our personal histories.

It is not difficult to see the attraction of physiological explanations of human sexual behavior. Some people in science and some people who were enamored of science have favored explanation in terms of quantifiable features of sexuality over aspects that are not easily quantifiable. It may even have seemed tough-minded to adopt an approach that focuses on biological and chemical matters, which lends some weight to the claim that science has tended to be overly masculine.[1]

What is wrong with a purely biological explanation of sexuality? Does it not provide clarity and focus? It does provide simplified theory, which might be taken for clarity, and it does provide focus, but it is also reductionistic in that it ignores some important data. Simple theory and narrow focus can be bought entirely too dearly when the definitions leave out too much of importance.

Have any philosophers actually been guilty of such reductionistic thinking? They have done this in a number of ways. Thinking of sexuality only in terms of reproduction was one kind of reductionism. The theologians were not the only ones guilty of this. Plato, Aristotle, and other classical philosophers did it, and even a modern philosopher, Schopenhauer, reduced sexuality to biological matters when he considered secondary the seeking of pleasure in sex and held that the real happening was nature achieving its purpose of reproduction.[2] There are several things wrong with Schopenhauer's view of sexuality. One thing is his talk of nature's acting with purpose. Sex certainly has the function of reproduction, along with other functions. This does not mean that there is a Mother Nature who is having her way with us. Of course, no one will admit to thinking such a thing. The talk of nature is figurative, but even talking figuratively about nature's acting with purpose can lead to careless thinking. It seems that the members of all species act in such ways as to preserve their species. This seems to be instinctual. Humans frequently act in ways that threaten the human species. We deliberately damage the natural environment, develop weapons that might become doomsday machines, and reproduce to the point that many people are concerned that our fruitfulness may be our downfall. Few people, if any, engage in sexual activity for the sake of the human species. We need to think clearly about this. When sexual things happen, people are doing them. Nature, the figurative abstraction, is not doing these things.

People engage in sex to realize a number of different kinds of purposes, and they often do this in spite of the possibility of reproduction. Sexual behavior results from many social and psychological factors, some of which we are not even conscious of when we engage in the intercourse that might result in reproduction. One of those human purposes is having children, and sex does have the function that makes this human purpose realizable in most cases. Other human purposes have nothing to do with reproduction, and those purposes are realized through other functions of sexuality. Some human purposes are realized seldom or maybe not at all. Sex cannot do all we want it to do.

Schopenhauer's putting aside as secondary all of the human reasons for engaging in sexual activity is hopelessly reductionistic. We cannot possibly understand sexuality if we ignore the reasons that lead people to engage in sex. A concept of sexuality that does not take account of the psychological and social aspects of human sexuality is not good science. It is not clearheadedness, and it is not a way of avoiding bias. It is unnecessarily reductionistic, which makes it an incomplete concept of sexuality. We need a more adequate understanding, one that comes to grips with the complexity of human sex.

It is not a complete view of sex to see it as "male evacuation lust" (D.H. Lawrence). It is not adequate to think of sex as nothing more than a release from tension. According to this view, sexual need is fulfilled in the discharge that relieves the person from the tension. This view is expressed in the description of sex as "scratching an itch."[3] There may be times when a sexual act does this for a person; there may be people for whom sex is never more than this. We do have a crude expression for sex acts, "getting your rocks off," that suggests such use of sex. The concept of sex as nothing more than relief from a painful tension is not a complete description of the role of sexuality in human life, however, because this is not all that people find in sex, or even the most important aspect of sex. Sexual attraction and response are usually much richer and more rewarding than any scratching of an itch. Such tension as there may be before sexual orgasm is not unpleasant in itself. It is not often a painful condition from which people act to secure relief. Often people go to considerable trouble to increase sexual arousal. Sexual stimulation can be pleasurable even when it is not expected to reach a climax. There are times when lust is its own reward.

Social and Psychological Aspects of Sexuality

To define sex as only a biological matter, an appetite such as hunger or thirst, is to ignore much of what sexuality is in people's lives. An interpretation of sex in chemical or biological terms alone ignores the psychological and social aspects that make human sexuality vastly different from sex in most other animals.

Explanations of sexuality in psychological or social terms might not all be adequate. Certainly the biological aspects should not be ignored. The problem is oversimplification that leaves out anything relevant. The psychological and social explanations are a valuable counterpoise to the other reductionistic approaches. We need to examine some of these views of sexuality to see what we can learn from them.

One of the views of sexuality that goes beyond a merely biological interpretation is the official Roman Catholic position, which holds that sexual union should be both unitive and procreative. Contrary to widespread, but mistaken, opinion, the Roman Catholic teaching does not hold that conjugal sex is only for reproduction; equally necessary is strengthening the union between husband and wife for their personal growth. The church's insistence that every act of intercourse be open to conception, except in grave circumstances, has been criticized as making sex too instrumental, thereby decreasing its value in promoting mental and emotional growth. This insistence also seems to contradict the freedom that the church says is necessary in marital love. The modern teaching of the church does have the virtue, however, of recognizing that sex has nonbiological aspects.

An important aspect of sexuality is what sex means to people. Sex is usually directed toward another person. We need to examine the nature of the intention toward the other person. Some interpretations of this may not see sexual attraction as all sweetness and light, but we need to explore this matter carefully and not accept uncritically a view that we might find pretty and uplifting.

Bernard H. Baumrin holds that sex is essentially manipulative, "physically, psychologically, emotionally, and even intellectually." He says that the idea that we should never use another person is an impossible ideal; we cannot avoid using other people. We use and manipulate another person in sex, according to Baumrin. He attacks our sentimental notions of perfect sexual harmony, with spontaneous coming together of minds and bodies, which he calls a myth. Rather than being spontaneous and free, we try to make ourselves desirable and to influence the feelings of the other. He says we deliberately plan to get a response from the sexual partner.[4]

This talk of manipulation may be a bit unpleasant, and it may not be a complete picture of a healthy relationship, but we may have to admit that there is some truth to Baumrin's perspective on sex. Part of what Baumrin says is obviously true; we must use other people. When a person says, "I don't want to be used," this person probably means that he or she does not want to be used unfairly or without reciprocity. The person who is never used will be an isolated person indeed. If we try to ignore the manipulation involved in sexual relationships, as in other relationships, we are likely to make mistakes that we could avoid.

To recognize the element of manipulation in sexual relations is not to justify treating all manipulation as warranted. Baumrin holds that even though we cannot avoid manipulating the other, we have responsibilities toward our sexual partner. He defends a sexual ethic based on mutuality and reciprocity. We must respect the wishes of the other and try to meet the needs of the other, as well as our own.[5]

Jean-Paul Sartre presents another interpretation of sex that focuses on the nature of sexual attraction. Sartre's explanation of sexual desire might seem negative and depressing. In his book *Being and Nothingness,* Sartre said that sex is a futile passion because it tries to possess the freedom of the other person. We are not simply caressing the body of the other, not simply trying to hold and possess the other person's body. Caressing and holding are expressive of desire to possess, but possession of the other person must include the will of the other, and it must be a will that is acting freely. We cannot possess what we want to possess; possession would destroy what we want. This makes sexual desire self-contradictory, since it has an impossible object. Freedom possessed would no longer be freedom.[6]

Sartre's view of sex as a futile passion might well strike us as exaggerated, but what is it exaggerating? In a healthy love relationship, we certainly want the other person to be responding to us freely. It would not be very meaningful if the response of the other were being forced. Without a free response, our attention to the other would be sadistic and cruel. It would not be satisfying to a person who was concerned about the relationship, a person acting in love. Of course, there are sexual acts that are not motivated by love, acts that are expressions of power and domination. The thought that all sexual relations involve attempts to possess and dominate is very depressing, but I do not think all sex is an attempt to dominate. We need to be aware of the role of power in sexual relationships, but I think Sartre was mistaken in understanding sexual attraction as a desire to possess. It seems to be this at times, and those times may involve the futility of which Sartre speaks.

The views of sexuality that we see in Baumrin and Sartre are depressing, but at least they are attempts to take into account the psychological, the distinctively human, aspects of sexuality. In considering the place of power and manipulation in sex, they are attempting to be honest about sex. Sex often involves the use of power, the demonstration of power over the other. Power might always be involved to some extent. With some people, the exercise of power might be the dominant aspect of sexual pleasure. Even when people are not consciously trying to be domineering, the element of power can be a serious barrier to equality and freedom in a relationship. A number of writers have discussed the question of whether the greater economic and social power that the male usually possesses can be kept out of the bedroom, and some of them are pessimistic about the possibility of two people's being equal in their sexual relationship when one is much more powerful economically or socially than the other. It is an important question, since sex does seem to involve an element of control and manipulation of the other person. There is considerable dispute, however, over the extent to which manipulation is a factor in all sexual relationships, and some writers believe it is something over which people can have control.[7]

Sartre's and Baumrin's descriptions of the psychological and social aspects of sex may unduly stress the elements of possession and manipulation. Possession and manipulation are never quite as simple as some talk of them might suggest. It might not be sex that is futile, but the idea of possession of a person. Both Sartre and Baumrin give incomplete accounts of sexual encounter in talking of possession and manipulation of another person without consideration of the changes that sexual encounters can make in the self. In sexual relationships, we are not simply acting upon another while remaining untouched ourselves. We bring what we are, our identities, into these encounters, and a significant sexual experience in which we do not totally objectify the other has an effect on our identity. We do not attempt to capture the subjectivity of the other without involving our own subjectivity. A copulation in which one objectifies the self and the other reflects little of what is distinctive in human sexuality, making it less interesting to talk about than sexuality that involves the personhood of two people, with all of the risks and possibilities that it offers.

Sartre's notion of the futility of sexual passion seems also to see the frustration of the desire to possess the freedom of the other as a bad thing. It would, however, be a terrible thing if we could possess a person in the way Sartre sees as the goal of sexuality. It is necessary for us that other people remain the other. Their otherness really is not the hell Sartre saw it to be. Even when it is frustrating for us, we are able to maintain our identity and grow intellectually and emotionally because we live among other beings like ourselves who can maintain their identity.

There is some insight in Sartre's observation that sexual attraction is not just to the flesh and bones of another. Maurice Merleau-Ponty agrees with Sartre that in sex we are not attracted simply to a body. "What we try to possess, then, is not just a body, but a body brought to life by consciousness."[8] This conscious body obviously has a life of its own, a life with its own standpoint and its freedom, as Sartre was well aware. Merleau-Ponty saw that sexuality is not something that can be separated from the total being of a person. "[S]exuality is not an autonomous cycle. It has internal links with the whole active and cognitive being."[9]

When we desire the sexuality of a person, a conscious body, we are being responsible and serious only if we desire the person as a complex being with thoughts, emotions, needs, and freedom. What it must mean to possess such a person must be thought about seriously. It cannot mean to take full control of that person, because this is the way of futility of which Sartre wrote. The only mode of possession must be reciprocal, because in this way only can sexual encounter satisfy the deepest needs that make us seek another person sexually. Possession in the case of rewarding sexual encounter is more nearly like possessing a cause, a mission, or a responsibility than it is like possessing a suit of clothes or an automobile.

Reciprocal Awareness of Body

Sartre's concept of sex as a futile passion is not all he has to say about sexual encounter. Also in *Being and Nothingness,* he describes a scene of two people responding to each other and being aware at the same time of their bodies. He describes a man who sees a woman a few tables away in a bar. Actually, he sees her in a mirror and finds her very attractive. Meanwhile, she has seen him in the mirror and finds him attractive. Each of them comes to realize that the other is looking, and each is pleased with the attention of the other. This makes each of them aware of themselves as the object of the other's admiration and interest. What this involves is awareness of the self as a body. As the man and woman become aware that they are objects of admiration and interest, they are acutely aware of being embodied, along with being aware of the body of the other.[10]

Sartre calls this awareness of oneself as body, which comes with the realization that the admired person is also admiring, a "double reciprocal incarnation." His notion of a double reciprocal incarnation shows that sexual attraction is not, at its best, a one-sided action. Being aware of being desired is an important aspect of being sexually aroused. This shows that sexual attraction can be a mutual activity in which both people enable the other to have a rich experience of his or her sexuality and body. Thomas Nagel and Sara Ruddick use Sartre's concept of a double reciprocal incarnation in their explanations of what they consider good sex, which they think involves a certain kind of completeness. Sex that is directed to an object, but is not a response to the attitude of the other, is incomplete. Extreme examples of incomplete sex would be fetishism, voyeurism, or masturbation.[11]

I think intercourse in which one partner is self-absorbed and does not care what the other partner is feeling would also be incomplete sex. To be complete, awareness of the desire of the other would be a necessary part of one's arousal. Sexual intercourse in which a person is psychically detached from the body, so that the body is not felt to be oneself, would be incomplete sex. This might happen when the person thinks of the body, or part of the body, as a tool. The completeness in which one's sexual arousal involves awareness that the other person is sexually aroused by one's body would, I believe, tend to avoid the seeing of the other as a mere sex object.

This interpretation of sexuality in terms of reciprocal incarnation is richer and fuller than an explanation of sex that sees only the biological aspect and ignores the psychological aspects. We may run into a danger, however, of becoming too judgmental. Although we might think of sex with reciprocal incarnation as more rewarding, more fulfilling, than sex without it, we can see that it is an ideal that is not realized in much sex that is good enough to be satisfying and worthwhile. Certainly, less than ideal sex is not to be seen as morally wrong. It would be cruel indeed to hold that sexual experiences that are the best of which a person is capable are not morally permissible. We will see more about this chapter 5, "Sexual Morality."

Robert Solomon presents a concept of sexuality that many of my students find attractive. He says that sex has its purposes apart from the biological function of reproduction. Sex, he says, is a kind of language, a kind of communication between two people. As a language, sex can express tenderness and affection. It can also express hostility and resentment. Sex is sometimes used to express superiority over the other or submission to the other. As language, sex is reciprocal.[12]

In chapter 5, we will see Lois Pineau's use of the concept of sex as language in describing mutuality in sex, with both partners sensitive to the responses of the other person, as happens in good conversation.[13]

Alan H. Goldman questions Solomon's analogy between sex and language and points out some significant differences between the gestoral nature of language and sexual activity.[14] Trying to understand the nature of sexuality through the use of any analogy must be done with care. An analogy points up a similarity between one thing and another, but we should not let an analogy limit our conception of sexuality. Sexuality is not exactly like any other aspect of life. It may be more like conversation than like other parts of life, but it has features that conversation does not have. Our concept of sexuality must allow for the possibility of procreation. It must make room for the changes, the growth and development, that people experience as they age. Our concept must be realistic. Solomon's analogy draws our attention to important aspects of sexuality that other concepts have neglected. That is its value. If Solomon is correct in using an analogy that stresses the interaction between two people and the desirability of mutuality in sexual encounters, we can see real meaning in the concept of intercourse. I believe that Solomon's analogy is better than alternative analogies. If we do not let the analogy limit our thinking, it can help us see that coitus can really be intercourse, that it can be making love and not just making sex.

The Lived Body

Part of our difficulty in trying to understand sex as both biological and psychological comes from confusion in our thoughts about the body. When we try to think in theoretical terms about the body, we tend to think of what I call the corpse body. This is the notion of body in the claim I heard years ago that the human body is worth about ninety-seven cents. This is the body seen as so much carbon, so much calcium, so much water. The corpse body is by its nature a dead thing, and we ponder over its having life. It is strange that we see the body this way, because we have never experienced ourselves as corpses. A much better concept of the body is that of the *lived body,* a term used by many phenomenological philosophers.[15]

The lived body is our way of being in the world, enabling us to perceive the world, to realize other people, and to act within the world. Merleau-Ponty said that having a body is "to be involved in a definite environment, to identify oneself with certain projects and be continually committed to them."[16]

Each of us lives his or her body, which involves many social and psychological functions, as well as those that are readily recognized by everyone as "bodily" functions. Actually, the psychological functions are bodily, as actions of the lived body, but some functions lend themselves better to biological and chemical explanations than do others, and we think of these as bodily actions. When we are sexually attracted to another person, it is a lived body, a body that is being lived, that realizes the attraction, and it is a lived body to which we are attracted. We only create confusion when we draw an ontological distinction between that which is bodily and that which is psychological. When we understand the concept of the lived body, we realize that there is more to body than people usually associate with the body. If we try to understand sexual attraction as desire for contact with a corpse body, we will not understand it properly. The idea of being attracted to a body becomes an unappealing matter, and we might feel negative about it or feel some need to justify doing something that seems unworthy of us. If we separate the psychological aspects from the body, we will have a poor notion of sexual attraction. We will not understand all that is involved in wanting the lover's body. We can understand our desire for the body of the other better when we see that it is the lived body with its biological and psychological functions, along with its social context, that makes a sexual encounter meaningful and important to us.

On Not Selling Sex Short

There is still much to be learned about the nature of sexuality. As helpful as they are, most theories about sexuality have been developed by men. These theories seem to have been made on the assumption that a nongendered, generic, concept of sexuality would be possible. Now we know that this may not be the case. Even if the female perspective on sex is not radically different from the male perspective, there may be significant nuances that should be considered. There may be other important differences in sexuality coming from differences in social class and educational background. Generational differences and nationality should not be ignored. It may turn out that the differences are minor, and a general concept of sexuality will be possible. We are all lived human bodies, living in the same world, and this might make our ways of comprehending sexuality more alike than different. I hope that is what we will find, but we must not just assume that this is the case.

For various reasons, people often have sold sex short. Some people seem to have been afraid of sex. One fear is that it is such a powerful thing that it will make people reject or neglect the more important things in life. Some people have had personal problems with entering a relationship of giving and sharing. Some people have believed that sex must be restricted for the sake of religion, but philosophers have been as guilty as the clergy of trying to suppress sexuality. One approach that has been used to keep sex from playing too large a role in people's lives has been to consider some behaviors natural and others un-natural. It seems that what has usually been considered natural sex is minimal sex.[17] John Barth, in his novel *Gile's Goat Boy,* described this proper kind of sex, efficient heterosexual intercourse, as "the two-minute emissionary missionary male-superior ejaculation service." A frequent result of minimal sex is that women received little pleasure in it, as was thought to be fitting. Another consequence of minimal sex is that very few people received the rich interpersonal rewards that sexuality can bring when it is properly understood and practiced in love, without fear.

If we can come to understand sexuality as a richly rewarding mutual sharing between two people, we will see how inadequate it has been to think of sex as merely a biological means to reproduction or as something to be repressed, whether as minimal sex used mainly to satisfy the unfortunate lusts of men or as something that people need when they are young but can escape from when they get older. If we can see that sexuality is an important part of a long relationship between two people, and a lifelong part of that relationship, even though its expression might change with the years, we can see that sex is truly something to celebrate. We can see that sexuality is one of the forces that make us social beings, that foster our aesthetic sensitivity, that, in short, make us human in more than a genetic sense.

~ 3 ~

Does Sex Have a Purpose?

Is Reproduction the Purpose of Sex?

Does sex have a purpose? Of course, people have various purposes for which they engage in sexual behaviors, but does sex have a purpose in and of itself? The answer to this question might seem a lot simpler than it is. We will need to examine the concept of sex's having a purpose, but first, let us look at some proposed notions of that purpose. We saw in chapter 1 that Schopenhauer thought that the purpose of sex was to reproduce the species. He wrote about nature's fulfilling its purpose, while people were deceived in thinking they were acting for the sake of pleasure.[1] Many people agree basically with Schopenhauer. They look at the biological function of sex throughout the animal kingdom and think that the purpose of sex is obvious. Yet sex among humans does a lot more than bring about the birth of babies. People often, perhaps most often, have sex without any intention of having a baby. Are they doing something unnatural or something wrong?

The claim is made, based on the theory of natural law, that sexual intercourse engaged in with the intention of avoiding pregnancy is morally wrong. On what is this claim based? Pope Paul VI published an encyclical, *Humanae Vitae,* in 1968 that states the doctrinal principle that the human person has a vocation, a calling from God, that is both natural and supernatural.[2] This vocation expresses the divine will for human beings and thereby gives the purpose of sexual union. Marriage is a matter of the senses and of the spirit. Ac-

30

cording to church doctrine, marriage is not an invention of human society or a product of evolution; it was instituted by God the creator. What was the purpose of God for sexual union? Actually, sex between husband and wife has a double purpose, or rather two aspects of a single purpose, because the two are inseparable. They are reproduction and a communion of the two persons, the procreative and the unitive functions. The marriage is to draw the man and woman closer together for their spiritual growth and for the generation of children. It is not true that the church considers reproduction the only legitimate purpose of marriage. Part of the purpose of marriage is to unite the couple as "one heart and one soul," in a "special form of personal friendship." This is an exclusive bond between them, and it lasts until death.

Even though reproduction is only part of the purpose of marriage, it is a requisite part. If the couple is able to have children, they must not do anything to prevent the sexual act from being fecund. No artificial means of birth control is allowed. The rhythm method, in which intercourse occurs only in periods of the woman's monthly cycle when she is expected to be unable to conceive, is allowed only for grave cause, such as a serious illness.

The teaching of *Humanae Vitae* is not just that a married couple is morally obligated to have children if they can. It is that every act of intercourse must be open to conception. Before the encyclical was issued, many people were hoping that the church would approve of "responsible parenthood," which called upon married couples to have children but allowed the use of contraception to space the children as the parents desired and to allow postponement of parenthood for economic, professional, or educational reasons. *Humanae Vitae* redefined responsible parenthood as knowledge of and respect for the biological processes of sex, which called for "the deliberate and generous decision to raise a large family" and allowed postponement of procreation only for "grave motives and with due respect for the moral law." The married couple are not free to act completely on their own wills.

Any sexual behavior that cannot result in conception is held by the church to be wrong. Same-sex intercourse, oral-genital sex, and masturbation are considered contrary to the purpose of sex and morally wrong. Sterilization is held to be illicit. Abortion is absolutely forbidden, even for therapeutic reasons, as a "means of regulating birth."[3]

Against Reproduction as the Purpose

Strong arguments can be raised against the position of *Humanae Vitae* from other theological positions. Some religious groups agree basically with the Roman Catholic position on the purpose of sex and its moral implications, whereas others differ in various respects. When we take a philosophical approach, what do we find? Philosophical arguments have been directed at the encyclical, including the observation that its teachings appeal to tradition but lack any attempt at a philosophical defense of the claims. It argues from the claimed authority of the church. Ethical arguments that could be recognized by thoughtful people outside the church are not attempted.[4]

When we examine the claims made in *Humanae Vitae* philosophically, we find at least two problems. One is the concept of purpose; the other is the claim that the unitive and reproductive functions of sex must be inseparable. Let us examine the inseparability thesis first; this will throw considerable light on the nature of sexuality.

Carl Cohen points up some of the philosophical problems with the principle of the inseparability of intercourse and procreation. The principle is not supported by respected ethical approaches. He shows how the principle turns out to be false when tested against the standards of utilitarianism, the ethical view holding that the morally correct behavior is that which brings the greatest good (or pleasure) to the persons concerned. The moral test of a sexual practice, such as use or nonuse of birth control, is the emotional and physical pleasure that is the consequence of the behavior. Moral rightness has nothing to do with fulfillment of an organic function. The practices that benefit the people involved are worthy in themselves.[5]

The inseparability principle is not supported by the requirement of Kantian ethics that people not be treated as merely means. If preventing conception is an expression of disrespect, it is so only because of the attitude of the person involved and, possibly, some flaw in the relationship. Other people express concern and respect by not risking an undesired conception.

The claim that use of contraception shows a lack of respect indicates a negative view of sex. An attitude of disgust toward sex is commonplace, and the origin of this attitude is ancient. Saint Augustine of Hippo thought that the sex act is shameful, which he saw as the reason that people do it in private. He does not seem to have considered that people want the act to be private because it is very personal and precious to them. Augustine shows that he thinks sexual intercourse wicked when he speculates that in paradise our first parents could have reproduced without lust had there been no sin.[6] The same derogation of sex can still be seen in the feeling that sex must be justified by something worthy enough to make up for its shame, something like the birth of a child. When people say of sex that one must pay the fiddler afterward, they appear to be thinking of sex as something for which amends must be made. Carl Cohen describes the concept of sex indicated in the inseparability principle as an unwholesome, instrumental view of sex. He says the encyclical rests on the view that sexual intercourse is unworthy in itself, that its value is only instrumental—good for achieving something else.[7] The instrumental view of sex and the more negative view that sex is shameful unless it is redeemed by childbirth are prejudiced views that no longer dominate thinking in our society. Many people, including many religious leaders, think of sex as worthy in itself and a source of much joy and good in people's lives. The inseparability principle does not rest on defensible ethical principles or insight into the nature of humans and their relationships.

Principles of morality that stress the importance of the development of human personality, of the potentialities of human beings, certainly do not give support to the inseparability principle. Being forced to bear children in the face of unfavorable financial, social, and medical conditions has kept many people, especially many women, from developing themselves educationally, artistically, and professionally. Even when the burden of a large number of children, coming at short intervals, was borne willingly, the mother sacrificed immeasurably in many cases, and often the children were not given the educational and cultural opportunities necessary to their full development. These judgments rest, of course, on different values from those the opponents of birth control might uphold. But long suffering, self-denial, humility, submission, and unquestioning obedience are more likely to be the virtues upheld by authoritarian religion than those supported by a system of personalistic morality, or personalistic religion, for that matter.

Opposition to birth control cannot be adequately supported by a claim that it is un-natural, hence immoral. To consider chemical and barrier methods of birth control un-natural runs into the confusion seen in other attempts to reject behaviors as un-natural (see chapter 7, "Homosexuality"). To hold that a bodily function is natural, with most concepts of something's being natural, would not entail that it is wrong to interfere with the function. In some situations, functions that could be called natural are destructive and can even cause death. The function of making the blood go from the extremities to the abdomen in the face of injury or great fear, a protective function, can lead to shock, which sometimes results in death. The function of blood clotting is beneficial in some situations and not in others. There is no normative connection with naturalness. The Roman Catholic natural law theory employs a concept of the natural that relates it to God's will, giving it normative significance for Catholics and other believers in versions of that doctrine. Cohen says that the belief that birth control is intrinsically wrong must be based on the notion that God intends for all natural functions to be completed.[8] This would have strange consequences, such as making much of the practice of modern medicine illicit. The treatment of shock and the dissolving of blood clots would be contrary to God's will.

The connection between sex and reproduction is one of the most important issues we face. The reproductive function of sex is separated from the unitive and other functions by most people, even members of religious bodies that teach that they are inseparable, but moral matters are not resolved by observation of majority behavior. Is the inseparability claim justified, or if not, why not?

It might be held that intercourse that is open to pregnancy is more unifying than sex that is not. How are we to determine this? We should be careful to avoid romanticism in thinking about sexual relations. What do we learn from experience? It seems to be that sexual intercourse is not the same in all situations and at all times. People can remember very tender and unifying moments when a baby was intended and wanted. But what shall we say of times when one partner wants a baby and the other, not wanting a baby, reluctantly, and maybe resentfully, agrees not to use contraception? What shall we say about the teenage couple who do not use contraception because that would seem to indicate that the romantic experience was planned and that they are morally responsible for what they are doing? What shall we say about intercourse through which one partner wants a pregnancy as a means of controlling the other? We can see that a close connection between the possibility of conception and unifying the couple is a matter of circumstances.

From the perspective of environmental ethics, we can see the peril of unlimited increase in the number of humans in the world. Objection to the limiting of births, so that fewer children are born but they are born into families with room for them and time for them, seems terribly wrongheaded. It is certainly better for the biosphere that there not be teeming masses of people who are desperate for food, fuel, and water. There should be some control over the number of people born, while at the same time the quality of life improves. To restrict the enjoyment of sex to fulfilling the reproductive function contributes nothing to protection of the natural environment and nothing to the improvement of human life.

Functions and Purposes

When we examine the concept of sex's having a purpose, we can see that the notion is problematical, whether we are talking about what God wills for people or are thinking about evolution or nature in the development of sexual reproduction. It is easy to become confused about the notion of sex's, or any other natural function's, having a purpose. What would it mean for sex to have a purpose? We need to be careful in our use of language in dealing with a subject as important as this. The common use of the word *purpose* is often careless. The notion of a purpose implies a conscious intention. For those who believe that God has a purpose for sex, God is the purposer, and the purpose is actually God's purpose. Sex itself has purpose only in a derivative sense. If the claim that God has a purpose for sex is not accepted, what sense can be made of a purpose for sex? Can there be impersonal purpose? Can nature or evolution have a purpose? The claim that evolution is directed, aiming at some predetermined end, is controversial, a matter of faith and hope more than a demonstrable claim. Purpose without a purposer is a difficult concept to defend. What could it be? It is important at this point that we distinguish between purpose and function. The reason we might think that sex has a purpose apart from a purposer is that we often confuse the concept of function and the concept of purpose.

Sex clearly has a function, or rather, a number of functions. It can lead to reproduction, it can serve to express affection and a feeling of unity between two people, it can give pleasure, it can be a means of showing power over another person, and it can be used to make money. Sex can be used for reasons with which almost everyone identifies, and it can be used for very individual reasons such as passing the time on a rainy day or running away from a problem. It can be used to express one's independence or to give in to one's dependency. Sex has all these functions and surely a few more, but does it have a purpose? People who use sex have purposes, that is clear enough. Sex has functions, and people have purposes. Some of these purposes are good, admirable, and constructive. Other purposes are bad, hurtful, and reprehensible. Sex lends itself to serving all of these functions.

This analysis of the functions of sex and the purposes of human beings shows that we cannot analyze sex, discover its purpose, and know thereby what we should and should not do. To understand what is right use of sex and what is wrong use, we must make moral judgments, using the tools of ethical analysis that we apply in the making of other moral decisions. There is no direct shortcut to understanding sexual behavior.

In chapter 5, we examine sexual ethics. Are there any reasons for engaging in sex that are not good reasons? We can see that something is wrong with sex engaged in to cause pain or to express anger, sex to dominate another person, and sex to secure an objective totally unrelated to the sex act itself and the other person involved. We can explain what is amiss in these sexual engagements using familiar ethical concepts, such as the moral wrongness of doing malicious harm to a person, using deception, being dishonest, and using a person as a mere means to an end in which that person does not share. Recognizing the wrongness of such acts does not require a notion of sex's having a purpose apart from the purposes of the people involved.

Engaging in a sexual act in order to have a baby is recognized as responsible behavior when that is what the couple want and when there are no significant reasons not to have a baby. Using sex to express love and affection is recognized as a good use of sex. Sexual union as a means of strengthening a relationship is almost universally approved. To show why these are good purposes for sexual activity, we use familiar moral principles, psychological principles of mental health, and our knowledge of what makes for pleasure and happiness for individuals and for families. To explain why engaging in sex just to avoid boredom or to avoid dealing with a problem are inferior uses of sex, we use the same knowledge of ethics and psychology. In making these judgments, we do not need to talk about the purpose of sex. We talk about the purposes of people, some of which are good, some of which are morally bad, and some of which are just ill-advised.

Thinking that sexuality has a purpose does not lead us to helpful insights. Holding that nature gives sex a purpose, that of procreation of our species, and that is the final word on sexuality, ignores all the richness that sexuality brings to human life. Accepting as the purpose of God the inseparability of sexual intercourse and procreation is not satisfactory philosophically or morally. We do well to think no more about the purpose of sexuality and to think about the purposes of people.

We will benefit from thinking about what sexuality has been in rich and fulfilling lives. Even though some people have seen sex as a burden, and others have seen it as a threat to their soul's salvation, sexuality has contributed much to people's lives. The contribution of sexuality to interpersonal relationships—enabling unions that join people in the physical, mental, and emotional aspects of their lives—makes it a great boon to humankind.

When we realize that the purpose of sexual activity is the purpose people bring to it, we can make some judgments of different purposes. Some purposes for sex are wrong, not for reasons that are specific to sex but because some motivations are wrong whatever the area of life in which they are pursued. Use of sex to dominate, to debase, to frighten, to bully, to hurt are bad. Use of economic power, social position, or physical strength for these purposes is also bad. When we make judgments about the purposes people have for sex, we need to remember that not all people are alike. They vary greatly in needs, abilities, imagination, energy, and opportunity. What one person wants from sex might not be right, or possible, for another. People have been too judgmental about sex in the past. Now that we have a liberating understanding of the place of sex in human life, we have an opportunity to avoid being judgmental. A few things we should condemn because they are causing harm and hurt to people. The rest of the differences between people's purposes for sex should be left to those people.

~ 4 ~

Feminism

Varieties of Feminist Theory

Feminism has developed over a long period of time. The goals of eighteenth- and nineteenth-century feminists were modest according to current standards. Allowing women to be educated and to hold property corrected injustices of long standing, and now we take such things for granted. We need to remember, however, that women won the right to vote in this century, and some legal barriers to women's holding and disposing of property were removed in the lifetime of people now living. Feminism now takes several forms and has various goals, so it might be confusing to people who have not kept up with its development. We might question whether feminism is one or several movements on behalf of women. Do the several approaches to feminism have anything in common?

Jane Flax holds that feminist theory has certain shared assumptions. It holds that men and women have different experiences, so that the world is not the same for them. Some feminists think that women and men should be able to have the same experiences, while some other feminists see special values in the experience of women. Flax says that feminists hold that the oppression of women is not a subset of some other social relationship, such as class struggle. This does not seem to be the case, however, with Marxist feminists. Another common belief that Flax identifies is that the oppression of women is not merely a case of "bad attitudes," such as sexism. It "is part of the way the structure of the world is organized." This structure is patriarchy, a system under which males have more power than females. Another common element is the belief that patriarchy is internalized, so that it affects the way people feel about themselves. The last shared assumption is that power should not be attached to gender.[1]

Flax holds that all kinds of feminists share certain purposes. One is to understand the "power differential" between men and women. How did it come to be? What maintains it? How does it relate to other power relations? All feminists, according to Flax, seek to understand the oppression of women, its history, its relationship to other forms of oppression, and how it operates in the family. All feminists seek to overcome oppression in the three basic realms of human experience: production, reproduction, and individual internal life, the "psychodynamic sphere."[2]

Even though feminists have much in common, there are some significant differences between them. One way to classify different approaches to feminist concerns is political. Alison Jaggar holds that feminists are united in rejection of a conservative ideology that denies that women are systematically oppressed and claims that the sexes are innately different and should have separate roles. There are, however, several distinct ideologies in the liberation movement, related to basic philosophical issues: the nature of freedom and equality; the function of the state; and the nature of the human person, especially the female.[3]

Liberal feminism sees women's liberation in terms of civil liberties and seeks the removal of restraints upon women. It holds that roles should be based not on sex but on the individual's ability to perform tasks. Race and sex are irrelevant criteria; each person should be considered separately. There should be a minimum of state intervention in personal affairs. Liberal feminists hold that discrimination should be illegal, but they support preferential hiring and oppose laws against contraception and abortion. Liberal feminism seeks reforms, but it does not try to change the whole social order.[4]

Classic Marxist feminism is based on the teachings of Marx and Engels. It sees the oppression of women as a result of the institution of private property and advocates the abolition of private property. Feminism is seen as part of a larger class struggle. Traditional monogamy and the family, with the double standard of behavior for men and women, are related to relations of property. Women should be in industry, and household duties should be socialized. The liberation of women is seen in economic terms rather than in terms of civil liberties.[5]

Radical feminism holds that the oppression of women results from women's biological and sexual nature. The economic dependence of women on men is related to women's reproductive role. Sexual oppression is more basic than economic oppression. Liberation of women will require a biological revolution, to be achieved through new reproductive technologies that free women from their biological role. Radical feminists attack heterosexuality as the exclusive norm. Leading radical feminists base their thought on Freudian psychology.[6]

Alison Jaggar describes some more recent developments in feminist thought. Lesbian separatism urges women to refrain from heterosexual relations. This is sometimes advocated as a matter of strategy in the struggle for women's independence. The choice of a sexual partner is seen as having political significance.[7] Some separatists support the goal of a matriarchy in which men would be excluded from their society.

Socialist feminism denies the radical feminist view that reproductive biology is the cause of the oppression of women. It stresses the need to change the economic basis of society, but it holds that economic change alone is not adequate; feminine consciousness must be developed. Socialist feminists hold that the Marxist view of the family is simplistic, and they reject the sexual puritanism that they associate with Marxism. They agree with Marxists that women should be in industry, but they should not be in low-level jobs.[8]

Nancy Hartsock argues for a socialist feminist approach. She sees feminism in terms of social revolution. She stresses practical action groups and the unity of theory and practice.[9]

An approach to feminism which largely developed outside the United States, primarily in France, has received increased attention in the last few years. It is called essentialist feminism. Essentialist feminists hold that women are essentially different from men. They stress the obvious aspects of female fertility, such as women's monthly cycle, pregnancy, childbirth, and nursing; fertility gives women, they say, unique power and a special role. They hold that women do not think and feel the way men do, that women have different sensibilities, because of their essential nature. Other feminists have acknowledged these differences but have held that they are culturally conditioned and are not universal in women.[10]

Feminist Consciousness

Sandra Lee Bartky holds that even though feminists are divided along political lines, something crucial to feminism is beyond the political aspects. To be a feminist, she says, one must become a feminist, which is a transforming experience, including an altered consciousness. Feminist consciousness is not universal, as is the oppression of women. Current features of society enable the emergence of feminist consciousness. Bartky points to contradictions in society (a Marxist concept) in existing property relations, attitudes, and values, which conflict with new social relations caused by changes in the mode of production. Other changes that enabled the development of a feminist consciousness are the availability of contraception, the larger number of women who work outside the home, the increased presence of women in education, changes in housekeeping and food preparation, a weaker role of the family, and the social upheaval of the 1960s.[11]

What is a feminist consciousness? Bartky describes it as an anguished consciousness that recognizes the possibility of the transformation of the intolerable condition of women. It is a consciousness of victimization of women that is undeserved and offensive. The feminist consciousness is a divided consciousness, conscious of weakness and of strength. Another dividedness within feminist consciousness produces confusion and guilt, for the victim knows that she is better off than most people in the world. The victim of oppression suffers a psychological oppression, which causes "harmless" things to become sinister; social reality becomes deceptive. Bartky describes this as category confusion; the victim is unsure how to categorize things, including her own behavior. The feminist becomes vigilant, suspicious, wary. Realization of the deceptive character of social reality shows many opportunities to struggle against the system, which makes many social occasions into tests. The feminist does not know what sort of person to be or what to do. Bartky says the picture is not totally dark, since there are opportunities for "raised" consciousness and personal growth. There can be liberating collective activity and a sense of solidarity with other women.[12]

The Male Feminist

So far we have been talking as if all feminists were women. There are men who consider themselves feminists. How does a man become a feminist? Perhaps no generalizations can be made about this, but some observations are in order. Even though men do not experience the same victimization that women experience, they might experience other forms of oppression, or they might be able to empathize with people who do experience oppression. A man can very well recognize the justice of feminism's call for an end to patriarchy.

There is not a substantial body of research on the factors that might bring about the acceptance of feminism by a man or the refusal to accept feminist claims. One could speculate about the man's relationship with his mother, the role of the father in the home. One could speculate about the man's socialization and participation in sports and other activities as a child and youth. I do not believe we would learn much by such speculation. There have been men who did not experience directly the pain of being oppressed but who sought the liberation of the victims. These men were among the abolitionists in nineteenth-century America. They supported the suffragettes early in this century, and now they side with feminists in today's struggle. What makes members of a privileged group side with the oppressed is not a well understood phenomenon.

Some people wonder whether male feminists are emotionally disturbed people, perhaps men who have trouble with the male side of their being. All I can say is that if nothing ever troubles the male feminists I know any more than their sexuality, their lives will be smooth and easy. They are concerned about the possibility of their being insensitive or overbearing, and they discuss the problem of being helpful without becoming the Mr. Fixit for the delicate women. They have no trouble being male.

It has been said that liberated women do not care for feminist men. Perhaps some women do not, and who expects to appeal to everyone? It has been my good fortune to have the respect, in some cases even the love, of strong and liberated women, and this seems to be the experience of other male feminists I know.

There have been some male organizations and movements in the past few years that seem to have arisen in reaction to the feminist movement. These movements have claimed that men have degenerated terribly since women exerted their power, and now the men need to reclaim their masculinity. Men have been led into the wilderness, undoubtedly not by a divinely inspired prophet, to beat drums and rouse up the wild man within them. Is there any benefit in organizing men in these ways? I am not sure about the drums. Making a bit of noise can be fun, and rhythm provides a basic pleasure, as even Aristotle noted. There are now women, as well as men, who seem to find a special value in drum beating, something spiritual and restoring. I get more pleasure from drums when a jazz band provides the sound, but there is power in meetings. Women have found not only solace but also power in meetings of like-minded women. Men can receive benefit from men's groups.

Men are not as accustomed to talking seriously with other men about what it is to be a man as women are to talking with other women about being a woman. Men tend to talk about sports or politics or occupational matters. To talk about sex usually means to brag, even lie, about one's experiences and adroitness. Men can do better than that. I have belonged to several groups from time to time in which men talked seriously about their lives. These were small groups, usually no more than five or six men. Larger groups fall into the male game of generalizing and dealing with abstractions. Male feminists, who usually feel like members of one of the smallest minority groups on earth, can receive significant benefit from small groups of men. The freedom and democracy in such groups is instructive in itself. The chance to be open about personal matters and receive the support of other men is invaluable. One sign of the effectiveness of these groups is that most of them do not continue for more than a year. Some of the groups I knew brought together men who were recently widowed, divorced, or "dumped" by a lover. These men soon gained from each other the strength not to need the group. The group that lasted longest was a group of male feminists who needed to talk about being a feminist, as well as help one another through griefs, job losses, and other situations.

Can male feminists contribute anything important to the feminist movement? This is difficult to answer. Women probably do not need men in the feminist movement to secure the success of the cause. They can reach their main goals by their own power. Some women may well wish that men would not become identified with the feminist movement. Other women, however, seem to want men to share their concerns. Feminist women are not all man haters, and some of them see the goal of feminism as securing a just and cooperative society of women and men.[13] I believe this is a most reasonable goal for women and men, and men can contribute to its realization.

There are feminists who do not want men to play a significant role in their society. They are separatists. We need to consider their viewpoint.

Feminist Separatism

Separatism is of several types. It can be fairly conservative, calling for temporary, even brief, separation of women into support groups or consciousness raising groups. Other approaches are more radical. Lesbian separatism probably strikes most people as the most radical approach.

Proposing that women separate themselves as much as possible from the family and work arrangements in which they are under the influence of men is a radical approach, but some feminists think this is the way women must secure freedom and growth. Marilyn Frye holds that women must separate themselves from men and male-dominated institutions and activities for the sake of independence, growth, sisterhood, and safety. She expects this call for separation to disturb men greatly because men are very dependent upon women, which Frye calls male parasitism on women. She thinks that separatism is a serious challenge to the "structure of power." Frye thinks that heterosexuality, marriage, and motherhood are the primary institutions for making women available to men. Separation, she says, is the way to pursue sexual equality.[14]

One call for separation asks women to become lesbians. Joyce Trebilcot holds that feminist women should take responsibility for their type of sexuality as a way of making a commitment to the equality of women. The type of sexuality may be lesbian, heterosexual, bisexual, or celibate, but Trebilcot favors lesbianism. Becoming a lesbian is, as she sees it, a process of discovery and creation. Bisexuality or pansexuality, she says, does not require a decision regarding sexuality and leads to the exploitation of women. Trebilcot rejects the view that one's sexuality is a given. She holds the pluralistic view that all orientations are natural and can be healthy if one adjusts well.[15]

Trebilcot realizes that many women believe that they cannot choose. She sees them as having a conflict between reason, which favors lesbianism, and feelings, which are heterosexual. Women should not, however, let sexual "twinges" determine their sexuality. She says that economic and social advantages lead women to heterosexuality, but there are reasons for taking responsibility. Women can be in control and be stronger, independent, and sex-creating. Consciousness is raised about sexuality; the woman has a better understanding of the working of patrimony. Another advantage Trebilcot sees is that there will be fewer heterosexuals, and women who decide for heterosexuality will be less antilesbian, less afraid of lesbianism.[16]

Sara Ann Ketchum and Christine Pierce say that a movement or theory is separatist to the extent that it fosters relationships or organizations of members of the oppressed group. The purpose of separation is to produce solidarity, pride, and a "noncontingent culture," which is a culture not determined or defined by the dominant group. Only in a "womanculture" do women get a noncontingent concept of being a woman. A separatist culture protects women from the prejudices, contempt, and hatred of the dominant group. One way this works is that it protects women from internalizing prejudice and hatred against them, so that they do not have consequent feelings of inferiority. This kind of association is not sexist, they say, because these separate organizations of the oppressed group are not the same as organizations of the dominant group.[17]

Separatist groups can range from minimal separation to more radical separation. The most minimal separation is interest-group separation to help women develop an understanding of their political or economic interests and to foster those interests. Ketchum and Pierce say that the only thing radical about these groups is the idea that women do have interests as a group. A middle level of separation is consciousness raising groups, which meet from time to time to foster group identity and understanding. Lesbian separatism is a more radical type of separatism. The extreme approaches are the conservative rejection of all separatism and "sexual nationalism," which advocates a total political and sexual separation, and "asexualism," which would avoid sexual relationships entirely.[18]

The value to women—and to members of any group that has been, or even feels that it has been, under the domination of another group—of a time of separation from the dominant group should be taken seriously. There is a well-attested phenomenon of internalizing the values and viewpoints of the dominant group. Only in a setting in which members of the dominant group are not present can members of a dominated group escape seeing themselves as they are seen by members of the dominant group. No matter how much we protest that it is not so, we are not totally unaffected by the views of others. It can be a valuable experience for women to be in a group where they are not seen by men and not judged by men. There is no agreement about how long the periods of separation must be to have their liberating effect.

The lesbian separatists seem to think that the separation must be for long periods of time and that it should include the sexual and affectional part of a person's life. Other people believe the time spent in consciousness raising or support groups is sufficient. Some people might need more time away from the dominant social group than other people need. That would not be surprising.

The claim of Ketchum and Pierce that same-sex groups need not be sexist is well taken. The purpose for which a group gathers is the determining factor. When a male group has as its goal the continued domination of women, the group is sexist. When a group gathers to plan harm to the other group, it is sexist. Gathering for the sake of greater self-understanding and mutual encouragement in a just cause should not be considered sexist.

Separatism might appear to be purely negative, a turning away from the society of men with no other well-defined goals. It would be a mistake to see it that way. As Ketchum and Pierce make clear, the separation is sought for definite purposes. The separated group life accomplishes a liberation and growth in women.

Feminists have given serious attention to the nature of the association women should have between themselves. Janice G. Raymond sees friendship between women as a help in escaping the effects of "hetero-reality," which is the tendency of people to think of women as existing only in relation to men. She says a group of women are perceived as being alone. She quotes Lily Tomlin's report of a man walking up to a group of women together in a bar and saying, "Hey, what are you doing here sitting all alone?"

Raymond does not see friendship simply as an escape. She writes of "Gyn/affection," her term for woman-to-woman "attraction, influence, and movement." She understands Gyn/affection to involve feelings between women but also mutual influence and empowerment.[19]

Raymond holds that Gyn/affection is not limited to lesbian relationships and does not require a withdrawal from society, which she rejects, calling it "dissociation," and sees as failure to be an effective member of society. At the same time, she is opposed to "assimilation to the world" by which women adapt themselves to "male-defined structures." She says that the assimilated woman is "the new androgyne," who has a "masculine" career and a "feminine" marriage.[20]

Raymond sees pitfalls in a stress on sexual liberation. She does not share a feminist openness to whatever sexual practices a woman wants to pursue. She objects to lesbian sadomasochism because it puts one of the women in a position of passivity and degradation. She warns of "the tyranny of tolerance."[21]

Other feminists have responded in different ways to Raymond's treatment of friendship between women. Claudia Card is not satisfied with her treatment of lesbianism and separatism. She thinks Raymond rejects separatism. Marilyn Friedman approves of Raymond's presenting a concept of the strong individual, the "Self," which does not degenerate into "liberal individualism." She praises Raymond's ideas on "Self-regard." The capitalization of "Self" is Raymond's.[22]

In her recent book, Marilyn Friedman continues to explore the meaning of friendship between women. She writes about the inadequacy of basing ethics on impartiality and examines the possibilities of ethics based on partiality, which recognizes obligations to those who are near and dear to one. There is a growing interest in partiality among moral philosophers, both feminist and nonfeminist, who recognize the value of special relationships. Friedman sees problems arising from nonfeminist versions of an ethics of partiality, which tend to be abstract. She supports a feminist approach that stresses the virtue of caring and the importance of context in commitment to particular persons. Friedman also considers the role of communities in friendships.[23]

Understanding separatism is important to understanding feminism. Separatism underscores two aspects of feminism that I believe to be necessary. One is the need for women to get away from understanding themselves in terms of how men perceive them. The other is the need for women to find strength, insight, and determination from their relations with each other.

Feminist Philosophy

Feminist philosophy is varied and exploratory, but several themes that most feminists share can be identified. Feminist philosophy is critical of what is seen as male bias in philosophy. Alison M. Jaggar identified several of these biases. She found male bias in the devaluation of women's philosophical work. She refers to the absence of women from the Western philosophical tradition, a result of social and educational conditions that limited women's contributions and of a virtual ignoring of the work that women did. Some of the bias Jaggar identifies was overt misogyny on the part of philosophers such as Aristotle, Thomas,

Kant, and Hegel. Another aspect of the bias was the omission of the concerns of women from philosophical inquiry. Jaggar said that philosophy has exhibited male bias in distorting categories and in the conception of philosophy. She says this grew out of "reflection only on men's lives—and only on some parts of men's lives," as can be seen in constructing ethical theory on a legislative model and the importance given impartiality in ethics.[24]

In the central areas of philosophy, metaphysics and epistemology, Jaggar found male bias in major categories: the concepts of human nature and the understanding of knowledge. One aspect of this is the dualistic manner of thinking with pairs of qualities or entities in opposition to each other. She cites body/mind, nature/culture, objective/subjective, emotion/reason, public/private, and others. She says a few of the male biases are the favored position of reason over other aspects of experience and the concept of rationality, the "fetishizing" of "objectivity" with the separation of the knower from what is known, and in the treatment of the body, nature, and passion as "a problematic to be transcended." She recognizes that feminism is not the only philosophical position from which these biases are criticized, but only feminism recognizes that they are male biases.[25]

Laura Sells sees feminist philosophy wrestling with the dualisms that male philosophy had settled by favoring one of the pairs of entities or qualities and devaluing the other. In a review essay on the philosophies of Lorraine Code, Sandra Harding, and Susan Hekman, she explains their struggles with objective knowledge and knowledge in relation to the knower and with the conflict between essentialism and antiessentialism (Code), the relationship between science and feminism and the methods of feminist empiricism and standpoint theory (Harding), and the issues of postmodernist feminism (Hekman). The dualisms with which they struggle are, according to Sells, rationality and irrationality, subject and object, and nature and culture.[26]

One of the main feminist objections to male bias has been that science operates according to masculine methods and values in its sharp separation of the knower and the known and its claims of "value neutrality." Evelyn Fox Keller called attention to male bias in science.[27] Feminists examine the social institutions of science and note that women are inhibited from entering some sciences. They examine the usually ignored social construction of science with its male biases. They urge a rejection of the supposedly "objective" approach and the adoption of an epistemology that would incorporate reason and emotion and unify theory and practice.[28]

The work of developing a feminist epistemology continues. In a review essay in *Hypatia,* Sara Ruddick[29] reports on the recent collections by Linda Alcoff and Elizabeth Potter (*Feminist Epistemologies*)[30] and by Louise Antony and Charlotte Witt (*A Mind of One's Own*).[31] The reference to feminist epistemologies (in the plural) is correct. Three leading approaches are feminist empiricism, feminist standpoint theory, and postmodern feminism. These three epistemological directions might be brought into a unified feminist epistemology. In a review essay, Nancy Tuanna[32] claims that Lynn H. Nelson's work[33] creates a bridge between the three favorite feminist epistemological approaches.

It would be a mistake to see feminist epistemology as some kind of special pleading or ad hoc way to support women's interests. Alison Jaggar has shown that feminist approaches are closely related to Marxist, American pragmatist, and poststructuralist traditions.[34] The spring 1993 issue of *Hypatia* is a special issue on feminism and pragmatism.[35] Not only is feminist epistemology not isolated from other approaches, feminists do not need to abandon standards of philosophical adequacy and rigorous criticism. For example, Beth A. Dixon, in a review of Lorraine Code's *What Can She Know?*[36] expressed concern over the importance Code gives the gender, race, class, and history of the knower in her analysis of knowledge. Dixon fears that this might make knowledge "idiosyncratic" in being too relative to the individual knower. She agrees with Code's critical comments about traditional epistemology, such as its "idealized conception of objectivity" and of "knowers as solitary and autonomous reasoners." She says that "the job of an epistemologist is to analyze how knowledge figures into particular people's lives" but holds that we should not "abandon the search for necessary and sufficient conditions for knowing."[37]

Feminists have taken a special interest in aesthetics. They have found in traditional aesthetic theory the same sorts of male biases they found in epistemology and metaphysics. The importance of sight and hearing, as opposed to the senses that are traditionally important to women in their work, is held to be a male perspective on art. The stress on reason in seeing art in terms of cognition and the detachment of aesthetic satisfaction from personal interest are like the stress on detachment in male oriented science.[38]

Hypatia had a special issue on feminist aesthetics with papers on several aspects of feminist interest in the arts and an annotated bibliography compiled by Linda Kruholz and Estelle Lauter.[39] The American Philosophical Association's *Newsletter on Philosophy and Feminism* had two special issues on aesthetics in 1990.

Feminists have been concerned with the male domination of the visual arts and sculpture. It is not that women produced no art; their works were usually ignored and seldom shown. Women were limited to the roles of muses and models. Many good artists were largely unknown until the National Museum of Women in the Arts was established in Washington, D.C. A few books helped to inform the art world about the contributions of women.[40]

Another feminist concern was the portrayal of women in the arts, the female nude in particular. In a book based on a BBC television series, John Berger explains the relation of the male, who is the implied viewer, and the female, who is the object of the male's perception, in terms of the objectification of the woman and power and possession on the part of the man.[41] This has been the concern expressed by a number of feminist writers.

One of the most important areas of feminist philosophy has been ethics. Feminist ethics presents serious challenges to traditional approaches to ethics. The abstractness of ethical theory and the stress on rules of conduct, along with the goal of definitive moral judgments based on one moral principle, made traditional ethics detached from the particular circumstances of life. Ethics was usually approached from the perspective of a moral judge, one who is impartial and able to look upon life as an "ideal observer." Too little attention was paid to the moral agent, the individual person who must make a moral decision in a particular set of circumstances. Feminist moral philosophers were attracted to contextualism, an approach to making moral judgments that takes into account everything morally relevant in a situation. This focus on the particular situation counteracts the detachment that can make ethical judgment so abstract that it becomes reductionistic. An ethical theory is reductionistic if it does not see human beings in their biological, psychological, cultural, legal, and other important dimensions. A Kantianism that plays down feeling and deals with human beings only as rational thinkers is ignoring much of what makes us human persons. The contractarian approach that pictures people as individuals making rational judgments about their self-interest is another reduction. It sees only one aspect of being human and does not take account of the many different motivations that lead to our behaviors.

Feminist thought was able to break through a formalistic approach to ethics that saw ethical reasoning only in terms of arguments, usually deductive arguments, addressed to general directions for conduct. The very idea of letting feelings influence moral thinking was abhorrent to most traditional moral philosophers. Feminist ethics stressed caring, nonhierarchical relationships, seeking of common consent, and other values that were largely ignored in traditional ethics. American pragmatism, with John Dewey the best-known advocate, practiced ethics as problem solving. This is one of the affinities feminism has with pragmatism. Feminism does not consider moral judgment primarily a matter of intellectual argument. As problem solving, moral judgment does not see being impersonal and detached helpful. Solving the moral problems of particular people in a specific situation does not aim at generalities to be applied to everyone in every place.

Feminist ethics was greatly influenced by Carol Gilligan's *In a Different Voice,* published in 1982, and later writings.[42] Gilligan, a psychologist, argued that female moral development is not like male development and women's moral thinking is not like that of men. She opposed Lawrence Kohlberg's theory of moral development in six stages.[43] She said women do not develop by these stages, but this does not mean that their moral development is defective or inferior. She held that most discussion of ethics has been limited to typically male ways of approaching ethics. She noted that Piaget[44] saw but largely ignored girls' differences, such as greater tolerance, innovative approaches to problems, and willingness to make exceptions to rules.[45]

Gilligan contrasts two alternative ways to see moral issues, in terms of justice and in terms of caring. Unlike the stress on impartiality in traditional ethics, feminist ethics recognizes the importance of relationships. She says that women and men tend to focus on "different dimensions" of a situation. This thinking in terms of attachment between two persons on the basis of equality changes the concepts of relationship "from hierarchy or balance to network or web." In the justice oriented approach, detachment is seen as the mature level, achieving the ability to separate oneself, to be "objective" in making judgments. In the caring approach, detachment is itself a moral problem. Feminists hold that care, attachments, attention to context, and responsibility have an important place in ethics. The goals of traditional ethics, depersonalized rationality and abstract justice, can be augmented with the alternative perspective provided by feminist ethics.[46]

Annette Baier combines elements from David Hume and Carol Gilligan to supplement traditional ethics. This gives her a broad and inclusive approach to ethics that she describes as a mosaic. It is ethics that is more open and more diverse than traditional ethics. It includes elements of virtue, such as caring, loving, trusting, and gentle helpfulness.[47]

Alison Jaggar thinks that feminist ethics needs to correct any male biases in traditional ethics and that it must take the moral experience of women seriously, though not uncritically. She warns against considering women as moral experts or "extrapolating directly from women's experiences" and substituting women's values for men's values. She does not think feminist ethics should focus just on what are called women's issues. She illustrates how a feminist ethics can approach issues of equality and difference between men and women, the question of impartiality, dealing with the particularity of moral judgments without succumbing to moral subjectivity, problems with the concept of autonomy, and issues of moral epistemology.[48]

I believe a contextualistic and pluralistic ethics—open to recognition of the varieties of moral thinking that are useful in making moral decisions, accepting the importance of special relationships, and able to realize the moral importance of virtues that were largely ignored in traditional ethics—can help solve some of the problems of ethical theory that have troubled moral philosophers for centuries. The careful philosophical work of thinkers like Annette Baier and Alison Jaggar shows that feminist ethics cannot be dismissed as trivial or as a fad. It is not just something to make women feel good. It can provide much of what has been missing from moral philosophy and correct much that has been wrong with moral philosophy.

Feminist ethics has been adopted in some practical areas of moral concern, especially in peace issues and environmental ethics. Peace and opposition to militarism grow directly out of feminist beliefs. Traditionally, women have been thought of as opposing war, which has been partly true. Feminism has added new dimensions to the pursuit of peace, since most feminist theory and most feminist concerns relate to the issue. The American Philosophical Association's *Newsletter on Feminism and Philosophy* for spring 1994 shows that this continues to be a productive area of feminist thought.

The practical area of feminist ethics with which I have been most familiar is ecological ethics. Thought in this field has contributed significantly to environmental ethics and to ethical theory generally. The mainstream, largely male, philosophical approaches to nature that dominated nineteenth- and early twentieth-century thought about the environment have been blamed as partly responsible for the environmental crisis. The usual approach to nature accepted as proper the domination and exploitation of nature, moderated, if at all, by a conservation that did not reject exploitation but advocated using natural resources carefully and making them last as long as possible. New approaches to nature were developed following Rachel Carson's warning about the dangers of DDT and increasing interest in Aldo Leopold's "Land Ethic," the concluding section of his *Sand County Almanac*.[49]

Most of the environmental philosophers were male, but female writers made significant contributions to the new ways of thinking about nature and the place of human beings in the system of nature. In the 1970s, Carolyn Merchant and a few other writers explored the significance of ecological feminism. The literature became more abundant in the 1980s and 1990s. *Environmental Ethics* has published significant work in this area.

Karen J. Warren reports that Françoise d'Eaubonne coined the term *ecofeminisme* in 1974 in an effort to make known the role that women could play in an environmental movement.[50] A movement with several emphases and from several feminist perspectives followed. Warren does not give a rigid definition of ecological feminism, but she does give some "boundary conditions," which she describes as being like those of a collage or of a quilt. She points out important features of a growing movement that she sees as a critique of previous weaknesses in earlier forms of feminism. She also sees changes that ecological feminism can make in environmental ethics. The ethical theory she supports is contextualistic and pluralistic, giving voice to oppressed people and to concerns usually overlooked in traditional ethics.[51] The image of feminist ethics as a mosaic was employed by Annette Baier.[52] Jim Cheney supports the pluralism of ecological feminism in terms of postmodernism and bioregionalism.[53]

Rosemary Ruether pointed out an important theme of ecological feminism, the historical connection between the domination of nature and the domination of women. Women were identified with nature and were exploited along with nature. The liberation of women and environmentalism both require a social revolution that overcomes the attitude of domination.[54] Other feminist writers built upon Ruether's identification of the oppression of women with the oppression of nature as the reason environmentalism and feminism are closely related. Some feminists are critical of deep ecologists who do not seem to realize the nature-woman connection. Michael E. Zimmerman says these critics accuse deep ecologists of opposing "anthropocentrism" (human-centeredness) as the root of the domination of nature, when actually androcentrism (male-centeredness) is the real root.[55]

Karen J. Warren strongly affirms Rosemary Ruether's belief that feminism and environmentalism are closely related and gives a clear explanation of the "conceptual frameworks" that supported the oppression of women and led to degradation of the natural environment. Warren holds that environmentalism is not complete without a feminist perspective. She sees feminism correcting male biases and shaping ethics that will oppose any kind of social domination.[56]

The American Philosophical Association's *Newsletter on Feminism and Philosophy* 90, no.3 (fall 1991) is devoted to articles on ecological feminism, curriculum materials, and a bibliography selected by Carol J. Adams and Karen J. Warren. The *Newsletter on Feminism and Philosophy* 91, no.1, (spring 1992) has additional articles on ecological feminism, along with comments on articles in the previous newsletter and more outlines of courses in environmental ethics taught from a feminist perspective.

Maria Mies, in Germany, and Vandana Shiva, in India, have shown that ecological ethics is a worldwide concern of women. Their book on ecofeminism explores issues of science and feminist research, poverty, the crisis in food and nutrition, nuclear hazards and other hazardous wastes, the effect upon women of globalism and nationalism, and population concerns. They explain the conflicting policies of subsistence culture and "catch-up" industrial development in the southern countries and the conflict between ecofeminism and biotechnologies and reproductive technologies.[57]

Feminism and Humanism

In the introduction, I mentioned the possibility that the concerns now expressed by feminism could one day be part of a more inclusive humanism. What would make this possible? Several developments would need to pave the way for this. The social and economic goals of feminism would need to be realized. As long as there are unfair social, political, and economic restrictions on women, there will need to be a movement specifically concerned with correcting these inequities. As we have seen, equality between men and women must include an appreciation of any special qualities that women can contribute to our culture. This means that a feminist movement will be needed until male biases in science, history, philosophy, ethics, the arts, and other important areas of life have been overcome.

Will we ever achieve this level of equality? That I do not know. I know that we have made significant progress. We can see that the good old days about which some people are nostalgic were actually the bad days without universal public education; Social Security; consumer protection; and many social, cultural, and economic opportunities that we might be taking for granted today. Without being so rash as to make predictions, I confess to some optimism about what we might achieve in American society.

We might never be able to enjoy a society in which the feminist movement and movements to protect and aid minorities will no longer be needed, but I think that such a society would be highly desirable. A society that is both "color-blind" and just would be a good thing, the realization of our desire for equal justice under the law. I believe a genderless society would also be a good thing. When our concern can be for people, as people, and for their social and natural environments, we will have made significant progress in solving the problems of our society and in realizing the dreams of our people.

~ 5 ~

Sexual Morality

Various questions about sexual morality continue to divide people and even cause social divisions. Many people consider sexual wrongdoing especially serious. Sexual behavior is an important aspect of ethics, but we need to be careful to avoid approaches to sexual ethics that are confused, simplistic, and misdirected.

The source of ethical guidance is one area we need to talk about. Many people rely on custom or religious authority to guide them, but philosophical ethics seeks rational grounds for approving of some behaviors and condemning others. These rational grounds, unlike authoritarian commands that must be accepted without question, can be discussed, criticized, and adapted to changing circumstances. Another difference between the sexual ethics of many people and philosophical ethics is the role of marriage in determining which conduct is right and which wrong. Many people consider marriage the most, or only, critical factor and hold that married people can engage in sexual activity and people outside a marriage cannot. As we will see, the presence or absence of a marriage is only one, and sometimes not the most crucial, thing to be considered. Marriage does not justify any and every form of sexual behavior, and the question of whether sexual activity outside of marriage is morally right is not always subject to a simple judgment.

The activities that are considered subject to moral judgment vary from culture to culture and even from time to time within a culture. When I was a young person, I knew people who argued over the morality of social dancing and mixed-sex swimming. Now these things are not widely discussed. There is more likely to be argument about

56

people's living together before marriage. Adultery, a married person's engaging in sex with a person other than the spouse, is generally treated as a more serious matter than sex between unmarried people, and the grounds for being concerned about adultery are not the same as those for premarital sex. For these reasons, adultery is considered in the next chapter. The issue of abortion is considered separately in chapter 8, and homosexuality is the subject of chapter 7.

What Is a Moral Issue?

Some of the argument about sexual ethics is whether certain questions are moral issues at all. Some years ago, I lived in a small town (it seemed the smallest town of its size in the country) in which the letters page of the small weekly newspaper was filled for a time with letters declaring the evil of women's going to market in what were then called short shorts and letters defending the practice. A few writers saw that this should be approached as an issue of fashion or etiquette, not a matter of morality. If a matter is not of moral concern, it should not be approached in terms of moral judgment. There can be serious disagreement about which behaviors are and are not properly subject to moral judgment. Some business practices might be of moral concern, even if the businessperson prefers to think of them as merely matters of business. Matters of dress are probably seldom, if ever, appropriate matters for moral judgment. Sexual acts are what most people seem to think of first when there is mention of morality. For some people, *morality* means sexual morality. The criteria on which matters of moral concern are distinguished from nonmoral matters are not simple; it is not surprising that reasonable people disagree about some matters. How can we recognize that an issue is a moral one, in distinction from legal issues and matters of custom?

One feature of morality is its recognized authority and importance. Morality tends to over-ride customs and good manners. Notice how most people criticize immoral behavior more severely than they would criticize breaches of custom or manners. Kurt Baier holds that morality over-rules self-interest for the good of all people in the society, and many moral philosophers agree with him on this point.[1] The law is held to be very important, and in some cases the law requires people to do what they believe is immoral, but we only allow this to happen in very significant cases in which there is some grave danger, as when we require vaccination of children contrary to parents' moral beliefs.

Another feature of morality is that it is created informally, unlike law. Morality is thought of as a product of personal belief and commitment. The use of the police to enforce morality is very controversial and seldom accepted in this country. Custom is like morality in this respect.

Morality tends to be more internalized and personal than law and custom. Motives are important to morality, and personal autonomy is an important aspect of morality.

More so than law or custom, morality is related to what is harmful or beneficial to people. Even though this aspect is more important in some ethical approaches than others, it is seldom ignored entirely.

Philosophers hold that morality must be based on reasons. It must be arguable. It always makes sense to ask why one should do something. The typical moral argument claims that an action is required by a general moral principle. Producing a greater balance of good over evil, being just and fair, not causing useless and unmerited pain or harm, and being conducive to preservation of the natural environment are cited as reasons for doing an action. They are never suggested as moral reasons against an action. Some principles are especially useful in understanding sexual morality, and they will be explored in a few pages. It is not expected of custom or etiquette that good reasons can be given for it. Sometimes a custom or the polite way of doing things will make things easier, quieter, or more graceful, but we do not insist on being given reasonable explanations for all customs, and we will accept explanations that no longer make a once-useful practice reasonable. It is desirable that good reasons be given for laws, but the lack of such reasons does not keep the law from being legal.

Most philosophers hold that morality must be impartial in the sense that morality is not a matter of private choice. What is wrong for one person in a situation is wrong for any person in those circumstances unless some relevant difference between the two people can be pointed out. There have been some second thoughts about the requirement of impartiality, especially on the part of feminist writers, as we saw in chapter 4. The critical comments on impartiality, which I think are justified, do not eliminate the requirement, but they clarify it and make it less abstract.

These are some of the features of morality. They can be clarified more than we have done here, and some aspects of the nature of morality are subject to debate, but this brief survey should serve our needs here.

Judging Actions Right or Wrong

In addition to deciding which acts are subject to moral judgment, sexual ethics must judge which sexual acts are morally right. This is not a simple matter because the context must be considered. When are certain acts right? With whom are they right? Does the rightness or wrongness depend on how the behaviors are done? When a moral judgment is made without consideration of the context, the judgment is too abstract. It becomes, at best, an exercise in more sharply defining moral principles and, at worst, a heedless application of principles to situations they do not fit.

Many people get the answers to moral questions from an authoritarian religious group, and they have definite and specific answers to the familiar questions, even though these answers may vary from group to group, and individual members of these sects might not always abide by the rules of the religion. Most members of these legalistic religious bodies do not think that nonreligious people have any basis for making moral decisions. This chapter examines the grounds on which people who are not under the direction of a religion make moral decisions regarding sexual behavior. This will be of value to many religious people who are members of religious groups that do not approach ethical questions in an authoritarian manner. For many people, religion gives a strong motivation toward morally right behavior and a sense of responsibility for doing what is morally right. The actual directions for conduct, however, are not found in literally interpreted scriptural passages or traditions of the religious group. The ethical direction is determined in the same way responsible nonreligious people determine which behaviors to approve and which to reject. Many religious people turn to philosophical ethics to answer questions about morality, including sexual morality. This is especially important when new issues arise, issues with which we do not have years of experience in dealing.

How can people who do not live by an authoritarian code of conduct decide what to do? Especially, how do they know which sexual behaviors are morally wrong and which morally right? There are a number of principles that are widely accepted because they have been tested in years of human experience. Some of them have directed people to behaviors that consistently result in greater happiness and human welfare. Some of them are trusted because they are compatible with the highest values that we know and help people realize these values in a rich way. Some of these principles have a certain attractiveness to people who are morally responsible and really want to live good lives. We will examine some of these familiar principles, and to keep our talk of principles from being too abstract, we will see how they provide guidance in actual situations. In addition to familiar values and principles, we can be guided in our moral judgments by the deeper understanding made possible by a philosophy of sexuality. We have considered the nature of sexuality, and this understanding of sexuality helps us see why some behaviors are constructive and some destructive.

Let us look at some principles that have long been recognized as ethically significant. Some of these principles are advocated in religious teachings, but they commend themselves to us for reasons that all thoughtful people can recognize. Some of these principles have been advocated by noted thinkers in the past, but we need not accept them on the authority of anyone. They stand on their own. It is interesting to many people to see how these principles developed in the past, and we can be grateful to those thinkers who understood these principles and explained them clearly for the first time, but our interest in these principles is not primarily historical.

Mutuality and Autonomy

Immanuel Kant (1724–1804) made a significant contribution to a rational perspective on sexual ethics two centuries ago when he held that it is morally wrong to treat people merely as means to what one desires and not also as ends in themselves. Kant realized, of course, that we cannot avoid using people as means. What is wrong is using them merely as means, without acknowledging their value as ends in themselves. There are many ways in which people can ignore the worth that people have as persons. The person who sees a servant as a mere thing to do work, something like a vacuum cleaner, is morally wrong. The rude customer who treats the clerk "like dirt" probably recognizes no worth in the clerk except as a means to the customer's convenience in shopping. If I do not mind the repair bills and am not afraid of being observed acting foolishly, I can yell at my laptop computer when the battery runs out and bang it up a bit; I cannot do the same thing to the secretaries, research assistants, and other helpful people at the university without great moral fault. In regard to sex, Kant said that outside of a loving relationship, people are treated as sex objects. He may have been the first person to denounce the use of people as sex objects. Kant held that outside of marriage, people will be used as mere objects of sexual desire.[2]

We do not need to agree with Kant that marriage is the only way to avoid using people as merely means. His condemnation of homosexual unions and relationships outside of wedlock seems to reflect his personal feelings more than an unbiased understanding of these relationships. The basic insight about the wrongness of using a person as a mere means can stand on its own.

The moral wrong about which Kant wrote is still a wrong. Why is it wrong? Using a person as a mere means to someone else's ends creates a relationship in which the person is not respected as a person, and his or her freedom and personal growth and development are not fostered. In such a relationship, there is a lack of reciprocity and mutuality. These failures make a sexual relationship wrong. Respecting fully the personhood and freedom of the other, helping the other grow in ability to realize his or her full potential, respecting the right of the other to be himself or herself and not a mere adjunct to oneself, avoiding anything that will be hurtful or detrimental to the other, learning to talk together and work out disagreements fairly—these are some of the things that make a sexual relationship morally right.

Our description of what is missing when a person is used as a mere means to another person's ends has revealed some more principles and values that guide our ethical judgments. Respect for the freedom and autonomy of other people, as well as our own, is an important aspect of acting morally. These principles show clearly why seduction or using force or pressure in securing sexual activity is morally wrong. By seduction, I refer to getting a person to do something the person does not want to do or something not in the person's interest. We sometimes use the word *seduce* for coaxing or tempting a person to do what the person really wants to do but is reluctant to do. This may be harmless, but even here we must be careful. Judging what is in a person's interest or anticipating a person's desires is tricky and invites the rationalization by which people come to justify doing what they want to do.

Some sexual practices, those in which a person's freedom is not respected, are probably wrong in any likely situation. Rape, which seems to be only incidentally a sexual matter, is an action in response to animosity toward women. It grows out of hatred and resentment, and its goal is to cause terror and pain. It is easy to see why this behavior is morally wrong; in addition to its bad motivation, it causes unjustified pain and harm. It is hard to conceive of a situation, even a fanciful one, in which rape would be morally justified. Seduction is a paradigm case of trying to use another person as a mere means. It is an attempt to overcome the freedom, as well as the good judgment, of the other person. A situation in which seduction is morally justified would be an unusual one indeed. Some people defend sexual encounters between adults and children, but I cannot see defense of such relationships as anything but romanticism or gross selfishness. Participating freely and with understanding in a sexual relationship requires a good bit of maturity. Before this maturity is acquired the child cannot be a real sexual partner but only an object to be used, probably by a person who is unable to relate to other adults.

Autonomy can be seen as a moral value in itself. Immanuel Kant considered it one of the features of a good moral will, which he held to be the only thing that is good in itself.[3] Many moral philosophers today would not link autonomy to the concept of reason that was crucial to Kant's ethics. Kant thought that reason would dictate specific and absolute obligations that any rational person would recognize. He rejected as without moral significance any action that grew out of feeling or inclination. For Kant, reason was the one thing that gave humans moral importance. Not only is this concept of reason very narrow, but it is based on a concept of the human person that few people would want to defend. Humans are much more complicated than Kant seemed to realize, and they have a richness of experiences and potentialities that he did not take into consideration.

What do I mean by *autonomy,* and why is it a moral value? Autonomy is the ability and the right that people have to make decisions about their lives. Autonomy is not absolute. People can enjoy it to varying degrees, and it would be difficult to determine what is a minimal level of autonomy below which it would not be morally significant. It might be necessary on occasion to ignore a person's claim to autonomy, and we must act responsibly as well as in freedom, but the moral importance of autonomy would be hard to deny. Acting responsibly does not require uncritical acquiescence to the wills of other people or the denial of our own personhood, including our desires, feelings, and emotions. Even though some emotional states can encourage people to make unwise decisions, decisions that are hurtful to the person or unfair to other persons, autonomy does not require us to ignore the way we feel about things. We exercise our autonomy best when we act as complete persons, bringing our thinking and our feeling together in the direction of our lives.

We must be careful in using personal autonomy as a moral criterion. Raymond Belliotti points out some problems with a libertarian approach, which stresses voluntary exchange and free interaction. The libertarian criteria have been faulted for not giving adequate consideration to the social context in which decisions are made, thereby treating the persons who make decisions too abstractly, as rational makers of choices in pursuit of their self-interest.[4]

If we are going to be realistic about human autonomy, we must recognize that it is limited in the lives of many people by customs and the circumstances of their lives. If we are to recognize the autonomy of people with whom we have dealings, including sexual relationships, we must take account of these limitations. Just getting a person to agree to something may not be enough; the consent may not be informed or freely given. A person who has been treated badly and is now very insecure, or who has been taught that it is necessary to please people always, might consent to something that is not beneficial or really what the person would prefer if not under duress or in circumstances that distort understanding of what is in the person's interest. Sharon Bishop Hill writes about the kind of education to which many girls were subjected and to which some girls might still be subjected. They were taught domestic skills and led away from combative sports, and they did not learn simple mechanical skills. They were not informed about work and professional opportunities for women outside the home. They were praised for being obedient, patient, and not demanding.[5] Under circumstances similar to these, a person's autonomy is severely limited, even when the person is doing what is desired and willed. Feminist critiques of romantic love and of marriage throw light on the problem some people find with liberal approaches to sexual morality.[6]

Cases in which a person cannot act freely pose special ethical problems. Cases in which a person is freely willing to do something that will be destructive might call for acting against the person's autonomy, but these are difficult situations. To act responsibly requires good judgment, integrity, adequate knowledge, and often courage.

If people often are not able to act with full autonomy, and if autonomous decisions are not always the wisest and most helpful ones, why is autonomy a moral value? It is a value because we are not treating people with respect and fairness unless we acknowledge their autonomy, even assisting them in acting more freely when they need this help. Not respecting a person's autonomy is failing to treat that individual as a human being. This aspect of respect for people plays a role in a number of moral issues.

In medical ethics it is generally agreed that medical procedures that might significantly affect a person should never be carried out without securing, if possible, that person's informed consent. Recently, when my wife and I refinanced the mortgage on our house, our agreement and the papers we signed did not take final effect for a period of time. Why was this? It was to make sure that we fully understood what we were agreeing to and that it was what we wanted. What applies to ethical medical and business practices also applies to sexual encounters. We can see readily that some sexual practices violate, while others respect, the autonomy of the person whom one is encountering. Autonomy can become one of our primary criteria in making moral judgments, including judgments about sexual actions.

Mutuality is closely related to the recognition of autonomy, which will usually be one aspect of the practice of mutuality. It is difficult to make any sense of the notion of two people's mutually enslaving each other. The double reciprocal incarnation of which Sartre wrote is an experience of mutuality and freedom. Becoming one's body does not take away one's freedom; it does not make one's glands more powerful than one's love of beauty and desire for companionship. The experience of double reciprocal incarnation involves both people in the same way. Each is aware of the self and responding to the other. The mutuality of the experience is a moral value that is realized in the response of each to the other. This kind of mutual responsiveness can be contrasted with other encounters in which one person is responding only to needs or desires of the self.

Lois Pineau explains what needs to follow the response to the other's desire. She writes of "communicative sexuality," in which each person is concerned that the desire be mutual. The sexual partners will be sensitive to the responses of the other, much as a good conversationalist is sensitive to the other person in the process of communication, not just concerned with the content of the talk. In a sexual encounter, the good lover will not be concerned just with having an orgasm but will value the other person's pleasure and will accept responsibility for knowing the other person's desire.[7]

One indication of how well a couple succeed in acting in mutual responsiveness and in respect for each other's autonomy is the way they feel after the encounter. When one of the people feels "used," which usually means used badly or unfairly or hurtfully, something has gone wrong or someone has behaved wrongly. When one or both of the people feel frustrated or angry, someone has been badly used, or the motivation for the encounter was to possess, to control, or to dominate the other person. This suggests the approach to sexual encounter that Sartre said is doomed to failure.

We have seen the moral importance of respect for the sexual partner, including respect for that person's freedom and right to make decisions about things that are important in the person's life. We have seen the moral significance of mutuality, with both people engaging in the encounter in response to the attractiveness of the other person and the other person's attraction to the sexual partner. In addition to these values in the relationship, we can see the importance of fairness, which should follow from respect and mutuality. Another important aspect of a morally good sexual encounter is that no harm is done to oneself or to the partner. In fact, both people should intend good for the other. Sara Ruddick writes of reciprocal benefits in good sexual experiences; certainly such benefits should be desired not only for oneself but for the partner.[8]

The ideal of a mutual relationship with both partners acting autonomously will probably be a basic part of any sound sexual morality, but we need to take a careful look at the level of mutuality that should be morally requisite. Belliotti examines the views of Vincent Punzo, John Hunter, and Roger Scrunton,[9] who argued in different ways that morally good sex is sex with love, an intimate sharing between two persons who are deeply concerned with each other. He sees a tendency in those who argue for sex with love to put forward a "false dichotomy" between love in which there is a unity of selves and the activity of "sexual marauders" who have no regard for the humanity of their partners.[10] Is sex without a complete unity of selves immoral? Surely there is a very broad area between the perfect intimacy, harmony, and mutuality that we can see as an ideal and the vicious sex of the marauder who treats the partner as a mere object. As Alan H. Goldman pointed out, sex can appropriately communicate other emotions than romantic love, or it can be "plain sex" that is not a means to anything else.[11] If a couple mutually desire physical contact with each other, and the reasons for this desire can be of many kinds, what might make their sexual encounter morally wrong would not be the fact that they are not in love. Brutality, deception, coercion, and a number of moral wrongs could make their intercourse wrong. We should be reasonable about this. Although brutality is almost always wrong, coercion is risky, but may be necessary in some cases, as we have seen. Wrongful deception should not be excused on the ground that some deceptions are harmless, even well meant. Common sense shows us the difference between exaggerated ascriptions of beauty or charm and lies about one's marital status, health, or intentions regarding the relationship.

Using being in love as the criterion of morally right sex fails in several ways. It fails as a justification of sexual engagement. Being in love does not justify any and every relationship. Concerns about commitments already made, the welfare of the couple and other people concerned, and other moral considerations must be faced. Being in love is also inadequate as a negative basis of judgment. To say that a sexual relationship is morally wrong because the man and woman are not in love is to fail to see that there is a difference between immoral sex and sex that is less than ideal, even poor and disappointing sex. Although love and intimate sharing can be the most rewarding basis for sex, failing to find such a happy relationship need not be seen as morally wrong. Belliotti suggests that sex without love can meet a person's need for adventure, emotional liberation, even shared risk. People who engage in sex without love need not be pictured as moral monsters who care nothing for their partners.[12]

There is no firm evidence that less than ideal sex prevents better sex later. Warnings of harm are based on speculation. As we will see in the chapter on pornography, the claim that immature approaches to sex prevent growth into more mature sexuality is not well founded. When people are not dealing wrongly with each other, they probably deserve no condemnation when their sex lives are not of the richest and most rewarding kind. Better sexual satisfaction, with love and intimacy, might come to them when circumstances are more fortunate.

The Body in Good Sex

Jean-Paul Sartre's concept of embodiment in sexual relationships indicates other criteria for evaluating sexual relationships. As we saw in chapter 2, Thomas Nagel used Sartre's concept of a double reciprocal incarnation in explaining his concepts of good sex. Sara Ruddick also employs Sartre's notion of double reciprocal incarnation to clarify her concept of completeness in a sexual relationship. Nagel and Ruddick both stress the aspects of doubleness and reciprocity, which are morally important and can be seen in relation to Kant's idea of not using a person as a sex object. Ruddick's concept of completeness is based on the importance of occasions when people "become" their bodies, when they are conscious of bodily activity. Sexual acts should involve such embodiment.[13] The basic aspect of embodiment, of consciously living our bodies, is important in itself, both for Sartre's understanding of sexuality and as a point of moral reference. Many people have a difficulty with accepting themselves as embodied persons, and this can have significant consequences. Sara Ruddick cites the work of psychologists who have documented the ill effects of dissociating oneself from one's body.[14]

Living one's body in sexual encounter, becoming one's body in a double reciprocal incarnation, is morally significant. Failure to become one's body through dissociation from the body in sex can be harmful emotionally, psychologically. It also stands in the way of receiving benefits that a sexual encounter can provide. It seems clear that the benefits to be received from sexual activity are morally significant. The moral principle is clear: activities should not cause harm and should lead to the realization of available benefits.

I have argued that it is a mistake to understand sexuality as merely biological, which is an incomplete view of human sexuality. In the same way, it is a mistake to deny the bodily aspects of sexuality. To deny the body leads to an incomplete view of sexuality. Being honest about our bodily nature is necessary if we are to realize our needs as human persons. Denying the importance of being living bodies can be morally damaging.[15]

Sex and Marriage

To many people, the only question of moral importance is whether the man and woman engaged in sexual activity are married. Sexual activity outside of marriage is often called promiscuity. The concept of promiscuity is somewhat vague, however, and for many people the term does not have a clear descriptive content but carries with it a great deal of emotive and hortatory force. Dictionary definitions do not clarify the moral aspects of the notion; the root notion in most dictionaries is that of being "indiscriminate." This hardly captures the sense of what seems to be involved. We might romanticize the love of one person, even if little discrimination went into selecting the object of affection, whereas the "choosy" person who might have high standards of beauty or social standing for his or her several love relationships is seen as a moral monster. The notion of promiscuity seems to refer to relationships outside of marriage, and usually it implies more than one partner. Frederick Elliston says that a numerical criterion is not adequate; some people call a person who has had one affair promiscuous, whereas others use the term to indicate that several or many partners have been involved with the person. Whether a person is considered promiscuous or not depends on current social standards and the moral codes in effect at the time. Elliston considers the terms *free love* and *recreational sex* misleading. He defines promiscuity as sex with a series of adults, outside of marriage, with no commitments.[16]

Elliston examines several arguments that seek to show that sex with a series of adults, outside of marriage, and with no commitments is morally wrong. One argument is based on the connection between sex and reproduction. Contraceptive technology has lessened the impact of that connection, and Elliston holds that promiscuity does not rule out commitment to care for offspring. The argument tends to focus on the question of whether the traditional family is the best place to rear children. Promiscuous relationships entered without intention of having children would be condemned by the Roman Catholic view of the two functions of sexual union. (See chapter 3 for discussion of this view.) One argument against promiscuity is that it is a threat to monogamous marriage. This argument assumes that promiscuity does actually have an adverse effect on marriage and that monogamy is morally superior to alternative arrangements, assumptions that Elliston does not treat as obviously true. He rejects the claim that promiscuity always involves lying, cheating, and exploiting. One claim is that personal emotional security and growth require monogamy, and promiscuity shows a lack of self-discipline, respect, and consideration for persons, claims that Elliston questions. He asks whether the promiscuous person is lacking in self-discipline for refusing to be guided by a principle he or she rejects. He does not think the promiscuous person is necessarily disrespectful. He is inclined to think the question of promiscuity is an aesthetic or prudential question more than a moral one.[17] Since adultery seems to many people to raise more serious issues than other forms of sex outside of marriage, adultery and the concept of marital fidelity are treated in chapter 6.

Does Sex Raise Moral Issues?

Are moral issues involved in sexual behavior? Because of the extent to which human personality, personal needs, the vulnerability of individuals, and social interests are involved, it seems to me that the burden of proof is on the person who claims that sexual behavior is not a matter of moral concern. Deciding which behaviors are morally right is seldom a simple matter, raising questions over which responsible people disagree, in part because our psychological knowledge is limited. Complicated social and economic issues are also involved.

One thing I am convinced we should not do is reduce questions of sexual morality to the one issue of whether the partners are married, even though marriage may be one aspect of the question. It seems very clear that being married does not make any and all behaviors morally right. Abusive or unfair behavior is not made right by benefit of clergy. Questions about sex outside of marriage are more difficult. Does it make any moral difference whether the two people in a sexual union are married or unmarried? It clearly makes a moral difference if it makes other sorts of difference. Does being unmarried make hurtful a situation that would not have been harmful if the two people were married? It could do so, in situations such as a pregnancy when the two people are unable to marry or should not marry.

The people primarily involved in a sexual relationship should consider the effect of their actions upon other people who rightfully have a role to play in their lives. Parents, children, and spouses may have strong moral claims. Weighing such claims requires the exercise of judgment, because things must be balanced against other things. There are times when the claims of other people should be over-ridden by the needs and legitimate interests of the couple, but the right to do this should not be assumed, just as it should not be assumed that the desires of parents or children should always have priority. When should the needs and desires of a couple take precedence over the wishes, even the moral principles, of parents? When should two older people refuse to restrict their activities to that which their grown children approve?

General answers to such questions will not be adequate for every situation. We have, however, a number of moral guidelines that can be applied to making these decisions. In using these guidelines, it is important not to become too abstract and lose sight of important factors in the particular situation. For example, we should be concerned about hurting other people by our actions. The hurts are not abstractions, but actual matters that can be considered in detail. We might consider what kind of hurt, how serious is the hurt, the consequences of the hurt, and the possibility of making amends. We can consider the difficult matter of how much another person has a right to expect of us. Previous commitments do not bind us absolutely, but they are concrete elements of a situation that we should not ignore. Saying that morally significant decisions require good judgment is not a way to avoid responsibility. Good judgment is employed within specific contexts in which there is usually enough information available and enough applicable moral guidelines to enable us to make judgments on which we can act with a high degree of confidence.

Sex and Adolescents

Does the sexuality of adolescents raise special issues? What kind of education should young people be given? Should they be expected to abide by special restrictions not required of mature adults? School boards and communities are sharply divided on these issues.

Some people feel more secure in simplifying the matter by teaching sexual abstinence to young people. As is the case with most simple solutions to complicated problems, this is likely to fail. One thing that is almost certain to do more harm than good is any form of telling children and young people anything that is not true. Fear is probably the least adequate motive for governing sexual behavior. Respect for people in positions of authority is lost when young people have any reason to think that they have not been told the full truth or that they have been manipulated in an effort to make them behave in a way that is pleasing to their elders.

It would help us to know more about the effects of sexual activity and sexual relationships upon young people. We have plenty of theories, but we need more scientific information. The opinions of social workers, psychological counselors, and physicians are not scientific information. These people, as honest and well intentioned as they may be, are not engaged in careful scientific research. The people with whom they work do not provide them an unbiased sample, and they do not have a good research design. These people are engaged primarily in helping people, not studying them. They are in a good position to suggest hypotheses about the effects of certain behaviors upon young people, but they are not in a good position to test these hypotheses scientifically.

What contributions can philosophy make to answering moral questions about the behavior of young people? Questions about respecting the freedom of those who have not reached full adulthood are philosophical issues. It seems obvious that it is appropriate to act paternalistically toward young children. At what age is a paternalistic approach a violation of freedom? The answer can be stated simply: it is no longer appropriate when the person is capable of responsible freedom. Recognizing that a person is capable of this freedom is not so simple, and it does not seem to come automatically with a certain age. A number of things seem to be involved. Knowledge and self-understanding are part of it. A reasonable degree of self-control and an ability to think ahead and to act for the sake of future goals are necessary parts of responsible freedom. There is no set age at which a person gets the ability to recognize what is in his or her best interest and the strength to act upon this understanding. Some people seem never to get it; others get it fairly early. Ability to handle emotions, including affection, does not come to everyone at the same age. In many people, a secure childhood with plenty of affection from parents and other family members gives the strength to handle affectional relationships early in life. For other people, deprivation in childhood creates a craving for affection that often leads the person to accept hurtful relationships.

The needs of young people, and the moral guidance they should be given, do seem to be different from what more adult people need. In general, there seems to be considerable advantage in not rushing into sexual relationships for which the person will be better prepared as an adult. It is important, however, that the moral guidance given young people not be negative. The same values that adults can realize in sexual relationships can be realized in a growing way by young people.

Moral admonition should focus on the positive factors of self-respect and respect for others, of affection and the enjoyment of other people, and of personal growth throughout one's life. Sexuality is one of the most significant aspects of being a person, in all phases of life. It is experienced differently in different periods of life, but it need not be thought of as something postponed while one is young, any more than it needs to be something to be abandoned when one is old.

Must We Be Relativists?

We can see that sexual ethics must deal with some complex issues. Applying old, familiar principles and new insights to matters of sexual morality can be difficult and demanding. Disagreements can arise even when intelligent and reasonable people confront certain issues.

It might seem easier to fall back on an authority and avoid having to make difficult decisions, but there is a price to pay for avoiding the acceptance of moral autonomy. Authoritarian codes of conduct often leave many people unfulfilled and unable to grow and develop. The codes often require not only the sacrifice of what would bring joy and pleasure to a person but the sacrifice of the means to become a stronger, wiser, more effective person.

We lose rich moral insights when we refuse to accept a number of values in making decisions about sexual behavior. There is no need to reduce all our values to one central value. Even if this can be done, we do not gain anything by it. Reducing the values of friendship, amity, trust, and love to pleasure, for example, does not give us a better understanding of the several values. It is an exercise once deemed necessary by philosophers who felt a need to reduce all values to one. We really have no such need to simplify our understanding of morals.

In addition to accepting a number of values, we can accept a number of moral principles without falling into relativism. We must justify using each moral principle by clear insight into the difference between one moral context and another, and one kind of moral judgment and another. We must understand why a principle that does not give significant guidance in one situation provides the needed guidance in another.[18]

Why should we be concerned about avoiding moral relativism? We do not need to review the philosophical discussions of the inadequacy of certain kinds of relativism to see why relativism is unacceptable.

We have only to think of the sexual practices of many cultures in the past to see that some of them were hideously wrong. In fact, we know of practices in the present that no right-thinking person can condone. Genital mutilation of young girls, which is practiced in a number of countries to keep women from enjoying sex and being tempted to stray from the husband's domain, is a clear example of a morally unacceptable custom. Some practices of our own culture are morally suspect. A few people refuse to criticize practices of cultures that permit slavery, subordination of women, and other behaviors that we would not accept at home, but there are very powerful philosophical arguments to rebut that kind of moral relativism.[19]

We must be clear about one thing. Accepting moral autonomy does not lead to accepting anything whatever as good behavior. In fact, it probably leads to even higher standards than those of the authoritarian, who often becomes quite clever at finding loopholes in the literal codes. To insist on personal autonomy, rejecting authoritarian moral codes, is not to accept the subjectivist view that morality is just a matter of personal opinion. When one behavior is deemed morally right in one circumstance, and another behavior is accepted as right in another situation, the difference rests on the actual differences in the situations. It is a matter not of opinion but of the different consequences of doing something in one context or in another. It is a matter of real differences between doing something that is hurtful, dishonest, or unfair in one situation and doing the same thing in a situation in which it is beneficial, fair, and honest. Jumping up and down and shouting is appropriate behavior when one is a cheerleader at the ball game. It would be awful behavior at a funeral. We simply cannot talk adequately about a behavior without revealing the context. Within the situation, the ambiguity associated with actions described abstractly usually disappears.

Sometimes people get confused when philosophical ethics does not uphold one and only one answer to a moral issue. It is possible that more than one behavior will be morally correct in a situation, but other actions in the situation will be wrong. There are sometimes several ways to do good, to be honest, to be fair. One interesting example is that we unanimously recognize the need to care for infants and young children. Can we say that the parents of the child have an inescapable moral responsibility of caring for their offspring? In our society, that seems to be the case, but there are societies in which the mother's brothers are given this responsibility, and it seems to work out well in those places. This does not make the matter one of personal opinion. It is a matter of what accomplishes the morally right goals of the society.

Can differing sexual practices be morally right within the same society? Can two different decisions about a situation be morally right? If both of the practices, if both decisions, stand up to sound moral criteria, why should they not both be right? Life is not so simple, and social norms are not so simple, that we must condemn every action that differs from the one we adopt. The couple who marry before engaging in sex and the couple who decide to marry when the woman becomes pregnant might both be acting responsibly. Before we say that one couple is not morally responsible, we need to identify the reason. Is the behavior harmful, a failure to respect the autonomy of one partner, based on lack of mutuality, dishonest? Then we are right to condemn it. If we can find no moral fault, we have no moral right to condemn behavior that is simply different from our own.

Sexual ethics, as other aspects of ethics, is not arbitrary or whimsical. Standards of sexual behavior should be based on the needs of humans, the needs of a just and democratic society, and the need to preserve the natural environment, along with widely accepted moral values such as justice, fairness, and respect for people. Codes of behavior developed to meet the needs of earlier societies are not adequate for our lives today. Some aspects of these old codes may well become parts of our contemporary moral practices, but this is not because they are old and revered but because they still work for us. Some aspects of old sexual codes were ways of preserving certain economic aspects of the old culture or social divisions within the society. Some of them we now find morally abhorrent because they were unjust or prevented some people from developing as human beings.

If we are to have adequate moral guidance, we must not rely on abstract and very general concepts that do not grow out of our experience and knowledge of human beings. We must not think of sexuality as separate from other aspects of life. Sexual ethics cannot be isolated from considerations of economic justice and political justice.

Many people are concerned about sexual morality in modern culture. There seems to be a lot of confusion about sexual ethics. Should sexual ethics be taught in schools? For many people, this is the only place where they might learn about sex. It is important, however, that teaching sexual ethics not be an attempt to indoctrinate. The kind of sex education some groups wish to see would preach the official code of some religious group, a code that might not reflect an adequate understanding of human nature and human needs. Some people advocate a sex education that is completely negative, telling people only what they ought not do, and possibly giving the impression that sex is a dubious part of life. This kind of teaching would do more harm than good. Sex is too important to leave it to those who are afraid of it.

Adequate teaching of sexual ethics must do more than advocate certain behaviors and warn against others. Especially in a pluralistic society such as ours, it is important that people learn why some practices are good and others bad. It is important that people understand the basic values involved, so that they will be able to make good judgments in new and unexpected situations. Sexuality is an important aspect of human life, and sexual ethics is an important aspect of living well.

~ 6 ~

Adultery and Fidelity

Although many people consider adultery to be morally wrong, without question, and many people have adultery in mind when they use the term *immorality,* some moral philosophers have seen the question of adultery as a complicated one. Joseph Fletcher held that the morality of adultery depends on the circumstances and the motivation of the people involved. Richard Wasserstrom recognized that the promise breaking and deception usually involved in adultery tend to make it a moral matter, but he saw that changing ideas of marriage and sex make the issue complicated. Richard Taylor espoused a code of ethics to be employed *within* an adulterous relationship.[1]

Originally the commandment against adultery in the Hebrew scriptures may have been a defense of the male's property right to the wife.[2] It became a law to defend the family and the relationship between the wife and husband, and traditional moral theology condemns adultery as "a moral violation against marriage."[3]

Richard Wasserstrom raises the question of what makes adultery a matter of moral significance. In what respects does adultery fall under the domain of morality? This question should be faced before we examine arguments that are made against adultery.

If we define adultery simply as extramarital sex by a married person, it would not be wrong by definition. The definition is "neutral" in that it does not state that the behavior is morally wrong or define it in terms of something generally considered wrong, such as promise breaking. Some acts, such as promise breaking, are wrong prima facie; they are taken as wrong immediately unless there are some extenuating

76

circumstances that make what is ordinarily a paradigm case of wrong-doing morally acceptable in the particular situation. If adultery is defined in terms of promise breaking, it might be wrong by definition. This might not mean that it is always wrong, in fact, but it would always be a matter of moral concern. Wasserstrom notes that adultery involves the breaking of what is generally recognized as a serious promise. The breach may be more serious than other promise breaking, because the promise is especially important to people, and breaking it can cause more pain and hurt than other broken promises. The "wronged" spouse may have had difficulty keeping the promise but kept it anyway. More important, adultery may be viewed by the spouse as rejection, as loss of affection. Our society makes a connection between affection and sexual intimacy; it sees a correlation between sex and love. Sex is taken to be more in our society than bodily enjoyment; it is taken as the confirmation of a special relationship.[4]

If adultery is defined in terms of deception, the reason for considering it a moral issue seems obvious. The adultery shares the wrongness of deception. Even if nothing is said by the adulterous spouse, there is a tacit deception because of the promise made at marriage. Adultery is viewed as a "deception of a deeper sort," since the love that is thought appropriate to sex is considered to be necessarily exclusive; in adultery either the spouse or the extramarital partner is deceived about feelings.[5]

Some people would take issue with viewing adultery as wrong by its very nature. It might be held that the connection between sex and love is no longer an accurate reflection of the way people understand sexual intimacy. It might be argued that sex should not have the meaning it has had. Perhaps sex and love should be separated. Perhaps love should not be exclusive. It is hard, however, to get around the fact that for most people sexual exclusiveness is still taken to be an essential part of the nature of marriage; it tends to establish the existence of marriage. The issues of a broken promise and deception cannot be avoided if the adulterous spouse professes a more modern view of sex than that of the other spouse. Even if both spouses and the partner in adultery have adopted a new view of sexual intimacy, there could still be problems, since marriage is a social, not just a private, arrangement.[6]

Adultery has been condemned on the grounds that it is destructive of the institution of marriage. A moral prohibition of adultery probably has helped hold some marriages together. It is not clear, however, that the argument based on supporting marriage is an argument for the immorality of extramarital sex. It is not clearly a moral argument like arguments based on breaking promises and deceiving. The argument shows an instrumental, but maybe not the moral, value of the prohibition of adultery. The argument supports a hypothetical imperative; it must be joined with arguments showing that marriage is morally necessary.[7]

Another argument against adultery claims that it threatens the institution of the family, which it well might do. Sexual exclusiveness has played a role in the development and maintenance of nuclear families. The moral prohibition of adultery may have held some families together. It is not clear, however, that an argument based on protecting the family is clearly a moral argument like arguments based on breaking promises and deceiving. As the argument about protecting marriage, the argument shows an instrumental, but maybe not an inherent moral, value of the prohibition of adultery, so it, too, supports only a hypothetical imperative. Of course, many people are convinced that the nuclear family is a critically significant moral necessity, but this needs to be shown, not taken for granted. The prohibition of adultery is good if some psychological theories are true, but it is a mistake if other theories are true.[8] In chapter 11, we examine arguments for and against the nuclear family.

Richard Taylor has written a book on love affairs in which he proposes ethical rules for those having affairs and the spouses of those having affairs. Many people find this shocking, but it is a serious book that raises important moral issues. Taylor holds that if love and affection are good, "free expression of passionate love cannot be bad, except for its effects." Society has restricted the free sexual expression of affection because it has seen the effects of unrestricted sexual expression as very bad. Society has imposed rules and insisted on ceremonies, but Taylor does not think that this has worked. He says that the government and the church do not create marriages. The view that marriage is created by church or government confuses morality and law. The government can make marriages legal, but it cannot determine the morality of marriage or of the love relationship.[9] Traditional pastoral theology supports Taylor's position in a way. According to traditional theology, the couple marry each other and the church blesses their union. Members of the clergy who talk about how many couples they have "married" are talking carelessly. The fact that husband and wife make the marriage does not lesson the proper concern that society has to protect the institution of marriage. Taylor does not recognize that the laws of society have a broader function than the coercion of individuals who feel repressed by their marriages. The law is one way society teaches its values and supports the moral codes it deems necessary to the functioning of civil life.

The question of whether the effects of free expression of affection are damaging enough to justify legal control of marriage and moral rules against adultery still remains. Undoubtedly, most moral philosophers consider the expression of affection a good thing, but many people believe that its expression in an adulterous relationship is immoral, and other people think adultery has harmful effects that make this expression of affection less than a complete good. Fletcher describes some situations in which he says an extramarital relationship is justified by being the most loving thing to do, but many people reject his approach, especially those who think that no sexual act of love is morally good unless it has the blessing of the church.[10]

Taylor makes some significant points that even those who are convinced that adultery is always wrong might find insightful. Those who think that adultery might be justified in some situations might benefit from his rules, which we will look at shortly.

Taylor attacks some misconceptions about fidelity. He opposes the view that sexual exclusiveness exhausts the ethic of marriage. He thinks it is a mistake to consider infidelity synonymous with adultery. He holds that a person who never commits adultery can be unfaithful to a spouse and gives the example of a husband who hides his affluence from the wife.[11] I have seen cases of this, one in which a wife became a laughingstock when, at a charity bazaar, she called her husband to ask if they could afford some small item. She was the only woman in the room who did not know that her husband could easily afford to buy and discard everything on the table. Unfaithfulness is the violation of any trust. One can be unfaithful to a child, and a person can be unfaithful to a spouse in many ways. I think it is unfaithfulness to a spouse to refuse to share some aspects of family life with him or her. Perhaps the most common thing is keeping the family finances secret. It is also unfaithfulness to a spouse to prevent that person from having the freedom, if not the encouragement, to develop as a person.

Of course, that there are numerous ways in which people are unfaithful to spouses does not make adultery any less an act of unfaithfulness. Whether adultery is ever justified is a difficult question that may never be resolved to the satisfaction of everyone. This does not mean that this is just a matter of individual opinion. What was said about the sources of moral guidance and the nature of moral judgment in the chapter on sexual ethics applies to adultery as it does to other issues of sexual ethics.

Taylor is right, I believe, in challenging some commonly held ideas about marriage and extramarital relationships. His belief that jealousy is a destructive passion, with no redeeming features, deserves careful consideration. He seems to be correct in thinking that the source of jealousy is possessiveness. In its crudest form, a person might consider the spouse as a possession. A person who would deny thinking of the spouse as a possession might feel that the spouse is obligated to give sexual congress only to the husband or wife. Some people seem to feel unfairly treated because what should be theirs has been taken by another. Even when the angry spouse might speak in terms of injustice done him or her, an element of possessiveness lies at the heart of the feeling of having been wronged. A spouse might think that punishing the offending spouse in some way is justified, even a moral duty; however, we should not accept the angry righteousness of the offended spouse uncritically. Taylor says the possessiveness and jealousy involve the wrongness of treating a person as an object, and he calls it a perversion of love.[12]

Raymond Belliotti pointed out to me another side of marital possessiveness that Taylor overlooks. The offended spouse has suffered a severe blow to self-identify. For most people, their marriages have an important place in their sense of who they are, and a threat to the marriage is also a serious threat to their personal security.

Taylor's rules for the spouses of those who are having love affairs counter what many offended spouses feel entitled to do. He says that they should not spy or pry; the right to know is only the right to ask. His rules oppose confrontations and entrapment, which he sees as efforts to humiliate. "Stay out of it," he advises as the most effective thing to do.[13]

Taylor's suggestions go along with the advice that many marital counselors give. Adultery does not always cause the end of a marriage; some couples report that their marriage is better after an affair than it was before, probably because the couple learned to talk about themselves and come to more self-understanding and understanding of the other. Only a small percentage of partners in adulterous affairs become the new spouses, and couples get back together for many reasons. In some cases it might just be easier to reconcile than to face making a new life, but in many cases there is real love between the spouses that is stronger than the attraction to the extramarital partner. An extramarital affair means different things to different people, and it would be a mistake to see adultery as always a signal that the spouse is no longer loved or is rejected. Taylor mentions that feelings between partners in adultery are seldom as rich or meaningful as those in the marriage. The married partners have many things holding them together: shared affection, memories, shared projects, and children.[14]

Taylor does not present his rules simply as the practical approach to the adultery of a spouse but proposes them as also the morally right thing to do, based on the wrongfulness of using a person as a thing and causing humiliation.[15] Although we can sympathize with the hurt and angry spouse, we need to see that there is nothing noble in the desire for revenge and that there might be a great deal morally wrong with it.

Taylor also offers rules for lovers. This is shocking to some people who cannot conceive of moral rules for people who are doing what they consider morally wrong in itself. Taylor's rules can be seen as insightful, however, even if the sexual union itself is not one to be approved of morally. Taylor writes of "extramarital fidelity," which calls for honesty and the avoidance of misrepresentation and concealment. He says lovers should be honest about other relationships and matters such as health and money. He says that lovers should not exhibit or boast (maybe this could apply also to taking a "trophy wife" or a husband for status), should never deliver ultimatums, and should not abandon.[16]

Some of my students find it strange that Taylor advises the straying lover to refrain from doing to the extramarital partner what is being done to the spouse. Raymond Belliotti sees this as calling for more moral integrity in the affair than in the marriage. Taylor's counsel is oddly structured, giving instructions to the offended spouse about moral treatment of the offender and to the straying spouse about moral treatment of the lover, but the right treatment of the offended by the offending spouse is neglected.

Is adultery a moral issue? Are there matters involved that are clearly of moral concern? It would be very hard to support the position that adultery is not a moral issue. The degree to which human personality, personal needs, the possibility of great hurt, and the possible effect of the behavior on children and other people closely related to those who enter an adulterous relationship make it unlikely that a strong case can be made for not seeing adultery as a moral issue. The burden of proof clearly falls on those who do not consider it a moral concern.

Establishing that adultery is a moral issue does not answer the question of which behaviors are morally right and which wrong. Responsible people can disagree about a particular case because a number of factors may need to be weighed, and different people might weigh them differently. An adequate knowledge of what the relationship between wife and husband has been like may be difficult to acquire. It is not a simple matter to make judgments about motivation or to understand how the participants see their situation. The values and the disvalues involved might not be easy to assess.

Responsible people might hesitate to generalize about adultery. They might not feel qualified to condemn all cases of adultery. In part this hesitation may stem from our limited psychological knowledge. There does not seem to be a consensus about the causes or the effects of adultery, and this might vary from case to case. Many people are still making up their minds about what marriage should be. The nature of the obligation people are accepting when they marry is not clear; the words of the ceremony might seem clear enough, but many people do not take these words literally or in a juridical sense or expect other people to take them so. A number of theoretical issues about male and female relationships, about the making of promises and depending upon promises, and about the stages in people's lives arise and deserve to be taken seriously.

The time when we could be satisfied with making general judgments and avoiding the need to examine particular cases may be over for thoughtful people. It seems that many people are hesitant to judge the behavior of other people whom they do not know well. Perhaps those who need to make a decision, especially decisions about one's own behavior, will be unable to avoid thinking about the many factors involved in the case at hand. We can know, I believe, that this and other aspects of relationships are important, morally important, and that adultery is nothing to take lightly. We might be entitled to consider adultery a prima facie wrong, but that would not make it wrong in all cases. There does not seem to be any justified way to escape the hard task of careful thinking and, we would hope, insightful decision making.

~ 7 ~

Homosexuality

The need to think clearly about homosexuality has never been greater. With many homosexual people daring to "come out," more and more people will knowingly come into contact with homosexuals. There will be many opportunities to act with intelligence and understanding or to do things that are stupid and hurtful. In this chapter, we will examine some of the notions that still have currency among people who would hesitate to consider themselves homophobic. Some people think that homosexuality is a perversion. Others consider it immoral. Even others, who do not consider homosexuals wicked, think that they are sick people who need to be cured. Each of these notions raises conceptual and ethical issues.

Perversion?

The concept of *perversion* is notoriously problematic. The term carries with it the sense of behavior that is vile, warped, hurtful, and inappropriate anywhere. Avoiding these questionable moralistic notions by defining perversion statistically, as uncommon behavior, does not accomplish much. It overlooks the fact that calling something a perversion has been a way of condemning it and expressing revulsion toward it, and it uses a troublesome word when straightforward words such as *unusual* or *uncommon* work much better. Beyond a doubt, homosexuality is statistically uncommon, with estimates of the extent of homosexuality ranging from 2 percent to 20 percent of the population of the United States. Just being uncommon, however, is not a reasonable ground for condemning a practice or condition; most people are in the minority in some respects. Even if they avoid wearing bow ties or lace gloves, being Unitarians or members of Mensa, or drinking tea for breakfast or calling their mothers every day, eye color alone will make most people members of a minority, not to mention those unique fingerprints.

When most people call homosexuality perverse, they seem to mean that it is un-natural. Identifying perversion as that which is un-natural is using one obscure concept to throw light on another dark subject, but people still do it and think they are saying something significant. People really think that they have a clear and significant concept of un-naturalness. Upon careful examination, however, we will find that most talk of behaviors' being natural or un-natural is confused and devoid of any moral significance. Burton M. Leiser says that "unnatural" is "an ambiguous word whose use proves nothing so far as moral issues are concerned."[1]

Leiser refers to several concepts of un-natural behavior and shows why they have no real meaning or have no moral significance. The concept of the natural as that which is according to the laws of nature leaves very little, if anything, that is not natural. This use of the natural in reference to the descriptive laws of nature should not be confused with the concept of normative rules to govern human behavior. The notion of the un-natural as the artificial has no moral significance. Many artificial things are morally blameless, and some may be morally necessary, as some people think about wearing clothes. Perhaps saving lives through medical interventions into natural processes provides a better example of the morality of artificial things. There is certainly no moral justification for condemning as un-natural behaviors that are uncommon. Leiser points out that some things are valued because they are uncommon, such as the work of great artists.[2]

Some people take seriously the argument that it is un-natural to use parts of the body for purposes for which they are not intended. The intended purposes can be thought of theologically, as the purposes God intended, but this is not necessary. Michael Levin holds that the process of evolution selected the penis for placing semen in the vagina.[3] This notion of the natural may seem to be significant, since it can be stated in scientific terms. Burton Leiser, however, shows that it does not have the moral significance it seems at first to have. Of course, some uses of body parts can be seen to be destructive, such as cracking nuts with the teeth, but many parts of the body lend themselves well to various uses. The eyes, which must have evolved for seeing, can be used expressively, and no harm is done. The ears help hold up eye-glasses as well as hear. The assumption that the evolutionary value of a part gives its only proper use would need to be defended. Some use of sexual organs might be seen to be destructive, but receiving pleasure apart from causing a union of sperm and ovum is well accepted by most people in heterosexual intercourse, and a strong argument would be needed to show that other pleasurable sexual practices deserve to be condemned as perverse.[4]

One concept of the un-natural is contrasting it with the behavior of nonhuman animals. At first, this seems straightforward enough, but it soon can be seen to be rife with problems. We can start with the fact that behavior among nonhuman animals is quite varied between and within species. Most of the behaviors that are sometimes looked upon as human perversions are practiced by nonhuman animals, perhaps especially those we would consider more "highly" developed. Mastur-bation, homosexual behavior, sex with members of other species, and other erotic doings, not to mention infidelity to mates, are found among our nonhuman cousins.[5]

If we are safe in doing whatever nonhumans do, our behavior may be practically unlimited. The most important point, however, is that the behavior of nonhumans tells us very little about what humans should and should not do. We humans must judge behaviors on the basis of their appropriateness for us, for our human condition and possibilities. We are able to act with understanding and deliberation, and we can achieve much that is not attainable by nonhumans.

Undoubtedly, the most influential use of a concept of nature in reference to human behavior is the Catholic version of natural law theory, which holds that humans are able to comprehend through rea-son part of God's eternal law that applies to humans. Knowledge that some behaviors are natural in that they are what God intended for humans and other behaviors un-natural in that they are contrary to God's purpose seems at first to be morally significant, but there are serious problems with this approach, which is based on a theological position that many people cannot accept; it is not the case that natural law theory is based purely on reason. A more serious difficulty is the logical problems confronting any theory that bases moral right and wrong on divine commands. Logically, a command does not create a moral obligation. If it is argued that God's goodness makes divine commands an exception to the logic of ordinary commands, there must be some basis for claiming that God is good other than God's commands. If there is another basis for distinguishing good from bad, then it is not God's will that makes things good or bad. God could still command that the good be done, but it would not be his will that makes it good. We would, in this case, need to discover what makes some behaviors bad enough to merit the disapproval of God, or of any moral being. This puts us back where we were before, looking for a reasonable concept of natural and un-natural behaviors. This is what many moral philosophers do not think we have found.

There have been some attempts to explain the notion of perversion without relating it to un-natural behaviors. Thomas Nagel developed a concept of perversion as incomplete sexuality, which lacks the feature of "double reciprocal incarnation" described by Jean-Paul Sartre. See chapter 2 for Nagel's concept of good sex. According to Nagel, perversions are sex without the reciprocal arousal that he describes, which involves a sort of incompleteness. Nagel does not, however, want to make the moral judgment that unperverted sex is morally superior to incomplete sex, and he does not think that homosexual unions are perverted according to his description. Sara Ruddick also uses Sartre's concept of a double reciprocal incarnation in her explanations of what she considers good sex, but she does not think that incomplete sex is the same thing as perversion. She says that the natural sexual object is the genitals of a living person of the opposite sex, which makes homosexuality perverse. She gives little significance to perversion, however, and, citing the polymorphous sexual perversity of children, she says that perverse sexual desires are as natural as nonperverse ones.[6]

Sara Ann Ketchum considers Nagel's notion of perversion seriously lacking. It would, she says, accept rape as unperverted sex; rape can be a matter of reciprocal arousal, with the victim's fear increasing the viciousness of the rapist and the rapist's wrath arousing greater terror in the victim. In addition to involving a reciprocal effect on each other's emotions, good sex needs to be mutual, as well as reciprocal. Perversion, however, is more than falling short of an ideal of good sex; it is a preference for the reverse of the ideal.[7] Ketchum does succeed in incorporating a basis for the disapproval and revulsion that are associated with the perversion, but there is little chance that her concept of perversion will affect the common use of the term very much. For one thing, some heterosexual intercourse of married couples would be perverse by her definition. I agree that such intercourse, lacking in genuine mutuality, should be subject to moral criticism, but I fear that few people have the moral sensitivity to see the wrongness of any heterosexual sex act between married people, especially in the missionary position, even if one of the partners is not a wholehearted participant.

Roger Scrunton finds fault with homosexuality on the basis of gender rather than sex. He claims that mature sexuality requires "the opening of the self to the mystery of another gender," an adventure and taking of risk that involve taking responsibility for the experience of sex and that leads to commitment. He suggests tentatively that this helps explain the common condemnation of homosexuality as perverse. He does not claim that it justifies the judgment.[8]

Scrunton acknowledges that gender is a cultural construction, but he sees it as an effort to understand biological differences, and he says the encounter with another gender, rather than sex, is the element of mystery in sexual encounter. Scrunton's concept of gender seems to be a product of cultural lore more than scientific study. He supports his remarks about attributes associated with gender with references to Greek poetry and other literary references.[9] What he says about the importance of opening the self to the mystery of another in a sexual encounter seems sound, but he does not make the case that this must involve another gender. Far beyond all gender differences is the difference of every person from other persons. Traditional gender roles might be an obstacle to establishing a relationship, as Robert Solomon suggests.[10]

It is easy to understand why many educated people accept a view such as that of Alan H. Goldman, who argues for a statistical notion of perversion. Goldman does not consider perverted all acts that are unusual but only those that "relate to the form of the desire itself," such as a desire, not for physical contact with another person, but merely to look, to harm or be harmed, or to have contact with an object, such as clothing. These desires are not merely unusual; they are a means of sexual gratification. To call them perverted is merely statistical in that it does not have any evaluative significance. If perverted acts are morally wrong, it is because of ill-treatment of a person, not because of their connection to sex.[11] An interpretation of perversion such as Goldman's is straightforward, and it avoids use of questionable concepts such as being natural and concepts such as completeness and mutuality, which demand interpretation themselves. The statistical analysis, however, does not account for the negative feelings associated with perversion. The word *perversion* interpreted as a statistical abnormality does no work that would not be done even more directly by terms like *uncommon* or *out of the ordinary* when applied to sexual desires and means of sexual gratification. Michael Ruse holds that that which is thought of as perverted goes against cultural norms, something not culturally comprehensible. For most people, the term definitely seems to involve a value judgment.[12]

Most people will probably continue to use *perversion* to condemn behaviors that they do not understand or find repulsive. It is probably going to be a term expressing deep bias, not a word with much descriptive power. For this reason, I think we would be better off not using the concept of perversion in serious discussions of sexual ethics. In discussions of homosexuality, it seems to have no legitimate use.

Immorality?

Can we make a good case for homosexuality's being immoral, even if it is not a perversion? This claim against homosexuality seems to have a long history. Jeremy Bentham wrote several articles on the subject in 1774, 1785, and 1814–1816. He defended homosexuality, which he referred to as paederasty, against some common arguments. He held that homosexuality does not cause harm but instead gives some people pleasure. It does no harm to society, except in cases of rape. Bentham rejected Sir W. Blackstone's claim that it is an offense against peace and security, an assertion that makes no distinction between rape, which is obviously unacceptable, and consensual sex. Bentham held that Montesquieu's accusation that homosexuality debilitates those who practice it is not supported by either *a priori* argument or evidence. Nothing in the history of the practice indicates that it is debilitating. The fear that homosexuality would annihilate humanity by limiting population he rejected as unfounded. The charge that it robs women of male companionship would be a serious charge, if true, but Bentham did not think it true, since males are willing and able to bestow more sexual activity than society allows women to receive. If homosexuality did rob women of sexual partners, any punishment should not do more harm than is done by the crime.[13]

Michael Ruse notes the different attitudes toward homosexuality in ancient Greece and ancient Israel and Plato's disapproval of overt homosexuality. Kant, in his *Lectures on Ethics,* held that outside of the marriage bond, sex is using a person as a mere means. Why did he limit the possibility of a union in which people are not being used as sex objects to heterosexual marriage? He claimed that homosexuality is un-natural sex, which is not procreative. We have dealt with the view that homosexuality is un-natural, so we need not go into that again. A more important question for us is whether homosexual men and women are able to treat each other as ends, and not merely means, in a sexual relationship. Ruse argues that homosexuals can treat each other as ends. Ruse rejects the claim that homosexuality is "biologically unnatural," in the sense of being unknown in the rest of the animal kingdom and not serving a biologically useful purpose for humans, but points out correctly, I believe—that even if it were biologically un-natural, that would not justify the claim that it is immoral. Ruse thinks that for some people homosexuality is not good sex, but he believes that both Kantians and utilitarians "can and should approve of homosexual activity *per se.*" Ruse thinks that we have an obligation to work to eliminate the hatred that is directed toward homosexuals in our society.[14] It seems to me that the one incontestable moral issue related to homosexuality is the abuse that is directed toward homosexuals. There does not seem to be any sound basis in philosophical ethics for a moral condemnation of homosexuality, but hatred and ill treatment of homosexuals are clearly immoral. This can be seen in the context of utilitarianism and Kantianism.

An examination of homosexuality in the light of philosophical schools of ethics does not provide grounds for a moral condemnation. Ruse is right in seeing that utilitarian criteria of moral rightness would support the right of homosexuals to enjoy sexual unions. To ask that nonheterosexual people abstain from sexual activity would be to deprive them of pleasure and subject them to emotional pain. It seems obvious that Kant's rejection of homosexuality as un-natural was not derived from his ethical insights. The requirements that one's moral rules be those that one can will to be universally obeyed and that people be treated respectfully do not stand in opposition to homosexuality. One would not will that everyone be homosexual, and I do not know anyone who does will this. One could will that everyone love and treat with respect the person desired as a partner and willing to be a partner. It can only be wished that this responsible behavior toward sexual partners were more common among heterosexuals and homosexuals.

The growing opinion that homosexuality is not voluntary raises a matter of moral significance.[15] Moral judgments are rightly made of behavior that is voluntary. If it turns out that homosexuality is not chosen, but is an orientation with which one is born, then discussion of the morality of being homosexual will be seen to be inappropriate. Any moral considerations regarding homosexual behavior will need to be seen in this light. This is not to say that homosexuality would be morally wrong if it were freely chosen, but we might eventually have information that shows that it is not a matter of choice at all. We must be clear about what is at issue. Overt behavior seems to be a matter over which persons have a choice. The issue is orientation. Many homosexuals have sired or borne children, many after having lived as heterosexuals, but their orientation was homosexual. Joyce Trebilcot urges women to live as homosexuals as a way to further the liberation of women. This might be taken as evidence that sexual orientation can be freely chosen. It should be noted, however, that Trebilcot asks women to ignore their real sexual inclinations, which she refers to as "twinges." What she seems to be asking is that some heterosexual women live overtly as lesbians.[16]

The issue of whether homosexuality is an orientation that the person has not chosen or is a chosen "lifestyle" is very controversial. In the absence of much real information, this is a much-discussed topic. Perhaps we should be careful not to give the matter unwarranted importance. Some decisions do not hinge on the matter. Persecuting homosexuals and depriving them of civil liberties are wrong regardless of the origin of homosexuality. Even if homosexuality is not chosen, the society might have reason to see it as a social problem if it is morally wrong or socially damaging. The wrongness or the harm would have to be demonstrated, of course, and efforts to show that homosexuality is immoral or that it is a danger to society have not been widely convincing.

Homosexuals can act immorally, just as heterosexuals can. This misbehavior does not show that the sexual orientation itself is morally wrong, any more than the bad behavior of heterosexuals shows that heterosexuality is morally wrong. The less constructive aspects of what some people refer to as the homosexual lifestyle are probably less the result of the sexual orientation itself than of the refusal of the society to give social and legal recognition to homosexual unions. In a sense, our society encourages the very behaviors that offend it. Later we will examine the issue of homosexual marriages.

Sickness?

Is homosexuality not a perversion and not properly seen as a moral wrong, but instead a sickness, a mental illness? The idea that homosexuals should be seen as sick people might have seemed a kindlier approach than moral condemnation, pity instead of persecution. If there is no scientific basis for considering homosexuality a sickness, this would be misplaced kindness, in fact, not kindness at all.

The American Psychiatric Association had to deal with the way homosexuality was classified in the *Diagnostic and Statistical Manual of Mental Disorders* (DSM). This body lagged behind other professional associations in recognizing a need to change the designation of homosexuality from that of a mental disorder, as it had been deemed for about a hundred years. Finally, in 1973, homosexuality was designated a "sexual orientation disturbance." Even though it had to be recognized that homosexuality was not an illness, there was a reluctance to remove mention of it from the DSM. Some psychologists continued to see homosexuals as somehow disfunctional. Joseph Margolis sees this as an example of "the extent to which our moral prejudices masquerade as medicine." The medical profession seems finally to have recognized that homosexuality per se is not an illness.[17]

There is a clinical concern about homosexual orientation or other orientation that causes the person distress. There remains a need for counseling on the part of homosexuals who are not able to adjust to their orientation, but this unhappiness does not meet an adequate definition of illness, as indicated in the omission in the DSM-III of any reference to homosexuality as an illness. It is not the sort of condition or syndrome that can be properly classified as an illness, and it does not have an etiology suitable for such classification. Unhappiness is simply not a recognizable illness, whether it comes from sexual orientation or from dissatisfaction with one's physical appearance or financial state.[18]

Some psychologists and some religious groups claim success in treating homosexuals. What can we say to these claims? Is the idea of treating people to alter their sexual orientation justified?

Frederick Suppe points out some of the reasons why there is objection to efforts to cure homosexuality. Some psychotherapists think it is wrong to attempt to convert homosexuals to heterosexuality because the treatment would not be truly voluntary. Other people think that the concept of a cure for homosexuality strengthens prejudice and fosters persecution. If homosexuals are pressured to enter treatment programs against their wishes, or if the practice of treating homosexuals promotes prejudicial behavior toward them, these consequences of treatment programs would be a strong moral argument against treatment.

Another argument against treatment is the belief of some psychologists that treatment cannot be done successfully. Outward behavior can be changed, but if the result of this is to make a person nonsexual, not truly heterosexual, the claim to have cured the person is exaggerated. The problem seen by those who oppose treatment is that sexual orientation is not fully changed. Sexual orientation involves a number of factors: biological sex and gender identity, social sex roles, sexual behavior, patterns of interpersonal affection, erotic fantasy structure, and arousal cue response patterns. Even if a person's outward behavior is changed, so that sexual activities with people of the same sex are avoided, if the cue response patterns and the fantasy structure do not change, the sexual orientation is still homosexual. If a "cured" homosexual does not respond sexually to the same images that arouse a heterosexual person, if dreams and fantasies will not be heterosexual, it is unlikely that the person will be able to function effectively as a heterosexual. This is why therapists' claims to have changed behavior are often met with doubt. Suppe holds that the evidence of the effect of attempts to change homosexuals is not very strong and that additional research could change the matter.[19]

Are Male and Female Homosexuals Different?

In a society in which there are gender differences, whether natural or cultural in origin, it would not be surprising if female homosexuals and male homosexuals were different in the same way that male and female heterosexuals are different. Unfortunately, many of the notions about differences between men and women are part of the cultural construction of gender, and people are inclined to generalize recklessly about these differences. It is important to keep in mind what our experience should tell us: differences within groups of people seem always to be greater than differences between groups. It may be the case that women are usually more concerned about relationships and finding lasting unions than men are, but some men are dedicated to a lasting union and some women enjoy adventure, exploration, and taking chances. It may be unusual, but women of both sexual orientations can be predatory and exploitive, whereas men can be domestic and concerned about establishing a lasting relationship.

What has not been demonstrated is that homosexuality itself is the basis of gender differences between homosexual women and men. If some significant evidence is forthcoming, I will change my mind about this. In the meanwhile, I see no basis for thinking of four basic genders, male and female heterosexuals and male and female homosexuals. In my experience, which does not seem to be unusual, some homosexual males are very masculine, and some are not. Some lesbians are very "mannish," whereas some are very feminine. Some male homosexuals are promiscuous and seek frequent new partners, but I have seen the same behavior in male heterosexuals. I have seen responsibility and gross irresponsibility in people of both orientations, male and female. When it comes to differences, it seems that we are put face to face with persons, not classes of people.

Homosexual Marriage

Much of the hatred and fear of homosexuals is the result of false notions about them. Many people think that homosexuals are more predatory than heterosexuals, but this does not seem to be the case. Other people are disturbed by what appears to be irresponsible behavior of homosexual men who have many sexual partners and seem to spend a great amount of time in bars and bathhouses making sexual contacts. Certainly, it is physically dangerous to have many sexual partners and to "pick up" strangers in bars. There are both homosexual and heterosexual persons who are attracted to an approach to sexuality that many people find unattractive or even reprehensible. There may be many reasons why people choose this way of life. It is less surprising that homosexuals turn to such a life, since marriage is not allowed them.

Some homosexuals do establish long-term relationships. I recently met two middle-aged men who had been in stable relationships, for more than thirty years in one case, twenty in the other. When their mates died they moved to Florida, discovered each other, and are beginning a new relationship. This is the same as the experience of many people in Florida, most of whom are heterosexuals. Why does it happen to all too few homosexuals? The reason seems obvious in a society that does not recognize such unions and even makes them more difficult than they need to be. Perhaps the interesting question is how some homosexuals manage to have long-lasting and responsible sexual unions in spite of the many difficulties.

Should homosexual marriages be recognized? Opposition to official acknowledgment of homosexual unions is in part a result of unthinking prejudice, but many religious people oppose giving recognition to these unions because they believe that marriage is a religious institution that requires that the mates be of different sexes. Perhaps these unions could be called something other than marriages, perhaps "domestic partnerships." There could even be a number of heterosexual couples who might find the concept of a domestic partnership attractive and a way to avoid going through a religious service, or a pale semblance of such a service. There are many homosexuals, however, who believe themselves to be true Jews or Christians and who feel entitled to a religious blessing upon their union. Some religious bodies seem to be willing to bless homosexual unions, and in time others might be willing. In the meantime, it is hard to justify the refusal of our society to give them the legal and social protections that heterosexual couples can take for granted.

Some people fear that homosexual marriage would weaken the moral fabric of the society and weaken the institution of marriage and the family. We need to approach these matters realistically. The so-called traditional family, a married couple and their biological issue, is becoming exceptional. In human history, there have been numerous patterns of married life. Aside from polygamous marriages, there have been marriages of single people and various other parings of single, widowed, and divorced people. There have been varieties of age levels and mixes of age levels. Marriages have crossed class and religious bounds. All of these different kinds of marriages and other living arrangements have not destroyed the institution of marriage, and it is hard to see how homosexual marriages would destroy marriage. Frederick Elliston holds that arguing against homosexual marriage on the grounds that traditionally marriage has been associated with reproduction is anachronistic. Marriage between partners who cannot have children has always been allowed, and modern contraceptive technology has made reproduction an option that many couples reject.[20]

The argument that homosexual marriage must remain illegal to protect children from a poor environment and from confusion about their sexual identities overlooks the fact that homosexuals do raise children even without homosexual marriage. There are children from earlier marriages, adopted children, orphans of relatives, and other children who live with one or a pair of homosexual adults. Elliston believes that children living in a legally and socially recognized union are better off than children living with adults who must be secretive about their relationship. As for the fear that living with two people of the same sex will limit the social growth of a child, Elliston points out that varied social contacts can be provided, just as single parents must provide social contacts.[21]

When some people talk of the welfare of children, they seem to have something in mind of which they seldom speak directly. There is widespread fear that homosexuals would convert children they adopt or have from previous marriages to homosexuality. A better understanding of homosexuality should relieve people of anxiety about this. Homosexuality does not seem to be something that people choose or to which they can be converted. The fear that homosexuals will sexually molest children in their care is unfounded. Most molestation of children is at the hands of heterosexual male parents and relatives. People do not molest children because of sexual orientation but because of psychological problems or personal inadequacies.

Persecuting or ostracizing homosexuals and not giving their unions legal and social recognition is an injustice in itself, and it undoubtedly contributes to a weakening of the social institutions and practices that make for stability and the general welfare. It cannot contribute to social health to keep a large portion of the citizens outside of significant areas of the life of the society. The positive values to be realized in legal recognition of homosexual marriages are social justice, the freedom for homosexual men and women to choose a partner and achieve a stable relationship, the encouragement of responsible love, and the practice of citizenship and community life in ways that have been forbidden or discouraged in the past. If there are sound reasons for continuing to forbid homosexual marriages, it is the responsibility of advocates of this position to make their reasons known.

Reaching a Consensus

I believe we have resolved philosophically the more important questions about homosexuality, but resolving an issue rationally and achieving popular consensus on it are two different matters. It may take a long time to reach agreement among the less scientific and philosophical elements of society. Better understanding of the nature of homosexuality may help many people deal more reasonably with the issues. I believe most people will come to realize that homosexuality is not a lifestyle but a basic orientation that is not chosen by the homosexual, any more than most of us had to choose to be heterosexual. This is uncertain, however, and not as much depends on it as we might first assume. As people get the opportunity to know more homosexual men and women, they will see that the irresponsible life of those who cannot establish good relationships is not inevitable or even typical. I think that many Jews and Christians will find within their own traditions the basis for accepting and respecting people who are different from themselves in sexual orientation. I see the current agitation for a return to "traditional" values and modes of behavior—not that such values and behaviors ever were widespread, except in certain sectors of American society—as a kind of last-ditch effort to stave off changes in attitudes that some people find distasteful or even frightening. We can reach wide agreement on this matter and bring an end to the fear of and abuse of homosexual people. The cause of justice must win out over prejudice, both because it is morally right and because a stable and progressive society can be built on no other foundation.

~ 8 ~

The Morality of Abortion

The Main Viewpoints

The two main positions on abortion are often referred to as the *conservative* and *liberal* views. These terms are not ideal. Believing that abortion is morally right or that abortion is not a moral issue does not necessarily indicate that the person takes a liberal position on political and social issues generally. Being opposed to abortion does not, of itself, make a person a conservative. Some of the actions taken in opposition to abortion are anything but conservative. Actually, I see no justification for considering a position respecting abortion liberal or conservative in itself. Other terms, such as *prolife* and *proabortion,* are also misleading. People who work to defend embryos are accused of being indifferent to other efforts in support of life, and in some cases this seems to be true. The people who advocate keeping abortion legal do not all think abortion is morally right. For the sake of convenience, I will use the designations *liberal* and *conservative,* but they should be understood as being limited to the holding of the view that abortion is morally justified, or that it should be legal whether morally right or not, and the view that abortion is morally wrong and should not be legal.

Conservative Arguments

The conservative view is usually based on the concept of a "right to life." What is this right? A minimum interpretation is that it is a right not to be deliberately killed. Few conservatives take the broader interpretation that it is a right to the necessities of life. What it comes down to is a right not to be aborted medically. This seems to be the principle to be examined. Having a right to life does not entail having a right to everything needed to preserve that life, as can be seen in discussions in medical ethics over the right to some medical procedures for the extremely old and terminally ill.

What would give an embryo this right not to be aborted? Many conservatives usually hold that embryos have the right not to be aborted because they have a full complement of human genetic materials. Some people describe them as potential persons, but this way of talking about zygotes and embryos is not common, perhaps because liberals hold that actual persons should have more standing than potential persons. The right is claimed, then, for what we might call genetic humans. The argument is that it is human genetic material that makes an organism a human. John T. Noonan claims that conception is the "decisive moment of humanization" because it is when the new being receives the genetic code.[1]

Noonan traces the developing opposition to abortion in the Christian church from the New Testament and the early Christian community to modern times, in which opposition to abortion intensified. He writes about opposition to *pharmakeia* (abortifacient drugs) in the early community, about the issue of ensoulment, about Thomas Aquinas's views, and modern arguments about therapeutic abortion and the principle of double effect. He says that in Christianity the fetus has always been given a value apart from that of the parents. He thinks the key principles of Christian thought were love of neighbor and the equality of all human lives.[2]

Another theological ground for disapproval of abortion comes from the tradition of natural law. In chapter 3, in discussing the question of whether sex has a purpose, we saw that the papal encyclical *Humanae Vitae* stated the traditional position that every act of sexual intercourse must be open to conception. Artificial birth control was condemned by the encyclical, along with other acts, including abortion for the purpose of birth control. The rejection of birth control is based on the belief that the human person has both a natural and a spiritual vocation, which gives the purpose of sex. It is a dual purpose, to be unitive and procreative.[3] Whether abortion is ever acceptable, for therapeutic reasons, and under what conditions it could be approved, have been debated by theologians. It has been agreed by church authorities that abortion must not be approved if the purpose of the medical procedure is to destroy the embryo. If loss of the embryo is coincidental to a procedure carried out for another purpose, it might be approved by employing the complicated and controversial principle of double effect.[4]

The conservative position is not always argued from religious principles or based on the sanctity of human life. Don Marquis holds that abortion is almost always "seriously immoral," the same morally as killing an adult human being. Rather than basing his argument on the sanctity of life or on the concept of personhood or potential personhood, he says that killing is wrong because it deprives the victim of "all the experiences, activities, projects, and enjoyments that would otherwise have constituted one's future." This, he says, is one of the greatest possible losses, loss of the value of a "future-like-ours." Marquis realizes that his argument might apply to killing some nonhuman animals, as well as to killing an embryo.[5]

Marquis's argument applies to the issue of abortion a principle that is very important to many approaches to environmental ethics. We can have moral duties to entities that cannot be meaningfully claimed to have a right to life. The issue of morally right treatment of late-term fetuses, for example, might not hinge on arguments about a right to life.

Some conservatives oppose all abortions, whereas some others hold that abortion is justified in cases of rape and incest. The rationale for allowing abortion of an embryo resulting from rape or incest is not consistent with the principles on which condemnation of abortion is usually based. The embryos in these cases are just as innocent as other embryos and would have the same right to life that other embryos have. If abortion is killing innocent human beings, the wrongdoing of a parent should not be a reason to kill the embryo. Some people still blame the offspring for parental sins and hold them in opprobrium, and this might be the underlying motive for not protecting embryos who are conceived in rape or incest. I think, however, that the exception to a blanket condemnation of abortion is made for reasons of political expediency or from pastoral concern for the pregnant woman. The pastoral concern is understandable, but approval of abortion in such cases does seem to contradict principles on which opposition to abortion is based.

Liberal Arguments

Liberals hold that a right not to be killed deliberately belongs to actual persons—that is, humans who have been born alive. This position stresses having certain characteristics that entitle one to membership in the moral community. Liberals take the position that abortion is a personal and private matter and should be legal. Liberals usually deny that fetuses are human persons, so abortion is not the moral equivalent to murder, as conservatives consider it.

Mary Anne Warren examines the question of what characteristics make a person a person. An interesting thought experiment is considering what qualities would make us accept an alien from space as a member of our moral community. Warren suggests the presence of consciousness and capacity to feel pain, ability to reason, self-motivated activity, capacity to communicate, the presence of a self-concept, and self-awareness.[6] Jane English divided the concept of a person into biological, psychological, rational, social, and legal factors. She said the fetus lies in a "penumbra region," so that the question of whether it is a person cannot be answered.[7]

Which of the characteristics suggested by Warren and English are necessary to the concept of a person, a member of the moral community? All of them? Some combination of them? It is interesting that Warren does not mention physical appearance, looking like a person. Careful thought will show that appearance is a very poor indicator of personhood. A realistic statue, even one of Duanne Hanson's figures, is not accepted as a human person, even though we have a funny feeling upon discovering that what looked like a person is not one. Some people would reject immediately an alien who did not look human, but most of us are less narrow-minded. That is why the poster pictures, supposedly of aborted embryos, do not convince thoughtful people that embryos are human persons.

Most of the liberal arguments for the justification of abortion rest on the decision that embryos lack the qualities on the basis of which a being can be accepted as a member of the human moral community. Could abortion be justified in some cases even if the embryo is a human person? Jane English made an argument based on the right to self-defense.[8] This argument would only apply to cases in which the pregnancy was a threat to the pregnant woman's life or health. As limited in application as it is, English's argument is not accepted by all conservatives. Baruch Brody holds that an abortion would be justified only if woman and embryo would both die if there were no abortion. He does not grant a woman's right to defend herself if the embryo would not die if not aborted.[9]

Judith Jarvis Thomson has a famous argument that goes beyond the self-defense plea. She says that even if the embryo were a human person (which she does not believe to be the case), the pregnant woman would not always be morally responsible for bringing the fetus to term. An abortion would not always be a wrongful killing. She uses several illustrations to make the point that a person is not duty-bound to meet everyone's legitimate needs. She uses the story of a person kidnapped by the Society of Music Lovers to keep a famous violinist alive. The kidnapped person, who wakes up beside the violinist in a hospital room, has the only kidneys in the world that can keep the musician alive, but the cure requires staying nine months in the hospital. Thompson holds that the kidnapped person has no moral responsibility to stay, even for a short period of time. It would be a good thing to do, but it is not a moral duty.[10]

A frequent criticism of Thomson's argument is that the analogy is faulty; the kidnapped person and the pregnant woman are in different situations. The argument is conclusive, it is claimed, only in cases of pregnancy from rape. Only in pregnancy for which the woman is not responsible would Thomson's argument apply.[11]

I think Thomson's argument might apply more widely than is generally thought. Thomson's article deals with the question of a woman's responsibility for being pregnant. She uses several illustrations to explore this point. She asks how far a person must go in home security to avoid being responsible for a burglary. When has a person taken enough precautions? Another example is so far-fetched that it has not captured much attention, but it explores an important point. If babies grew from spores, like ferns, would a person who does not want to be responsible for a child have to cover all the windows and do away with carpets and all soft and plush material in the house to prevent any spores from becoming established in the house? There are people who think that any "indulgence" in sexual intercourse makes the woman responsible for pregnancy, no matter how carefully she has taken the prescribed birth control measures. I am not sure of this, and I do not like the snide "pay the piper" attitude many people express about sex. I think we should examine the violinist analogy a bit more carefully.

What would the person who wakes up in the hospital room have had to do to be responsible and obligated to help the violinist? Certainly the kidnapped person was not responsible, but what of less extreme cases? Would being a music lover make the person responsible? Of course not, even if the person had joined the Society of Music Lovers. Even if the person knew the musician and had visited in the hospital the day before, there would be no obligation to stay. Nothing short of full informed consent would make a person responsible for helping the violinist.

What would be analogous to informed consent in the case of pregnancy? This can be seen to be more complicated than it might first seem. I think we might get some light on this from the legal matter of contributory negligence. If a person's automobile explodes without warning and injures someone, what would make the owner responsible? Would it be necessary to have the automobile inspected by a certified mechanic every day to avoid responsibility? Would it be necessary to keep the car locked away in a fireproof garage and never drive it? Would not the routine care recommended by the manufacturer show that the owner is not guilty of contributory negligence? The couple who use state-of-the art contraception, and use it carefully, because they do not want a child are responsible for the pregnancy in a causal sense, but in a moral sense, they might not be responsible. Life cannot be lived without some uncertainty, but we are usually careful when it comes to assigning legal responsibility in what are seen as cases of accident. Perhaps we should be just as careful in respect to moral responsibility. I see no justification for assigning responsibility more quickly because sex is involved.

We cannot assume that responsibility toward the conceptus will be the same during all stages of pregnancy. To do so is to treat the matter very abstractly. There might well be a higher level of responsibility in the late stages of pregnancy. Some moderate views on abortion would support such a notion of progressive levels of responsibility. Note especially Jane English's moderate view as explained below.

When Does It Become a Person?

Most liberals on the abortion issue do not think the embryo is a human person, and most argument deals with this matter. Unfortunately it is frequently argued badly, from both sides of the issue.

The question of whether a fertilized ovum or an embryo is a human person is often argued in confused ways. It is sometimes treated as if it were a factual issue, one to be settled by more medical knowledge. We already have considerable knowledge of embryology. We know that an embryo has all the necessary parts of a human early in its development but that these are not fully developed or functional until the third trimester. We know that an embryo can experience pain in some sense but that it has not had the experiences necessary for most thought processes. Even if we learn a great deal more, medical knowledge will not tell us whether the embryo is a human person and a holder of certain rights that are guaranteed to U. S. citizens. This is not a factual issue, but a matter of decision. We will need to decide whether it is a human person. More scientific research cannot resolve the issue of when a fetus becomes a human person because this is not a scientific issue, not a factual issue. The society will resolve this issue by the way it decides certain legal questions.

A futile approach to the question of whether an embryo is a person was to identify a stage at which an embryo becomes a human person. At one time, people thought it was quickening, the time when the embryo was felt to move within the womb, that was the significant stage. We now realize, however, that the time of this movement is of little medical significance. The time of ensoulment receives little attention now, even though many people think the concept of a soul is significant. One problem was that theologians could not agree about when an embryo got a soul, and some even held that females are ensouled later than males. The main reason little is said of ensoulment now is that the conservative claim is that the fertilized ovum should be considered a human being, even if traditional theological texts held that ensoulment did not occur this soon. The major conflicting claims are that personhood begins at conception or that it begins at birth.

The one intermediate time between conception and birth that some people consider significant is the time when a fetus is viable—that is, able to survive outside the womb. Some people who think abortion is justified earlier in embryonic development object to abortion after a fetus is viable. The thinking behind this is obvious; the pregnant woman can be separated from the fetus without killing the fetus. The *Roe* v. *Wade* decision sees abortion in different light depending on the trimester for several reasons. The medical difficulty of abortion is much greater in the third trimester, so that very few abortions take place then, and these are for serious medical indications. Also, the fetus has a chance of survival outside the womb in the third trimester. The time of viability is not simple and cannot be established apart from the situation. In a large medical center, a fetus is viable sooner than it would be in more primitive conditions. With present medical knowledge, viability is not possible under any conditions before twentysome weeks. Before this time, the fetus has not developed sufficiently to survive even with medical assistance. This stage of development may set an absolute limit on viability. Further medical advances are not clearly foreseen. Babies born prematurely often have severe medical problems, and many of them do not survive.

Badly Stated Questions, Bad Arguments

If a question is put badly, the chances of answering it are decreased. People often use careless terminology in asking about the status of the embryo. This makes it unlikely that the issue will be seen clearly. A person may ask, "When does life begin?" The problem here is that the right question is not being asked. We all know that the fertilized ovum is alive, as were the sperm and unfertilized egg before it. The questioner might be trying to ask when it becomes an organism, but that is not what we need to determine. We want to know whether it is a human person, one of our fellow citizens.

Many people ask, "When does it become human?" This is not the right question either. In one sense, it is obviously human from the beginning, but the important sense still eludes us. Human genetic material identifies the embryo (or the zygote) as human, but only in an adjectival sense. It is obviously human, but only in the way a vermiform appendix is human or hair is human. The genetic material does not show that the embryo is a human person. The term *human* is ambiguous, with two distinct meanings. As an adjective, it associates something with the human species, but it need not be a person. We speak of human clothing, human customs, human habitations. As a noun, it refers to a human person, a human being. We need to consider our use of words if we want our thoughts to be clear. Badly worded questions do not address the significant concern clearly.

Mary Anne Warren shows how people on both sides of the issue use bad arguments. A traditional argument against abortion goes like this:

1. It is wrong to kill humans.
2. A fetus is human.
3. Therefore, it is wrong to kill a fetus.

What is bad logically is the "slide" of meaning, the equivocation. The first premise is self-evident only if *human* means full member of the moral community (this is the moral sense of *human,* not to be confused with the genetic sense). The first premise is acceptable only in the moral sense of *human.* The second premise is not question begging only if the genetic sense alone is intended.[12]

Warren also identifies logical weakness in common arguments used to justify abortion. Trying to justify abortion by pointing to deaths caused by illegal abortions does not face the issue of whether an embryo is a human person and whether abortion is tantamount to murder. Basing an argument for abortion on the suffering of poor women faces the same problems as the argument based on botched abortions. Poverty does not give license to act wrongly or illegally.[13]

Warren thinks that a widely employed liberal argument is faulty. That is the claim that a woman has a right to do as she will with her body. What Warren sees wrong with this argument is that it is stated as a property right. She says that a person's relation to his or her body is not the same as the relation one has to a property. Properties can be rented or sold, destroyed, or given away. Bodies are different. What we are concerned with in the abortion issue is not what a woman may do with a piece of property, but what she may legitimately do. Whatever we do, we do with our bodies, and it is precisely actions involving our bodies about which ethical questions arise. This is a special problem when another person has an interest in the action. If the embryo is a person, it might be morally wrong to take certain bodily actions.[14]

Warren would not deny that people have some kinds of rights in respect to their own bodies. The problem lies in deciding what these rights are in questions of abortion, euthanasia, use of certain medical procedures, and so forth. The fact that a woman's body is intimately involved in child bearing and in abortion makes her relation to the decision different from anyone else's. We do not need to use a bad argument to make this point.

Moderate Positions on the Issue of Abortion

The two absolute positions on the moral issue of abortion seem to make a middle ground between moral condemnation of all abortion and moral justification of any abortion the woman desires impossible. Many people, however, are not willing to denounce all abortions or to approve of all. Judith Lichtenberg points to three ways in which a middle ground is developed. A position that leans toward the conservative side in recognizing the force of arguments against abortion can also justify some exceptions to a general condemnation of abortion. Pregnancy from rape or incest, a serious threat to the health of the pregnant woman, or serious problems with the fetus can be taken as excusing conditions. The adamant conservative does not let these factors play any role in decisions about abortion. Another approach is based on the degree of development of the embryo. This is often expressed in terms of viability. Abortion, for significant cause, of an embryo too undeveloped to be viable would be approved in this approach, but causing the death of a fetus that could be delivered alive would not be accepted. With a third compromise position, a person who does not believe that abortion is morally right could argue that this is a matter of personal morality and that the government should not interfere. Lichtenberg says this position could be adopted for practical reasons, to prevent abortion from going underground with bad health consequences for pregnant women, to avoid having babies born to mothers who do not want them, or to keep government from adopting undesirable measures of enforcement.[15]

The late Jane English took a moderate position on abortion. She did not base her view of abortion on the embryo's being or not being a person or being a potential person. She recognized the great difficulty of resolving that issue. English did not adopt without reservation a conservative or liberal position. She held that abortion is sometimes justified. She found abortion, especially late in the pregnancy, to be problematical, even if the fetus is not considered a person. It is enough like a person to make killing it problematical.[16]

Daniel Callahan, director of the Hastings Institute, supports liberal abortion laws, but he takes a moderate position on the personal morality of abortion. He makes an interesting point about moral attitude. He holds that even if an abortion is justified, there should be some regret about it, a degree of moral tension.[17] I believe this is a fitting response to the ambiguity of the issue. It also indicates something important about the purpose of morality. Some people seem to think that the goal of morality is to have a good conscience. The desire for a good conscience can lead people to oversimplify important issues. Albert Schweitzer said, "We must never let ourselves become blunted. We are living in truth, when we experience . . . conflicts more profoundly. The good conscience is an invention of the devil."[18] Life is complicated, and an element of tragedy haunts our best efforts to do what is right. We need to remember this, not try to escape from it.

The Legal Issue—Choice

Most of the public discussion of abortion deals with the legal issue. Should abortion be legal? Should women have a legal right to choose abortion? If legal, should abortion be restricted? Liberals hold that the personal decision and the legal issue are separate matters. A woman should have the legal right to an abortion, regardless of the morality of the action. Conservatives do not believe that the two matters can be separated. They hold that abortion is an unjust killing and should be illegal. Strictly speaking, abortion is not murder when it is not illegal, since murder is illegal killing. Conservatives believe that abortion is tantamount to murder and is, morally speaking, murder.

These two approaches to the legal issues related to abortion seem diametrically opposed. The issue does not lend itself to easy compromise. The liberals see the conservatives as people who are trying to force their moral beliefs on other people who do not share these beliefs. They think it is quite reasonable to ask conservatives to abide by their beliefs and to allow liberals to act upon their own. The conservatives, however, see the liberals as people who are supporting the unjust killing of innocent human life. It is a violation of the rights of the embryo, and allowing abortion to occur without moral protest is unthinkable. Liberals have a hard time understanding the reason why conservatives will not allow them freedom of conscience, but with the conservative view of abortion as murder, the conservative cannot accept abortion any more than the liberals would accept the murder of living babies or adult humans. Liberals, on the other hand, do not believe that an embryo is a human person and that abortion is murder. Liberals believe that abortion is a personal and private matter that is no business of the law, except for the setting of certain medical standards. Not allowing women the choice of an abortion is restricting them unjustly and is putting some women in physical danger.

The law of the land allows abortion, restricted only by certain medical standards, for the first trimester. The medical requirements are stricter during the second trimester. In the third trimester, abortions are limited more, and seldom is an abortion performed unless there is serious threat to the woman or there are serious problems with the fetus. Most liberals do not take exception to limitations on abortion in the second and third trimesters. Conservatives, of course, believe that the law allows what is morally wrong and a violation of rights, so they attempt to make changes in the law.

The liberal, prochoice position does not require belief in the moral rightness of abortion or belief that abortion is not a moral issue. It is possible for a person who believes abortion is morally wrong to support a woman's choice in regard to abortion. This may not be a common position, but it is an interesting one because it points up some principles that are important to the liberal position. The liberal approach to legal and social issues has generally not supported legal moralism, the view holding that a government may legitimately restrict a citizen's freedom to prevent the doing of moral wrong. It has usually been conservatives who advocated restrictive laws that support a moral principle. Moral legalism has been the basis for advocacy of censorship, laws against nude dancing, laws against use of profanity, and similar matters. Liberals, on the other hand, have usually recognized only the harm principle, which holds that a government may legitimately keep people from harming other people. Less often, liberals have advocated measures based on the principle of legal paternalism, which holds that people may legitimately be restrained from hurting themselves. In respect to abortion, liberals do not consider an embryo to be a person, so the harm principle is not seen to apply to abortion. The conservative opposition to abortion might be based on the harm principle, since the embryo is considered a person. It could be based on legal moralism. Liberals, thinking about the conservatives' effort to make abortion illegal, might think that it is based only on legal moralism. Liberals consider the conservatives' action an unwarranted interference with individual freedom. If the conservatives are basing the demand for legal protection of embryos on the harm principle, the liberals' demand for freedom seems unreasonable to the conservatives. Both liberals and conservatives see themselves as defending the proper legal and moral approach.

Some prochoice advocates do not consider decisions about having an abortion to be moral decisions. Barbara Ehrenreich says that if men were subject to the discomfort of pregnancy, "pregnancy would be classified as a sexually transmitted disease and abortion would be no more controversial than emergency appendectomies." She thinks people have chosen to consider abortion a moral issue.[19] Many advocates of choice, however, do see abortion as a moral issue. From a liberal perspective, what are the moral factors to be weighed? One factor would be the consequences of giving birth or having an abortion. Endangering the health of the woman or risking serious financial or other harm to the family would be considerations. Giving birth to a seriously defective child would be a consideration. These do not automatically lead to a decision to abort, but they are matters to consider and weigh against other considerations. These are quality-of-life concerns, in terms of both of the quality of life of the family that would be affected and the probable quality of life that the embryo could expect if carried to term. The conservative position does not recognize quality-of-life concerns as morally significant in the matter of abortion.

Another factor in the moral evaluation of a prospective abortion is the motives and reasons on the basis of which the decision would be made. Mere convenience would probably not weigh heavily with a responsible person but being able to continue with one's education would be considered a sound reason for abortion. As with other moral decisions, a decision for abortion can be judged by liberals to be selfish, trivial, shortsighted, unjust, irresponsible. The decision can be judged to be fair, responsible, reasonable, and serious. The moral decision is more complicated for the liberal than for the conservative, since it requires the weighing of a number of contextual considerations and moral values.

The key difference between conservatives and liberals is that liberals may hold that a woman has a right to decide even if her reasons are not admirable, whereas conservatives are generally less likely to accept a separation of private morality from the law. This is especially so in the case of abortion, since they do not see abortion as a victimless act.

For liberals, the legal question should focus on the rights of the pregnant woman and possibly other people. Also, the effect on society of allowing, forbidding, or restricting abortion must be considered. The liberal sees social and personal harm done by laws against abortion. The possibility of back-alley and coat-hanger abortions is not a sound moral argument for a personal decision about abortion, as Mary Ann Warren explains, but it can be a good argument for not outlawing abortion. The fact that the poor would suffer most hardship can be a good argument for not outlawing abortion. What is not germane in making a personal moral decision can be relevant to a legal argument.

The conflict over the law rests primarily on the embryo's right to life, as claimed by conservatives, and the woman's right to an abortion, as claimed by liberals. The right to life claim is most often based on the possession by the embryo of the human genetic code. The right to an abortion is more complicated. The *Roe* v. *Wade* decision is based on a claimed right to privacy.The Supreme Court interpreted the Constitution as protecting this right. Some state constitutions, such as that of Florida, clearly spell out the right to privacy. The right to privacy is perhaps best understood as a right of the citizen to be free of interference unless there is a compelling need of the state to control the citizens' activity. Freedom from unjustified interference in one's personal life seems to underlie the thinking of many prochoice people.

Some restrictions on abortion are probably inevitable, such as the requirement that trained personnel in medical facilities perform the abortion. There will be a need for licenses and inspections of facilities. Many liberals are opposed to restrictions presented as health protection measures that actually are used as antiabortion measures, such as requiring clinics to have the same facilities as general hospitals. Other kinds of restrictions are controversial, with liberals generally opposed to them or skeptical of them. Requirements that minors inform their parents and that wives inform husbands are seen by many liberals as subtle ways to prevent abortion in some cases. Liberals question the motives of proponents of such measures.

Who Has the Right to Decide?

An important issue for supporters of choice is who should make the decision regarding an abortion. Should it be the pregnant woman, the husband or lover, or the medical personnel? Should all three be involved? In an ideal situation, all those who are involved will agree on the best course of action. When this agreement is lacking, who is entitled to choose? Is it always the woman?

Allison Jaggar holds that the issue of who should decide depends on the social situation. The responsibility that society takes toward infants would affect the issue. In our society, the responsibility for getting prenatal care and for caring for the offspring falls most heavily on the pregnant woman. This would indicate that the woman, as the person most involved, should decide. In some extended families, and with some very rich women, the matter might be different.[20]

Jaggar's position rests on two key principles: (1) the right to life means a right to a full human life, and (2) decisions should be made by those most importantly affected by them. The first principle suggests that no person or group is a protector of the fetus's right to life if it does not attempt to provide the sufficient conditions for life. The second principle must take account of the social context and the economic situation. Jaggar says that in our society the right of the woman to decide rests on inadequate provision by the state for pre- and postnatal care (placing child-raising responsibility on the mother) and the small proportion of resources devoted to welfare.[21]

The father, says Jaggar, has less right to choose because he is affected less by the birth. He has more options regarding the effect of the birth on his life.[22] Jaggar is right about the possibility of fathers' avoiding responsibility. Even though some states are trying to make fathers assume at least a financial role in caring for the child, these efforts have not been very successful so far. The sad case is the father who deeply wants a child or is too honorable and responsible to avoid meeting his obligations to the child, but the laws that are to govern abortions cannot rest on judgments about each individual father, so the woman's claim must be given most weight.

Jaggar says that claims of medical personnel to control abortion decisions are even weaker than claims of fathers, since medical personnel are even less affected. Claims of the state would be based on the effect on community members of birth and an alleged duty to protect the right to life. Jaggar considers these claims weak in this society because the effect of a birth on society is minimal, and the state does not accept much responsibility for providing the sufficient conditions for life. Jaggar sees important limitations in giving the woman only a legal right to decide to have an abortion. She thinks a meaningful right to decide should include a right to have a child, with a full life for the child guaranteed by society. She says also that the right to decide requires cheap and convenient abortion. The choice should not be coerced by economic stringency. She sees a paradox in this whole matter. If the society provided sufficient conditions for life, the right to decide might be restricted, even though a woman's wishes should carry special weight, since she carries the fetus and goes through the birth process. The resolution of the paradox is that it may be more fruitful to shift the emphasis from individual rights to the fulfillment of human needs.[23]

Abortion and Infanticide

If liberals justify abortion on the grounds that an embryo is not a human person, do their arguments also justify infanticide? It might seem that they would, since the qualities that make one a human person are not well developed in a newborn baby. The level of consciousness, the sense of self, the moral sense, and the ability to communicate are beneath those of most family dogs and cats. Why, then, should killing an infant be considered murder?

Alison Jaggar puts this matter in clear perspective. A pregnant woman cannot sever her ties with an embryo except by abortion, but she can sever relation with a child without killing it. To kill a child is doing gratuitous harm. A right to practice infanticide does not follow from arguments supporting a right of abortion. The two issues are quite different.[24] Jane English gave a similar explanation of the difference between abortion and infanticide in terms of her self-defense argument: the fetus can threaten the woman in ways that the neonate does not.[25]

Can the Abortion Issue Be Resolved?

Can we reach any accord on the issue of abortion? This will be difficult. The two sides come at the issue with diametrically opposed basic beliefs. There are some beliefs that are germane to the abortion issue that most people share. Daniel Callahan says that we have a consensus on three grounds: that life should be protected and enhanced, that human rights are involved in abortion decisions, and that people should be morally responsible in their decisions. He realizes that this consensus is broad and vague, and it does not get us very far in reaching an accord on abortion.[26]

Is the situation hopeless, and can philosophy make no contribution toward resolution? Philosophical discussion can make significant contributions for those who seek help in rational discourse. Recognition that some arguments are not sound and that some ways of talking about the issue are not productive can help reasonable people come together. Much of the confrontation between liberals and conservatives is sloganistic and blindly emotional. It deepens divisions and does not foster serious thought about abortion. It does not help to use such terms as *unborn babies,* which begs the question and serves only to heighten the emotions. It does not help that liberals do not understand that conservatives are not just trying to force their opinions upon others.

We need not expect any scientific findings to resolve the issue for us. The question before us is not a factual matter. It is a matter of judgment regarding the moral standing of an embryo and, in rare cases, a fetus. As a society, we will have to decide about this matter. We will probably have to decide without the help of an overwhelming argument. We will be able to recognize the better arguments. We will be able to resolve this issue philosophically and rationally, but that is not the same thing as achieving total popular consensus. Our society will make a decision. When it becomes clear that the strongest arguments, along with the most important moral values, call for the adoption of one position, a democratic society will make its decision. Fortunately, it will not be necessary for every single person to agree with the decision of the society. Such full and complete agreement is not necessary, since rationally and legally resolving a moral question and achieving complete consensus are different matters. Those who cannot go along will be a steadily decreasing minority, which should be treated with respect and kindness, but the issue will have been resolved.

~ 9 ~

Pornography

What Is Pornography?

What is pornography? The word *pornography* comes from a Greek word for *whore* and the verb *to write* or *to draw,* but etymologies often do not take us very far. In the current use of the term, pornography can be drawings or something written, but it might just as well be a photograph, a movie, or a video. It might even be a stage play. What makes a specific example of these various media pornographic? Attempts to define pornography have usually been associated with issues of censorship or restriction on the availability of pornography. Finding a definition of pornography that will stand up in court is so difficult that we can sympathize with Supreme Court Associate Justice Potter Stewart, who said that he could not define pornography but he recognized it when he saw it. Legal definitions have proved very difficult; because of legal requirements, they tend to be general and vague, lacking the substance of specific description. Later in this chapter, we will deal with the issue of censorship. First, let us approach the issue from the perspectives of philosophy and feminist thought.

Philosophers and feminist writers have not approached the matter of defining pornography the same way as legal minds tried to define it. They have defined it in moral terms or in terms of its effects on individuals and society. The main idea in feminist definitions is that pornography is material that degrades and demeans women, portraying them as sex objects. Ann Garry broadens this concern to include the degradation not only of women but of people of both sexes, which is

114

important, since pornography portrays the sexuality of men as well as that of women. She says the only moral ground on which pornography could be condemned would be if it degrades people. Helen E. Longino adds the important point that pornography shows approval of the degradation, endorses it.[1]

These definitions certainly say something important about at least some types of pornography, but I do not think the definition is the best place to express a normative judgment. A neutral definition—that is, one that does not include a normative evaluation—facilitates the discussion of issues related to pornography. Is pornography sometimes good? Are all types of pornography degrading? It is difficult to discuss these matters if we begin with a definition that has already condemned pornography. It is important to discuss these matters because some people claim that pornography is of value to some people. Other people say that only some pornography degrades women by picturing them as merely sex objects. Ann Garry writes about good types of pornography. She says that there can be pornography that pictures mutual and reciprocal relationships.[2] Garry's paper shows the advantage of a neutral definition of pornography. Such a definition would include purely descriptive elements: pornography responds to and might stimulate interest in sex; it pictures or describes sexual activity or nudity; it might be provocative, or it might be playful or funny; it can be ugly or beautiful; and it might be either good or bad morally.

Susan Brownmiller rejects the concept of nonsexist pornography, arguing that there can be no equality in pornography, all of which is antifemale propaganda.[3] Some feminist critics of pornography seem to agree with Garry that some material that would be called pornography by unsophisticated people because of its depiction of sexual situations does not deserve the condemnation that they level at sexual material that degrades women. Gloria Steinem distinguished the pornographic from the erotic, with the erotic picturing compassionate love, freedom, and desire for a particular person, whereas the pornographic is associated with impersonal domination and violence against women. Steinem is aware, however, of cultural and personal differences about what is erotic. She says that in a male-dominated world, it is "almost futuristic" to debate what is and is not erotic.[4]

Longino uses the term *erotic* to describe material that others might refer to as "good" pornography.[5] Rosemary Tong thinks that "taking sensual delight in the erotic celebration of the body" and mutual sexual expression by people who are acting freely, which she calls "erotica," should be distinguished from "thanatica," which is degrading and endorses the degradation.[6]

Calling some sexual material erotic, rather than pornographic, will probably mean little to most people. Stipulations about using particular words to convey specific meanings are seldom effective, and only a few people seem to be adopting Steinem's usage. *Erotic* does not have for many people the meaning it has for Longino and Tong. It has probably been used as a derogatory term more often than it has carried the more sophisticated meaning. Some people think of the erotic as the obscene, possibly because too many obscene things have been called erotic, such as girlie shows and table dancing in tawdry bars. Ellen Willis does not think that a distinction between pornography and the erotic will hold up. She thinks that the distinction relates to social class or even to personal preference.[7] Alan Sobel says that making the distinction between pornography and the erotic will be ineffective, not convincing either the conservatives who might oppose sexual material the feminists favor or the liberals who do not look favorably on any restriction of expression.[8]

Pornography and Violence

One of the claims made against pornography is that it leads to sexual assault. Interestingly, this claim is made by some feminists and by conservatives who express no support of feminism.[9] We need to examine what is being claimed, since one understanding of the claim may be correct and important, even if another is lacking in supporting evidence. The claim that pornography incites individual men to engage in assault upon women is frequently made, but evidence to support it is lacking. Some of the claimed evidence is questionable. Ellen Willis objects to the "inverted logic" in arguments that make much of Charles Manson's and David Berkowitz's pornography collections.[10]

Research on pornography can be misleading. Donnerstein and Linz report experiments in which a high percentage of male research subjects who were shown pornographic films expressed a willingness to commit rape if they had no fear of discovery. When acceptance of rape was determined before the subjects saw the films, however, there was no change in the percentage of subjects who expressed acceptance of rape after seeing the material.[11]

Fred R. Berger cites the studies of Michael J. Goldstein and Harold S. Kant, which indicate that people inclined to deviant behavior seem to generate their own stimuli from various sorts of material, some of which no one would consider pornographic.[12]

Another claim about pornography is significant and should be investigated. It is that pornography helps create and sustain a social climate in which women are vulnerable to assault and other abusive treatment.[13] Pornography can portray abusive treatment of women and imply approval of such treatment. It can even indicate that women enjoy being abused and expect it. Such ideas might make the world a more dangerous place for women by making assault more acceptable. Is this claim sound?

Several clarifications of the claim are needed. Is the claim that all kinds of pornography, or just certain types, have the effect of legitimizing assault in the minds of some men? The kind of pornography that research indicates might have this effect would be that which pictures women as objects, especially if they seem to be accepting or even enjoying abusive treatment. Portrayal of violence is a significant factor. Some research indicates that picturing violence has an effect upon some people that picturing of sexual activity without violence does not have. It is still not determined how long this effect lasts.[14]

Some parents and educators are concerned about the effect of violent television shows upon children. Perhaps there should be some concern about the effect of violence upon some adults. It is ironical that some of the strongest opponents of pornography are not concerned about, or may even like, nonsexual violence in movies and television shows. The research we now have indicates that the nonsexual portrayals of violence may be dangerous to women. If they tend to give legitimacy to violent behavior, hostile people may direct their violence toward easy targets, women and children. The question of a connection between pornography and sexual assault is important, but it is not the only issue to be discussed. Donnerstein and Linz think that portrayals of violence, with or without sex, are a greater danger to society than pornography as such.[15]

If pornography does help create a dangerous social climate, the most irresponsible pornography would be that picturing women being violently abused. Some pornography pictures women being beaten, raped, held in bondage, and even murdered. This is degrading and dehumanizing, especially when women are pictured as willing victims. Such portrayals support harmful myths about female sexuality. In some minds, this sort of portrayal might legitimize violence. The type of person who will act violently toward women might act antisocially even without any encouragement from violent pornography, but many people are concerned about the picturing of violence, and for them the possible danger is an adequate basis for objecting to pornography of some types and in some situations. If such pornography does help create and sustain a climate that can be harmful to women, an arguable point, opposition to it is justified.

Some attacks on pornography might give the impression that most pornography is of this abusive type. Definite claims have been made that pornography is becoming increasingly violent. Fred R. Berger does not think that this is the case.[16] Donnerstein and Linz challenge the claim of the 1986 U. S. Attorney General's Commission on Pornography that most pornography is of the violent type. They cite sociological and psychological studies that show that violence in pornography peaked around 1977.[17]

It is hard to say exactly how prevalent violent pornography is. Not everyone will interpret a picture the same way. It is possible that a person who is quite concerned about pornography will see as violent or demeaning toward women a picture or a story that many other people will not see that way. One person might be offended or even frightened by pornography that other people will see as just silly or as funny.

The issue of violent pornography is complicated by the insistence of some feminists that all pornography is violence against women. Susan Brownmiller and Andrea Dworkin see pornography as psychic violence against women. Dworkin equates both the production and use of pornography to rape.[18] Some nonfeminist thought seems to support the view that pornography is connected to violence and male aggression. Robert D'Amico finds this understanding of pornography in some of Freud's writing and in some sociobiological writing.[19]

If all pornography should be seen as violent, there would be no point in distinguishing between kinds of pornography, but considering all pornography violent is far from general acceptance. There is significant disagreement between women over the interpretation of pornography. Ellen Willis contends that it is a mistake to hold that all pornography is violent, as the movement Women against Pornography does in claiming that pornography depicts violence rather than sex, thereby claiming a closer connection between pornography and rape than some feminists think is justified. Willis says that pornography is by definition overtly sexual, and much of it is not overtly violent.[20]

Lisa Duggan, Nan D. Hunter, and Carole S. Vance also object to the project of reclassifying all sexist images as violent or aggressive, which blurs the distinction between the assault of a wife beater and the visual "assault" of a sexist advertisement.[21]

Some feminists think it is a mistake to call all pornography violent on the ground that it is a product of patriarchy and that patriarchal sexuality is violent. Ellen Willis asks why this would call for condemnation of pornography and not romance novels. She says that considering all pornography violent does not allow women to distinguish between rape and consensual sex; it condemns all sex with men.[22]

Is pornography closely akin to rape? An examination of sexual assault might throw some light on this question.

Sexual assault is almost universally condemned and is considered an especially terrible experience for the victim. Carolyn M. Shafer and Marilyn Frye have written on the reason for rape's being held to be especially awful. They hold that what makes rape more horrible than other forms of assault is that the victim is violated at the center of her personal domain, the traits and properties that make one a person. Anything that affects one's person-properties comes near the center of her domain. Rape does this without the woman's consent, in violation of her will. Rape represents to a woman a man's sexual perception of her as a being who is in someone's domain with no control over her own domain. It is an ultimate expression of disrespect.[23]

Pamela Foa also notes that the wrongness of rape goes beyond its criminal character as an assault and is awful in a way assault is not. She rejects the view of Marilyn Frye and Carolyn Shafer that rape is a consequence of women's not being viewed as persons with moral equality, which deprives them of freedom and self-direction in their own domain. She says such an argument suggests that rape is wrong the same way other assaults are wrong. She finds the explanation of the awfulness of rape in the suggestion that the rape victim is an accomplice, is implicated in the rape. She holds that society's perception is that the victim desired and enjoyed the rape. Foa relates the "guilt" of rape victims in the eyes of society to Victorian sexual attitudes that hold that sex should be intimate and women should not enjoy it. The result of this, according to Foa, is that rape is the model of sex in our society. She points to the training of middle-class children: girls are taught to ignore feelings, while boys are taught to ignore what a girl says. This, she says, makes a woman's resistance the ultimate sexual turn-on.[24]

Shafer and Frye also are aware of the inability of society to deal with rape and to treat the victim of rape properly. They point out that our society holds rape in low regard yet tends to sympathize with men accused of rape. It believes real rape—that is, rape for which the woman shares no responsibility—is rare. They ask what "unsavory social purpose" can be served by the hypocrisy of the general public pretense that rape seldom occurs.[25] We all know how the police and the courts, even some medical personnel, have treated victims of rape. Things may have improved in this respect, but there are still problem areas. There are still those who blame the woman. Perhaps the worst aspect of this is that some victims internalize this judgment of society and feel guilty and unworthy. Fry and Shafer are right in seeing rape as a violation of something very central to a person's being a person. It might not be so much a denial of the personhood of the victim as an attack on that personhood. The role of society in the suffering of the victim is an important aspect of the awfulness of sexual assault. I believe Shafer and Frye and Foa contribute to our understanding of sexual assault.

Foa's claim about the rapelike character of ordinary sexual relationships needs a careful examination. It can hardly be denied that some coitus is very much like rape, but to generalize this to all sexual engagements would need evidence that Foa does not supply. Her claim, if sound, would have tremendous bearing on our understanding of sexuality. Is it a true picture? One problem with her claim is that much, if not most, sexual congress is motivated by sexual desire. It is generally agreed that rape by strangers is motivated by hatred or resentment and the desire to cause pain and terror. So-called date rape may be motivated in large part by an effort to exert control, to display power, or even to exact a revenge from the uncooperative female sex. If Foa's claim is accepted, it would mean that all sexual activity is an effort to dominate, harm, or cause pain. It would mean that love, caring, and tenderness could play no role in sex between men and women. This is not a belief to be accepted without much more reason to believe it true. We do not need to deny that often sexual activity is used as a weapon or tool of domination to assert that sex can be an expression of love. There will be further examination of the nature of love in chapter 13.

There have been rare cases of men who claimed to have been raped by a woman. I have no information about such events, and I also wonder whether talk about them is not an effort to blunt concern about rape of women by men. There are rapes of men by other men. These seem most often to occur in prison. The reasons for which they occur might relate more directly to the prison situation than to the motivations that lead to rape of women by men. I cannot see now how they will add to our understanding of human sexuality, so I do not discuss them further.

With the understanding of rape provided by Shafer and Frye and by Foa, we can see why some women see pornography as being very much like rape. They can see both rape and pornography as putting women into the position of persons with no control over central aspects of their being as persons. Foa's view that all coitus is rapelike is too questionable to be a reasonable basis for the condemnation of pornography.

Fred R. Berger holds that conservative arguments against pornography presuppose views of sex that many people reject. They also promote an un-necessary amount of social control.[26] Willis also sees opposition to all pornography as a reflection of sexual attitudes that not all women share. She says, "If feminists define pornography, per se, as the enemy, the result will be to make a lot of women ashamed of their sexual feelings and afraid to be honest about them."[27] Willis acknowledges that pornography can be a "psychic assault," but she says that women as well as men can find pornography a source of erotic pleasure. She denies that all women are made victims by pornography; some women may be rebels, who reject "sexual repression and hypocrisy."[28]

Lisa Duggan, Nan D. Hunter, and Carole S. Vance hold that blurring the boundaries between violence and nonviolent sexual expression appeals to a traditional view that sex is degrading to women. They say, "It is ironic that a feminist position on pornography incorporates most of the myths about sexuality that feminism has struggled to displace."[29] Regarding images of casual sex, sex outside of marriage, group sex, and so forth, they say, "Some of these ideas appeal to women reading or seeing pornography, who may interpret some images as legitimizing their own sense of sexual urgency or desire to be sexually aggressive. Women's experience of pornography is not universally victimizing," as antipornography laws would have it.[30]

Does Pornography Harm Men?

The question of harmful effects of pornography upon men does not receive much attention, but some concern about this has been expressed. Harry Brod holds that it is a mistake to think of pornography as a benefit to men and a loss to women. Giving up pornography would be a gain for men. He sees pornography not as an expression of Eros, the life affirming force, but as an expression of Thanatos, the force that seeks to remove all tension from life, resulting ultimately in death. Brod thinks that pornography corrupts male sexuality by objectifying the female so that the individual and personal is lost. This leads to standardizing the concepts of beauty and giving unrealistic ideas of sexuality. The concept of woman as something to possess, the goal of sex as focused on the genitalia and limited to orgasm, and impossible ideals of male sexual performance rob men of freedom and satisfaction in sexual relations.[31]

In support of his claims about the effect of pornography on men, Brod cites the views of Michael Betzold, Rollo May, Herbert Marcuse, and others. Freud, Hegel, and John Stuart Mill provide concepts from which Brod's analysis is constructed.[32]

The issues raised by Brod are important and deserve more careful attention than they have received. The claims made by Brod need to be examined critically. The impersonalization, focus on orgasm, unrealistic notions of male sexual performance, and attitude toward women as objects to be possessed are sufficiently common to be mentioned in magazine articles. Brod does not demonstrate that these features of male sexuality are products of pornography. It might be the case that men have always manifested these unsavory qualities and will continue to do so, with or without pornography. Male sexuality may have produced pornography, which has little effect on men. Brod does not show that a male campaign against pornography, which he advocates,[33] would be effective.

One thing that troubles me about Brod's paper and other efforts to describe male sexuality is that few of them consider the differences in male sexuality in different countries, different regions of the United States, and different American ethnic groups. National heritage, religious influence, and racial differences seem to influence sexual attitudes. Writers on male sexuality tend to be ethnocentric without being aware of it. Taking the various differences into account would detract from a neat picture that can be forcefully presented. It should be done, however, in the interest of accuracy and because it may throw some light on the issue of how biologically determined male sexuality is. Can male sexuality be improved? Can men be taught better attitudes and manners? Seeing male sexuality in all its varieties may help us approach these questions more adequately.

Is Pornography Immoral?

Is pornography morally objectionable, even if it does not lead to assault? Many people think pornography is morally unacceptable regardless of its effects. Can this be supported? What would be morally objectionable about pornography?

Some people have moral objections to nudity. It is difficult to pin down the feeling that nudity is immoral. It may be a feeling that nudity is sexually arousing, but nudity excites sexual desire only in certain contexts. Partial nudity is usually more exciting than full nudity, which can be anything but pornographic. Some people think that nudity is degrading, and in some cultures it might have this signification. In other cultures, however, nudity is not degrading. The gods and goddesses of ancient Greece were often pictured as nude. The athletes also competed in the nude. This seems quite reasonable when one considers that gods, goddesses, and athletes look much better without clothing than most people do. In some cultures, nudity was a mark of glorification. Antonio Canova's neoclassical statue of Napoleon in Apsley House in London is an interesting example. It is several stories tall, which makes the stairwell of Apsley House one of the few suitable places for it. In addition to its size, most people notice another feature of Canova's statue. Napoleon is nude. This was not degrading to Napoleon. Quite the opposite; he is pictured as a Greek god. In fact, Napoleon's sister, Paulina Borghese, was envious and had Canova make a nude statue of her. This statue, smaller than Napoleon's, is in the Galleria Borghese in Rome. Nudity is degrading only when the culture associates it with something degrading, such as slavery or military defeat. Moral objection to pornography on the basis of its nudity seems to be a culturally conditioned bias that many people do not share.

A more substantial objection to pornography is not to nudity itself, but to the portrayal of genitals. Some people feel that the portrayal of female genitals is degrading to women generally. Some claim that it "violates" them. Susan Brownmiller claims that it dehumanizes women by picturing them as objects, as pieces of sexual equipment. Kathleen Barry, Robin Morgan, Audre Lord, and others object on the ground that it is intimacy without the proper basis for it; lacking affection, it violates the private and personal nature of sex. It has been compared to prostitution as an impersonalized sexual experience. Certainly, an impersonal experience is less than ideal, but this might not be adequate grounds for condemning it morally. Some people might need to settle for less than ideal sex. Should this be subject to moral condemnation? Does it, in fact, degrade women generally?

Perhaps the cheapness and shallowness of the picturing of sex organs in an obscene fashion is the main objection. Jean-Paul Sartre writes about obscenity, finding the awkward lack of grace to be the objectionable aspect of it.[34] It is easy to see this in some pornographic pictures in which a woman (usually) is posed in an awkward and unusual position in order to display the genitals. This is an obvious basis for aesthetic objection to the material. Is there an obvious basis for moral objection? Degrading, belittling, or humiliating a person is morally wrong, but we would need to demonstrate that the portrayal does in fact do this in picturing the genitals.

Moral objection to the way sexual encounters are portrayed is more readily understood than is objection to portrayal of genitals. One does not need to accept a view such as that of Pamela Foa, who holds that ordinary sexual intercourse is rapelike,[35] to see that sexual encounters can be presented in ways that are obviously sexist and misrepresent the nature of female sexuality. Picturing women as sexually passive and submissive is not telling the truth about women. Women were once expected to be passive, and some women might prefer that role, but it is not true of women generally, and many women resent the perpetuation of myths about females. Ann Garry says that showing women as passive and enjoying being at the service of a dominating male helps to reinforce sexism in the society. Women are pictured as sex objects in a society in which being a sex object is associated with being hurt.[36]

The reasons on the basis of which some people object to any sort of portrayal of the unclothed human body or any portrayal of sexual activity seem to be cultural norms that are not shared by other cultures or to be individual tastes and standards that are not held by many other people. On the other hand, it is not difficult to see that it is morally irresponsible to portray women as enjoying being harmed if the portrayal is meant to give the impression that women are like that. Objection to picturing women as enjoying abuse that very few women might enjoy is not based on a narrow cultural perspective. It is here that the immorality of pornography might be found. Eva Feder Kittay claims that pornography is hate literature and is immoral because it contributes to political and moral injustice. More than that, it makes hatred and injustice enjoyable to the perpetrator.[37]

The claims made against pornography are serious. Are they justified? Alan Sobel examines the claims that pornography lies about women, that it degrades women, and that it endorses the degradation. He finds serious problems with all of these claims. There is considerable dispute about what pornography is saying or even that it makes any statements at all. It arouses sexual interest, but not by advancing any propositions. The claim that pornography degrades women is sometimes treated as true by definition. Descriptions of pornography as degrading often rely on exaggerated reports of the nature of pornography, with the use of extreme examples as though they were the usual content. Another approach, which Sobel calls "metaphysical," is more subtle and finds the degradation implicit in the latent meaning of the portrayals. This involves a kind of analysis in which users of pornography are not likely to engage, but the main weakness of this approach is that the interpretations preferred by the critic of pornography can be contested.[38]

Portraying degradation is hardly an immoral act. It can be used in good causes, on behalf of oppressed people who might be helped if their condition were known. The claim against pornography is that it approves of the degrading that it pictures. Those who make the claim do not explain, however, how the portrayal recommends what it shows. What is taken as indicating approval is that the activity is pictured as being pleasurable and there is no expression of disapproval of it. Sobel holds that these factors together do not explain how the work in question is an implicit endorsement. An added statement might disavow approval, but this would be too easy for pornographers to do to get around legal threats. There remains the question of whether any endorsement would actually lead to an increase in practice of the offensive behavior.[39]

Sobel does not show that pornography is not immoral, nor do I think that was his aim. He does show that the claim needs much stronger argument if it is to convince people in the society who are reluctant to restrict expression. The claim will need to be more strongly supported before it justifies legal defense against pornography.

The claim that pornography is immoral is a serious one, and it should be examined carefully. Some grounds for calling pornography immoral can be seen to be matters of cultural and personal taste; these do not provide substantial grounds for condemning pornography. It would not serve the cause of feminists to become water carriers for those who are uneasy with sex. People who appear to be fearful of sex know that it cannot be banished from human society, but they would like to limit it to the marriage bed, with the wife being too much a lady to enjoy or seek it, with little time spent at it, and with no talk about it inside or outside the home. This is hardly the feminist agenda.

The claims of feminist writers that pornography degrades women and helps create a climate in which they are subject to harm are far more serious than the protests of prudes, but the seriousness of the claims does not justify them. They merit close examination, which will be facilitated by their being presented in a way that avoids distracting shrillness and is more carefully elucidated. As we move beyond the expression of outrage to the needed study and analysis, we can determine which portrayals of sexual behavior are a threat to our welfare and which are celebrations of our sexuality or are just simple fun.

Does Pornography Have Any Value?

Pornography has its defenders among women as well as men. Most of the defense has come from men in the past. It has been defended as having educational value during certain stages of sexual development. James A. Gould credits *Playboy* and other magazines with helping overcome sexual ignorance, although he also gives credit to other factors, such as the feminist movement. G.L. Simons held that pornography is a harmless substitute for sex with another person and can help people overcome sexual problems.[40] Conservatives on the issue of pornography do not welcome pornographic literature as an educational tool. Irving Kristol wrote that pornography "appeals to and provokes a kind of sexual regression" that is autoerotic and infantile. He compared pornography to masturbation, saying it can become "a permanent self-reinforcing neurosis."[41] It has not been demonstrated, however, that immature sexual attitudes in the immature interfere with growth of mature attitudes later. Gould seems to think that ignorance is the most significant danger to young people, and he believes that there is still a surprising amount of ignorance on the part of both males and females. Gould also thinks that pornography helps prevent sex crimes.[42] This is a difficult claim to evaluate. The debate over the possible good effects of pornography involves comparing of statistics from countries that differ culturally, in size, and in the homogeneity of their populations. The debate also generates a great deal of strong feeling. The claim that pornography helps prevent violence is firmly denied by Susan Brownmiller and others who think that pornography is itself violence against women.[43]

Pornography might be more helpful to some people than it is to others. There is no advantage in teaching false ideas about sexuality while one's curiosity is being satisfied, so it would be important that people who might benefit from pornography be exposed only to pornography that is not sexist and not violent.

Pornography has been defended also for people who cannot have active sexual encounters. Vicarious sexual experience might be better than nothing at all.

Opponents of pornography do not seem much impressed with the possibility of good pornography, and they do not recognize it as having value for anyone. Some of this opposition may be based upon prudery, but with some of the conservative and feminist writers, pornography is seen as oppression of women. Irving Kristol saw it not only as a conspiracy against women but as a broader threat, "inherently and purposefully subversive of civilization and its institutions." He saw its infantile view of sex as so corrupting "that what is at stake is civilization and humanity, nothing less."[44]

Censorship and Restriction of Pornography

If pornography is oppressing women and threatening civilization, how should it be dealt with? Kristol advocated "liberal" rather than "oppressive" censorship. He saw as examples of liberal censorship the restricting of certain plays to theater clubs, composed only of people who are very serious about theater, and restricting the use of certain books to the reading rooms of libraries, where the reading can be supervised.[45] Feminists have been divided on the issue of censorship, with some opposing it, some advocating it, and others wanting to control pornography without actual censorship. The main difficulty facing proposals of censorship is the First Amendment to the U.S. Constitution, but its protection of free expression is not absolute. The U.S. Supreme Court has not supported the purveyors of material that could be considered obscene. One of its best known decisions, *Roth* v. *United States,* gave a three-part test: a book is not protected by the First Amendment if "(a) the dominant theme of the material taken as a whole appeals to a prurient interest in sex; (b) the material is patently offensive because it affronts contemporary community standards relating to the description or representation of sexual matters; and (c) the material is utterly without redeeming social value."[46]

The first part of the *Roth* test of obscene and unprotected material is that it is intended to arouse a high degree of interest in sex or to create sexual excitement. An important aspect of this test is that the purpose of the material is the stimulation of sexual desire or interest. Almost anything can excite sexual thoughts in a particular person. Two students of my acquaintance were known to use medical book illustrations for this purpose, but that does not make the pictures pornographic.

Another aspect of the *Roth* test is that the material is offensive according to community standards. The problem with this definition is obvious. The community in which there is a profitable market for pornography will find it difficult to establish clearly what the community standards are.

Another aspect of the *Roth* definition is that the sexually explicit material in question does not have serious social value, such as literary or artistic merit. Some vigorous opponents of pornography would gladly destroy books like *The Canterbury Tales* and *Tropic of Cancer* or artworks such as those of Boucher and Balthus, but laws proposed for the control of pornography usually protect serious art. There are several problems with this. The judgment of literary or aesthetic value can be controversial. Also, exempting literary works and art from the ban seems to rest on the assumption that what is harmful if it is not artistic will not be harmful if it is art. Is there any reason why this would be so?

I fear that there is a social bias behind this treatment of pornography; the thought seems to be that the more cultured classes of people can be trusted with a good bit of naughtiness to which the lower classes must not be exposed. Kristol, who advocated a kind of limited censorship of pornography that would allow the cultured and affluent to have limited access to pornographic materials, was concerned only that his proposal might be thought elitist, and he said he would rather be elitist than be what he calls an "egalitarian maniac."[47] Kristol did not explain why the elites were not affected badly by pornography, as he expected the masses to be affected. If it is the case that cultivated people respond to the obscene one way and the uneducated another, some explanation of this should be given.

Susan Brownmiller and Helen E. Longino have offered additional grounds for denying pornography protection of the First Amendment. Brownmiller claims that free expression applies only to political speech.[48]

Critics of Brownmiller's view hold that this is not historically correct. There are various justifications for the protection of free expression in various areas of life. For the citizen to act intelligently in a free society, there must be access to ideas and information, which requires the broad protection of free expression. There cannot be a firm line drawn between personal and political expression. Personal expression can be political, and even pornographic material can be political.[49]

Cynthia Stark supports a position similar to Brownmiller's view that only political speech is protected. She argues that freedom of expression has no worth in itself. To be protected, it must "promote some further moral or political good, such as being a means of determining the truth about matters, or serving to better the status of women."[50] Of course, one reason for supporting freedom of expression is that it is necessary for the preservation of political freedom. If an exercise of this freedom is working counter to the cause of political freedom, it would seem reasonable to curtail that expression, and this is what Stark claims that pornography is doing. The problem with this is the difficulty of making laws to govern the way to distinguish good expression from bad expression. Developing criteria to determine whether an expression is a contribution to our common good will be no more simple than the attempts to determine which expressions were obscene. Lisa Duggan, Nan Hunter, and Carole S. Vance object to letting the government decide such matters.[51]

The notion of political value would need to be extended greatly to cover our concern about protection of expression. It might be better not to see aesthetic value, the pleasure received from the arts, and the satisfaction of curiosity about numerous things as a political matter in all cases. At times, a political aspect of these things is clear, but these forms of expression do not become worthless when they are not serving directly a political purpose.

Helen E. Longino appeals to the distinction between freedom as license and freedom as independence. She says the right of independence must not be used to deny independence to others, as she claims is the case with pornography, which overturns the political independence of women. Pornography, Longino says, is a type of group defamation that is harmful to women; it is not protected speech, as libel and slander are not.[52] Critics of her view point out that laws protecting people from libel and slander have not been applied to the protection of large groups of people. Laws against defamation of individual persons pose many legal problems, and laws against defaming a large group of people would court greater dangers.[53]

One need not take an absolute position against any censorship to realize the need to be cautious about adopting measures that would censor or seriously restrict any form of expression. What would justify censorship of pornography? Fred R. Berger suggests necessary conditions for censorship—that is, conditions that must hold for the censorship to be justified. There would need to be evidence of serious harm that is closely related to the expression in question. It would also be necessary that counterexpression would not combat the harm.[54] Rosemary Tong holds that all women are harmed by degrading pornography, what she calls thanatica, but she believes that seeking a legal remedy should be a last resort to be used only after education or other efforts fail.[55] Ann Garry suggests that a nonsexist type of pornography might replace degrading pornography, as we saw above. Other people would be more comfortable with educational programs about sex and sexual relationships.

Berger points to dangers in limiting expression. He says that well-financed forces are attacking free expression, and liberal principles should not be abandoned without "compelling evidence of a clear and present danger."[56] What is there to fear from censorship? Feminist expression itself could be censored, and causes that are important to women could become taboo. We should not forget that antiobscenity laws were used to prevent Margaret Sanger from distributing information on contraception. With conservative courts, contraceptive literature and counseling could be made illegal. Sex education has frequently come under attack from people who would be delighted to censor any information about sex. Many significant works of art and literature have been banned from certain schools and public libraries and in some cases from any public access. We could lose a significant part of our liberty and of our artistic heritage if we play loose with censorship.[57]

Portrayal of violence, with or without a sexual angle, seems to pose dangers to society. Education and the development of good character seem the most promising approaches to the problem, but this will be difficult, and the problem might become so serious that regulation of some media might be necessary. Many people are disturbed about young people's having access to violence and pornography through computer networks, especially the Internet. Other people fear measures that might be taken to control the networks.

Pornography that pictures men or women in ways that a large number of people would interpret as demeaning is distasteful to most mature and educated people. Perhaps the only safe way to oppose these kinds of expression is to produce more people who will not be attracted to them. How can we do this? It all seems to depend on good education to foster correct thinking and mental health to foster good attitudes and desires, but except in the broadest outlines, these are concepts about which thoughtful people can disagree. What, specifically, will a good education be, and what are the bounds of attitude and behavior outside of which a person will be known to lack mental health? Of course, we can identify some people as ignorant and others as lacking mental stability, but these are the extreme cases. Not all of the people who enjoy pornography are among these.

Pornography will probably be seen as an urgent problem by many people, but we need not accept their assessment of the matter or heed the call for censorship without some definite evidence of harm. The harm would need to be as great as the harm that can be done by censorship. At this point, it seems that the harm done by pornography is largely speculative, whereas the history of censorship shows tangible damage. Mark R. Wicclair says that the "strong *prima facie* case against censorship" should weigh more heavily than the speculative connection between pornography and harm to women.[58]

I think that what we cannot do about pornography through sex education, cultivation of appreciation for literature and art, and other improvements in the society generally will not happen effectively. We can understand why some people find pornography offensive, even threatening, but we will do well to stand firm against dangerous and ill-considered measures. We must avoid exaggerating the dangers and the offensiveness of pornography. Unless we find evidence that it does threaten the security of women, I do not believe it is the sort of thing that should divide those who are working for the improvement of human society or distract them from their efforts, including efforts on behalf of equality for women and members of minority groups.

∼ 10 ∼

Sex Differences

Are men and women different? Obviously, they are. They dress differently, walk and talk differently, and might even think about things differently. But this is to give an uninteresting answer to what many people believe to be an interesting question. So what do they really want to know? Are men and women naturally different? Are there any differences that are not results of training and culture? That is an interesting question, but it is not as simple as we might assume; we are not too clear about how to answer it. John Stuart Mill saw the problem clearly more than a century ago. We never see men and women apart from cultural influences, which means that we may never be able to answer the question.[1]

Mill saw no need to answer the question about natural differences between the sexes. He saw that subjection of women was unjust and was a loss to society, which was depriving itself of the use of human resources. He held that the dominant role of men was a result of superior muscular strength, a social practice that converted "a mere physical fact into a legal right."[2] He did not think the dominance of men over women ever had social value. He wrote, "[t]he generality of a practice is in some cases a strong presumption that it is, or . . . once was, conducive to laudable ends. . . . If the authority of men over women . . . had been the result of a conscientious comparison between different modes of government of society" and was found to be "the arrangement most conducive to the happiness and well being" of both sexes, it might have some evidence in its favor. Alternative social arrangements have never been tried; the choice of male dominance was never "the result of deliberation, or forethought, or any social ideas, or any notion whatever of what conduced to the benefit of humanity or the good order of society." [3] Since Mill's time, we have seen additional evidence of the loss to society that results from the subjection of women. Have we achieved anything more in understanding the nature of the sexes?

Research on Sexual Differences

Some scientists have tried to discover the nature of males and females, and some of them think they have discovered the differences, even though other scientists have opposing opinions. There are some widely accepted opinions about sex differences, other than the obvious primary sexual characteristics. Only four differences are commonly considered well established: verbal ability in females and visual-spatial and mathematical ability and aggressiveness in males. These claims appear more impressive when they are explained in right/left-brain terminology, based on the theory that functions such as visual acuity, spatial sense, mathematical ability, and linguistic ability are dependent on separate sides of the brain. Some researchers hold that men are more right-brain, therefore more efficient in dealing with mathematics and spatial relationships, with more laterality (separate functioning of each side). Ultimately, such theory might or might not be recognized as significant.

There is no unanimity about the claimed differences, however, as some researchers question the significance of research showing differences between males and females. The Harvard biologist Richard Lewontin holds that, beyond the generally larger size of males and differences of primary sexual functions, there are no features that unambiguously distinguish men and women. He points out that the mathematical ability differential is less than half a standard deviation. [4]

Joyce Trebilcot points out the significant matter: men and women fall along the whole continuum of test scores for all qualities. There may be more tall men than tall women, but many women are taller than most men. [5]

Will more research eliminate the ambiguity surrounding questions of sex differences? I see no reason to expect it to. The nature of research on such matters does not give us much reason to expect clear and unambiguous answers to questions about sex differences. What is the nature of such research? We should see several aspects of this kind of research.

Research on sex and gender differences is analogical. A sample that is taken to represent a large population gives an accurate picture of the population if the sample and the population are analogous. If the sample is not representative of the population, the conclusions drawn from the sample will not be accurate. Since we cannot examine every human being, much research must be of this analogical type. It is not just a matter of luck whether we use a sample that is closely analogous with the broader population. The ways to increase the likelihood of getting a representative sample are well known; they are described in logic textbooks, such as Irving Copi's widely used introduction to logic.[6]

There are six factors that tend to make an analogical argument strong: (1) A large number in the sample helps to remove the danger of having a nonrepresentative sample. (2) A large number of respects in which the things in the sample are analogous to the population also helps. For example, for research on high school seniors, the sample should contain males and females from different socioeconomic, ethnic, racial, and regional groups. (3) Disanalogies between the sample and the population should be avoided. Recently, some medical research has been criticized because there were no women in the researchers' samples. (4) A significant number of differences among the members of the sample minimizes the likelihood of disanalogies between sample and population. Prediction of graduation rates of entering college students should not be based on a sample from one high school or one economic or ethnic background. (5) This kind of research is inductive, with its distinctive logic. Characteristics cited in the premises of an inductive argument must be relevant to the conclusion drawn. In some cases, this is obvious, such as knowing that the color of an automobile is not relevant to research on gasoline mileage. (6) The strength of the conclusion must be "modest" in relation to the strength of the premises. It does not do to predict low fuel consumption for a fleet of automobiles on the basis of one vehicle that was much more efficient than the other test cars.

Carefully following the six logical principles will not guarantee a representative sample, but failure to follow them will make getting a good sample a most lucky accident.

The research on sex differences is statistical. The conclusion does not necessarily describe any particular individual in the population. It only gives a percentage of probability. This has important implications for making hiring and school admissions policies. It should be kept in mind even when dealing with informal practices. We may question both the wisdom and the justice of electing a woman secretary of the PTA, as a matter of course, just because women usually write more neatly than men, just as we might hesitate to elect a man president, as a matter of course, because men usually exert more control.

J.R. Lucas does not see a problem with excluding women as a group. He thinks that excluding all women from activities for which most women have little talent has advantages that make up for any unfairness. The social benefits outweigh individual rights. "Because you are a woman" is a relevant explanation in many social situations.[7] Lucas is allowing efficiency in social situations to outweigh considerations of justice, self-realization of women, and the contributions that unusually talented women can make to society. The policy he advocates could well cost the society more than it contributes, and a moral defense of this systematic exclusion of some women would be very difficult. Contrary to what Lucas holds, I believe we should be concerned about justice for people who are not typical of their sex.

The most important thing to say about the findings of research on sex differences is that they do not solve our ethical and political problems immediately. We must still weigh the values involved and make decisions.

The question of whether differences between the sexes are innate or products of culture can lead us astray. Not only do we run into problems when we try to define *nature* and *culture*. Not only do we have difficulty in discovering which characteristics should be considered "natural" and which conventional. We can make the serious mistake of assuming that whatever results from inculturation can be changed and what people are born with cannot. We easily jump to the conclusion that innate characteristics make certain social patterns inevitable. That which can be considered natural does not carry inevitability with it, and cultural traits can be very difficult to alter. In fact, the innate traits may be easier to handle.[8]

Even if it turns out to be inevitable that men or women, on the average, will score higher on certain tests of skill, we still have to make up our minds about the significance of these matters. Inevitable things, such as the connection between the malfunctioning of certain glands and distressing physical symptoms, are not considered desirable conditions, so we take pains to overcome the effects of the inevitable.

If we had to give up in the face of natural characteristics, many of us would not be able to read or to hear ordinary conversations, but eyeglasses and hearing aids prevent these deprivations from being inevitable. In the same way, women are not precluded from doing "heavy work," since they can be assisted by various lifts, dollies, and other devices that men should use also, to prevent avoidable injuries. We cannot overcome all weaknesses and incapacities, but neither sex is, as a whole, unable to do what is required in most jobs and professions.

Gender Roles

Separate roles for men and women still have ardent supporters, who use their little arsenal of arguments to fight against changes in our social and employment practices. There are arguments from social history, which claim that what has been in the past is inevitable in the future. Steven Goldberg holds that authority and leadership have always been associated with the male. Male roles, he claims, have always had higher status. Male dominance is universal. Child-care roles are universally female.[9]

Margaret Mead and other anthropologists have studied cultures in which Goldberg's claims do not hold, but even if such patterns of culture were found to have been universal, this would not show that the old patterns are inevitable. A significant part of our cultural history has been the development of skills, machines, medicines, and social institutions that give people increasing choice about human events.

Goldberg does not rest his arguments solely on cultural history. He gives an explanation of why the universal patterns were inevitable. He believes sexually differentiated behavior is determined by nature. The determining agent is testosterone. Goldberg refers to animal experiments with testosterone and holds that fetal testosterone prepares the male brain to respond to endogenous testosterone.[10] There has been experimentation that indicates that androgens affect behavior, but the role of testosterone is not clear. An effect on brain structures has not been clearly established in animals larger than rats. Arguing from animal experiments to the inevitability of human behaviors is problematic.

Research on neonates and young children does not give the researcher access to subjects untouched by human culture. Some cultural influences might begin in the womb. Lewontin cites the blue, pink, and yellow diaper experiment. In a hospital, male babies were dressed in blue, females in pink. The color of the diapers affected the way babies were handled and the way they were described. When all the babies were dressed in yellow diapers, observers "got upset"; some even peeked inside the diapers.[11] It seems that many people cannot be comfortable unless even neonates are gendered.

Other arguments in support of gender roles come from psychology. Sigmund Freud claimed—based, he said, on the medical histories of his patients—that girls have penis envy and a castration complex, while boys suffer the Oedipus complex and rejection of the mother. The basis of such claims is highly dubious. Claims about the psychology of women made by well-known psychologists such as Bruno Bettelheim, Eric Erikson, and Joseph Rheingold have been challenged by feminist authors. Naomi Weisstein writes, "Psychologists have set about describing the true nature of women with a certainty and a sense of their own infallibility rarely found in the secular world."[12]

Weisstein correctly points out that claims made by psychologists on the basis of what they have observed in their clinical practice are not adequately tested and should not be accepted as scientific findings.[13] The clinical experience provides a rich ground for developing hypotheses, but the clinical counselor works with a biased sample. Even now, the people who go to psychologists do not represent the whole of society. While I was in college, I heard a psychologist claim that promiscuous girls are always unhappy and maladjusted people. He had learned this from his practice. I realized that this was not scientifically sound, since only the unhappy young women would be likely to go to a psychologist for help, whereas there may have been many women who were happily enjoying their escapades. What the doctor said might have been true, but his grounds for believing it true were not adequate. For psychology to determine whether there are significant psychological differences between men and women, the work will have to be done by trained academic psychological researchers who know how to test hypotheses about human personality. Just as philosophers largely reflected the dominant social views for hundreds of years (see chapter 1), psychologists in clinical practice tend to reflect a cultural consensus. Trusting one's sensitivity and intuition will not do, since these notoriously confirm the cultural consensus with which one began.[14]

We could argue for a long time over the question of whether any of the differences that are observed, or just claimed, between men and women are natural differences. This would not be the most profitable way for us to use the time. A more significant question, a question with which we can accomplish something, is the consequences of such biologically founded differences.

Approaches to Sex Differences

One approach to sex differences has been to assume, or to fear, that such differences would require distinct gender roles for men and women. To facilitate political equality, it was advantageous to stress similarity. If women and men are in fact basically the same, the injustice of requiring different gender roles would be obvious.[15] Gender roles have limited the activities of women and restricted their opportunities for personal development. Although sexual differences do not make different gender roles necessary, they are used by those who want to limit the activities of women to justify distinct roles for men and women.

What would be the consequence of some differences traceable to biology? Would the discovery of natural differences in regard to personality traits or abilities be good reasons to limit men and women to sex-specific roles? It is important to see that the enforcing of sex roles would not be inevitable. It would be a matter of social decision, and the basis for deciding should be determination of what is just and what is productive for the society. Small differences that do not prevent a person from doing a job effectively should not be a bar to that person's employment. To restrict the person because of something that does not make a significant difference would be a breach of justice. It would also be depriving the society of the contribution the person could make. For too long a time, women were not allowed to make contributions to society that they were capable of making. This robbed them and robbed the society. At the same time, men were robbed of opportunities to take part in the nurture of their children and of relationships that many men would have greatly enjoyed.

Mary Midgley holds that we should not be afraid of natural sex differences. Even though women have stressed similarities between men and women as a ground for gender equality, other feminists think that women have special interests, needs, and ideals. She objects to the ethical paradigm that has dominated the thinking of moral philosophers since the Enlightenment, the social contract, which sees individual persons as egoistic "social atoms." Even though some feminists simply put women into this old paradigm and see them as individual egoists who are no better or worse than men, other feminists stress "the distinctive value of women's insights, and also the special bond of sisterhood which is binding women together, rather than letting them be absorbed and assimilated into the wider human group." Midgley is opposed to equating political equality with a need for standardizing. She argues that difference is not always inferiority.[16]

An acceptance of differences is important. Differences can add much more than interest to the social scene. Differences can add a greater variety of talents for greater productivity in the society, and they can add a variety of perspectives on the issues facing the society to give a richer array of options from which to select the best social policies. Will this advantage still hold if some of the differences are related to sex? Midgley does not think we have anything to fear from sex differences, and I believe she is right.

I would go beyond what Midgley says about differences' not always implying inferiority. Even if some of the differences can be interpreted as inferiority, there will probably be no justification for disqualifying people from jobs and social roles on the basis of sex. Even if men are not as gifted linguistically as women, it would not be just or productive to limit all jobs that use linguistic skills to women. Even if women, on the whole, do not learn mathematics as easily or quickly as most men, there would be no justice and no economic advantage to the society in removing women from all jobs that require a knowledge of mathematics. Of course, people who are seriously lacking in certain abilities should not be in certain positions, but this is an individual matter. If it should turn out that one sex is seriously lacking in an ability, something of which there is no indication now, we would simply have to make accommodation for this newly discovered fact. It would not be just, however, to keep all members of a sex out of certain employment because most members of the sex are seriously lacking in the abilities needed. It is hard to imagine anything in which a whole sex is deficient except for male inability to give birth, and we have already learned to live with that. We have made some progress in allowing men to share significantly in child care. It does not matter whether they are as good at it as women. The point is that they are good enough, and roles in the family are not dictated to us by nature but are up to our choice. That is the important thing about all gender-related roles: we can choose which roles people will fill, and that allows us to be fair, to foster personal growth, and to accept the best that anyone can contribute to the common good.

If we are going to allow both men and women the opportunity to live personally rewarding lives and to make the greatest contribution they can to human society, will the approach that we have taken to sexual differences be the best way to face these differences? Christine A. Littleton calls this approach a symmetrical model of sexual equality and describes it as the way of assimilation. She says this is based on the notion that women, if given the chance, can be like men.[17] Alison Jagger describes this approach to sexual differences as blindness to sexual differences and points out that this is not always beneficial to women. The frequent discrepancy following no-fault divorce in the woman's income and the man's and problems with joint custody of children are cited as examples.[18]

Littleton contrasts symmetrical models with approaches that hold that differences between men and women should not be ignored. Asymmetrical models of equality can be based on concepts of "special rights," "accommodation," "acceptance," and "empowerment." She favors an "acceptance" model and argues that society must take account of actual differences without punishing women for them. Whether a difference is biological or social in origin is not important. The important matter is that women be treated as full members of society and differences not be the basis of unjust treatment.[19]

Jaggar writes of equality in terms of responsiveness to sexual difference. It can include special legal protection for women, a kind of institutional recognition of sexual differences. She recognizes that this approach to sexual differences can bring some advantages to women, but it is not without its dangers. It is controversial among feminists because it can protect women from some benefits. In the past, women have been limited by laws and work rules that protected them from certain dangers and hardships, keeping them from well-paying jobs that would subject them to overtime and night work. Also, Jaggar sees that special treatment of women could reinforce sexual stereotypes that are harmful to women. It could encourage a type of essentialism that holds that women are all alike. This could force on some women protection that they do not need or want. It could force all women to pay for medical insurance coverage for which they have no need. Both blindness to sexual differences and official recognition of these differences can threaten the social and economic status of women. Jaggar sees the present discussion between those who stress and those who minimize sexual differences as a debate over strategy.[20]

The question of sexual differences is now seen to be more complex than it appeared a few years ago. The attempt to minimize sex differences in the interest of promoting equal civil rights for women is now questioned by feminists who believe that some ways in which women are not like men should be valued, not covered up as if they were faults or weaknesses. Other feminists are disturbed by the failure of the civil rights approach to benefit women under certain conditions, such as divorce. Stressing the differences between men and women and asking for different treatment for women does not seem a sound approach to other feminists, who remember the history of special treatment of women as a hindrance to many women. They see a danger of sex stereotypes that would be of significant disadvantage to many women. Although recognition of differences between men and women, whether they be biological or social in origin, seems to be more widely accepted by feminists than it once was, the way to interpret those differences has not been settled with much consensus, especially as the interpretation relates to the issue of sexual or gender equality. Equality is a widely supported goal, but there are competing ideas about what it would be. Littleton, Jaggar, and others propose new concepts of equality, taking account of the distinctive needs of women. Some of the older ideas, such as justice for all persons and economic and social equality, will need to be incorporated into the newer concepts of equality. Concepts of gender equality and efforts to achieve it are the subject of the next chapter.

~ 11 ~

Gender Equality

Whether the sexes are alike in all except the generally larger size of men and the primary sexual functions is hard to determine, and as interesting as the issue might be, we do not need to settle it before we decide what kind of society we want. We can see that gender equality is just and that it will be good for human society.

The word *gender* has undergone some big changes in the way it is used, and this has happened so quickly that many dictionaries recognize only the use of the word in grammar to classify nouns as masculine, feminine, or neuter. Larger dictionaries might report an archaic use as a verb referring to parenting and an obsolete use to refer to copulating. Some people insist, often with considerable and surprising heatedness, that that is all the word means and that it should not be used any other way. The word is widely used in other ways, however, so I will explain how I use it. I try to avoid using *gender* as a euphemism for *sex*. Use of the word to refer to social patterns and behaviors associated with sex seems to me to be the most useful way to employ the word. Being a male person or a female person, the biological aspects, is sex. Giving different names for boys and girls, wearing different clothes, having different social roles, and other behaviors connected with one's sex is gender. It has been said that sex is given biologically, whereas gender is what society does in regard to sex.

The kind of equality I am concerned about is gender equality, which involves economic equality, equal freedom for self-realization, and of course, equal civil rights.

The Concept of Equality

There are several notions of equality, and most of them do not work well when we speak of humans' being equal. What sense can we make of the notion that all people are equal? Many people who profess a belief in equality are not able to articulate a concept of equality appropriate for describing humans. Stanley I. Benn explains three notions of equality. We will quickly put aside the two definitions that do not work well when we attempt to apply them to all humans, then we will examine a concept of human equality that can be applied to men and women.[1]

A qualitative or descriptive notion of equality claims that two or more things are equal in respect to some property or properties that can be possessed in varying degree. With this concept of equality, several oranges can be equal in size, sugar content, price, taste, or other quality. It is even possible to compare apples and oranges in respect to size, vitamin content, popularity, or some other quality that can be possessed in varying degree. This type of equality does not work very well, however, in claiming that men and women are equal. It is impossible to specify an important respect in which they are equal: if the property is specific, it will not apply equally to both sexes; if it is very general, it does not say anything significant.

An evaluative concept of equality claims that two or more things are equal according to some standard of value or merit. Two student essays might be of equal merit, even though they are different. One paper might reflect an outstanding knowledge of research done in a field, whereas another might do a brilliant job of explaining an issue and describing the information needed to resolve it. Here the excellence by which the papers are judged is broad enough to include several kinds of achievement. Two comedians, however, might be equally highly praised just on their being funny. How do we apply this to equality of the sexes? We will have a problem in explaining the nature of merit in a way that will not make it vague or prejudicial. We probably cannot apply the notion of evaluative equality in a way that will be meaningful to most people. A religious believer might claim that all people are equally precious to God, but that will seem vague or meaningless to many thoughtful people. It is sometimes said that all people are equal by virtue of being people, that they are equal as persons. This would, if it is a significant claim, eliminate any problem of gender inequality.

The claim sounds, unfortunately, more like reiterating the claim than explaining it. Actually, claiming that people are equal by virtue of being people is not logical as it stands. "All people are people; they are equally people; therefore, they are all equal." We can see that this does not follow logically when we use the same argument with numbers: "All numbers are numbers; they are equally numbers; therefore, all numbers are equal." We might wonder how something that seems so right as claiming that humans are all equally valuable can be illogical, and we might be able to approach the claim more subtly and make it say something important, but first, let us examine a notion of equality with which we should begin our effort to justify gender equality.

The distributive or prescriptive concept of equality is a policy of treating people, or the sexes, equally. Even if we admit that there is no way to describe a quality that can be had in varying degrees that all men and women have to the same degree, and if we cannot find a meaningful way to employ the notion of equal merit, we can commit ourselves to treating the sexes equally. As a nation, we have tried to commit ourselves to treating equally people of all classes, races, and other groupings. That is the prescriptive (S.I. Benn calls it distributive) sense of equality. We are finally trying to treat the sexes equally in school admissions, employment, access to medical care, and other areas of life. This is an important and understandable concept of equality.

Some people are bothered by an attempt to treat people equally, claiming an aversion to treating every person uniformly. Since people are not all alike, to treat them alike would be to treat many people inappropriately. Equality of treatment, however, need not mean identical treatment. William Frankena has explained that treating people equally is making an equal contribution to each one's life.[2] S.I. Benn explains that this means giving an equal consideration to the interests of everyone. Benn defines interests as "conditions necessary to a way of life or to forms of activity that are endorsed as worthwhile, or . . . as conditions necessary to the process of making of oneself something worthy of respect."[3] I think of interests as the needs, wants, and possible benefits and enrichments that the person values or would value with more knowledge and clearer understanding. Considering interests equally does not require giving people whatever they want. A person's wants might not coincide with the person's interests; what a person desires might go counter to the person's real welfare. After considering the interests of some people, we realize that the interests cannot be satisfied. A prisoner's interest in being set free might have to be answered by treating the prisoner as a person insofar as it can be done reasonably. Interests that are harmful to other people must be denied or redirected.

With the prescriptive understanding of gender equality, we commit ourselves to making an equal contribution to the lives of people regardless of gender. This would involve equal access to schooling, employment, legal standing, cultural enrichments, medical care, and any other aspect of life that can involve gender. Whether we are acting upon our commitment successfully will be seen in the way men and women are faring in the areas of life usually affected by gender. It will not result in uniformity of income, social success, or happiness. Making an equal contribution to every person's life does not equalize the success of each person. People have different abilities, social skills, mental acuity, and even appearance. One person will make more of the equal contribution than another, but we have voiced a commitment to treat people equally, and we are now trying to do it.

Why Treat People as Equals?

We need to think more deeply about the commitment to treat people as equals. There are at least two problems that we should face and resolve. One problem is providing a justification for treating people equally (as a policy) when they are not descriptively equal (in fact). We should be able to give a satisfactory explanation of why we should commit ourselves to equality in practice. Our explanation should be better than the fear of what might happen if we do not pacify the groups that are protesting their economic status. That might have been some of the reason in the past, but we can do better. We can find philosophical and moral reasons for equal treatment. Another problem with which we must deal later is possible conflicts between equal treatment and justice and freedom. Now we will focus on the first problem.

We can seek to base equal treatment on a moral justification. If we approach the issue morally, we find meaning in the fact that all people are people. Bernard Williams holds that "All people are people" is a useful tautology. Tautologies do not get us very far as premises in a logical argument, but this tautology has other uses. It is a reminder: we are all members of the same species and have significant things in common.[4] Our common humanity gives us a capacity to feel emotional as well as physical pain. We can all suffer from frustration and broken dreams. We all need affection, a degree of self-respect, and a sense of worth. We have moral capacities and a sense of justice. The useful tautology reminds us of things that are different from what we were looking for in trying to apply descriptive equality to humans. Descriptive equality requires equal possession of qualities that can be had in varying degree. Our common humanity, on the other hand, reminds us of another dimension of human qualities: whether they are had in varying degrees does not matter. These are qualities that make a moral difference when they are had in any degree, and some of them do not admit significantly of difference in degree.

When we see the demand for equal treatment as a moral matter, several moral principles add weight to the rightness of equal treatment. Kant's practical imperative (treat all people as ends, never merely as means), the principle of utility (accomplish the greatest balance of pleasure over pain), and the demands of justice converge on this issue. The moral basis for treating men and women equally in respect to gender matters is so strong that very strong arguments would be needed to justify continuing practices and gender roles that women consider unfair to them. Women claim that gender roles that restrict them in career choices are grossly unjust. Gender roles that restrict them in dress and personal deportment are frustrating and irritating. Are there any arguments that justify continuing gender roles?

Are Separate Sex Roles Defensible?

Several arguments are commonly made in support of continuing gender roles that many women see as continuation of patriarchy. Most of these arguments for gender roles are criticized by Christine Pierce and Joyce Trebilcot. Let us examine some of them.[5]

One argument for gender roles is that they are inevitable. We have already looked at claims that patriarchal practices are inevitable in the previous chapter. Arguments that gender differences cannot be avoided were based on cultural history, endocrinology, and certain psychological theories. It seems, however, to belie the professed certainty that gender roles are inevitable when social pressure and various regulations are employed in support of such roles. That which is inevitable certainly needs no efforts on its behalf. John Stuart Mill wrote that the "anxiety of mankind to interfere in behalf of nature, lest nature should not succeed in effecting its purpose, is an altogether unnecessary solic- itude." Mill understood, of course, the reason for the appeal to nature. Men do not want women as unwilling slaves, so they "turned the whole force of education" to persuade women that their character is not like that of men, but "it is their nature" to live for others.[6] Now women know that it is not their nature and they do not need to live for others; patriarchy is not inevitable.

A commonly used argument for gender roles appeals to nature. The problematic use of appeals to nature is examined in chapter 3. There we see that there are problems with the meaning of *natural* and the use of nature as a normative concept. Most of the notions of what is natural and un-natural do not have any normative significance, especially moral significance. Other concepts of what is natural are meaningful only in theological or metaphysical contexts that are defended by ap- peals to tradition rather than with arguments that would be accepted by reasonable people outside a particular religion. Concepts of nature that are not accepted by large numbers of people do not provide a strong enough basis for establishing social policy and practice in pluralistic and democratic countries.

Separate gender roles have been defended on the grounds that they are efficient. Christine Pierce counters the argument that it is efficient to have women in subservient roles with the question "efficient for whom?"[7] Restricting people according to gender might well be effi- cient for some people, at least in making their jobs simpler as employers. Running military establishments might be simpler. Efficiency in people's pursuit of a richly rewarding life would hardly be fostered by gender roles. Women who have professional or career goals that women in times past were discouraged from pursuing will not find gender roles efficient. Men and women who do not want their lives restricted by the patterns of cultures of the past will not find gender roles efficient. Efficiency must be seen in relation to goals. Only those who are satisfied with the life goals of previous generations will find gender roles efficient.

An even stronger counter of the argument from efficiency points out that efficiency is not the only, nor the highest, value that we should consider. Even if gender roles did turn out to be more efficient for our present society than allowing people to choose more freely their style of life, the gender roles would not be justified on such grounds. Justice and freedom to develop individual talents and capacities should over- ride considerations of efficiency.[8]

A benevolent-sounding defense of gender roles is that they foster the well-being and happiness of women. This defense implies that women are especially weak and vulnerable because of physical and psychological differences between men and women. The claim that there are significant differences between the sexes that require different roles is highly dubious. Even if the claims of such differences could be demonstrated, there are problems with this defense of gender roles. There is no evidence that gender roles create more happiness for women generally. Many women have spoken of the unhappiness caused by limiting roles. Imposed roles that do not allow for personal choice and fulfillment cause unhappiness. The welfare and happiness that are claimed to come from gender roles are not as apparent.[9]

The most significant objection to this defense of gender roles does not rest on factual claims and counterclaims. We must see that other values than happiness are at stake. Using one's special talents, making an important contribution in some area of life, being free to do something new and unusual for a woman to do, and taking leadership in a family, community, or nation when one has the ability are values for which a person might sacrifice some security and happiness. Women should not be denied personal responsibility for their lives. Women can decide the trade-off (if any) between happiness and other values.[10]

Gender roles have even been defended on the grounds of the attractiveness of certain differences between men and women.[11] This has usually been a case of men's finding women attractive in roles that were very costly to the women. In some periods of the past, women of certain classes spent a large part of each day in dressing. Even now women are put under pressure to meet a standard of beauty that can be costly and troublesome. High heels are only a cut above foot binding, and reducing diets are almost as painful as whalebone stays. The real problem with defending gender roles on the grounds of attractiveness is that the charm of the gender differences is related to notions of women as weak creatures who are valued for physical beauty and not for the same kinds of achievement a man would value in himself. The charm of the different roles rests on inequality and limitation of ability.

What Should Replace Sex Roles?

None of the arguments for maintaining separate gender roles can justify the practice. What should take the place of male and female roles?

Several feminist writers advocate androgyny. *Androgyny* is another term used with a meaning still not given in many dictionaries, which define the word only as "hermaphroditism." Some feminists use the term to refer to people's having a mixture of personality traits that includes some traits that have been considered masculine and some considered feminine. Androgyny in this sense has been held to be the ideal for both men and women.[12]

Joyce Trebilcot points out vagueness in the concept of androgyny. One notion, which she calls "monoandrogynism," is that there is one set of desirable traits that all persons should have. Another concept, which she calls "polyandrogynism," is that each person should be free to choose any traits regardless of their previous gender association.[13] Having all people limited to one set of personality traits is not realistic and would be unduly restrictive even if it were possible. Polyandrogynism is much more appealing, but there might be some reasonable limits set on characteristics that would be approved. Some aspects of the "macho" personality might be discouraged, along with some aspects of the overly submissive "clinging vine."

The concept of androgyny is not accepted wholeheartedly by all feminists. In *Beyond God the Father* (1973), Mary Daly described "reaching out toward completeness of human being in the members of both sexes" as "moving toward androgynous being," and she mentions androgynous being favorably in numerous passages. In one passage, however, she says that the word *androgynous* will become meaningless "because the word reflects the archaic heritage of psycho-sexual dualism," and in a paper published two years later, she rejects the concept of androgyny because it seems to give some acknowledgment to the association of some traits with maleness and others with femaleness.[14] Being part female and part male may not be what we will look for when we transcend the inequality of patriarchal culture. Especially since some feminists find special value in some female traits, we might develop new types of masculine and feminine personalities, equal but different types of each gender, something that will be possible when patriarchy has been surpassed. We look forward to people who will be free and whole and able to realize their full potential as human beings. What follows restrictive gender roles need not make people all alike in dress, manners, and ways of thinking. It should make people more interesting, sex more rewarding, and our lives happier.

We would do well to drop the often-confusing concept of androgyny and specify what should take the place of gender roles. Sharon Bishop (Hill) holds that self-determination, a choice of ways to develop their capacities and pursue their interests, is what women want.[15] Is there a right to self-determination? Such a right has long been recognized for men. There is no justification for denying to women the freedom that men have enjoyed. All rights are limited, of course, and the right of men to self-realization is limited by the rights of other people and the requirement that we not injure other people unjustly, so we might expect the right of women to self-realization to have limits, as Bishop recognizes. These will need to be reasonable limits, however, not the old limits under which women have long suffered. For women, the right to determine their own lives has been limited in both subtle and obvious ways that have not been used to limit (systematically) the rights of men. The autonomy of women has been limited by educational practices, family and social pressures, customs, religious teachings, and economic factors that kept mature individuals from exercising autonomy. Some laws that limited women socially and economically have only recently been changed. Even with no legal barriers to their self-determination, people can be given a limited view of their possibilities. This can start at a very young age; children's toys and games can limit the vision both girls and boys can have of their lives, and parental expectations can narrow the range of children's expectations.[16]

Abandoning gender roles should give men and women greater freedom for personal development and self-realization. Achievement of self-realization will certainly result in a variety of personalities, ways of life, and levels of success, since people are not all alike. Some differences might be primarily sex differences, but I expect differences within each sex to be more pronounced than differences between the sexes. The important thing is to achieve equality without destroying all personal difference and sexual differences, if there are any significant ones. Christine A. Littleton speaks of "equality of acceptance," which accepts differences and makes them less costly.[17]

Alison Jaggar points out a need to go beyond thinking about equality in terms of male experience, which tends to make equality mean the masculinization of women. We need, she says, to be critical of the ways in which equality is measured. She envisions a world in which justice and equality are united in a goal of mutual care, but it will not be the "feminized, sentimentalized, privatized care with which we are familiar." It will not be care as an irrational or nonrational feeling or care as self-sacrifice. It will not be care in contrast to justice. She says, "Feminists need to develop a distinctive conception of care, one that draws on but transcends women's traditional practice." The goal of this care is not to produce uniformity. Jaggar says, "Feminist care must be responsive both to our common humanity and our inevitable particularity."[18]

With any adequate concept of gender equality, there will need to be changes in social and business practices. Many people have not changed appreciably in response to the growing concern over equality. There are still people, men and women, who have not gone beyond the pattern of the man's asking for the date, deciding what to do, and paying for everything. These people are certainly not prepared to accept changes in the role of parents in child rearing or the matter of family decisions about money.

I do not want to suggest that dating patterns are a trivial matter. This might be the first time in a young person's life to come to grips with gender equality. Equality can be reconciled with differences fairly easily in this aspect of male and female relations. Some of us have found that dignity and autonomy on both sides can be preserved by sharing, perhaps with the more affluent person paying for dinners and the one with less income paying for lunches. (It might be difficult for many males if the female has the better income, but an insecure man might have difficulty with successful women no matter who pays for dinner.) Until there is no disparity of incomes, this may be the best we can do. Either person must be free to initiate a date, lovemaking, even marriage. When we are really equal, the woman proposing marriage will no longer be the subject of a joke.

Since I open doors for people of either sex who have an armful of books or would otherwise be helped if I held the door, and people of both sexes often do the same for me, I hope we get over common courtesies being an issue. They may be an obvious matter, but they are just a starting point. From there we can move on to more significant equality in the home, the workplace, the school, and the political arena. The ultimate point is equality, not politeness. When women no longer need doors opened and packages carried because the fashions to which they must conform force them to dress awkwardly, we will be able to practice real courtesy and show signs of respect for people as people. That is a worthy goal, respect for people because they are people and acceptance of their differences.

Greater economic justice must be a primary goal of a less gendered society. The latest reports of the economic differential between the earnings of men and women show continuing repression of women. Most of the people living in poverty in the United States are women and children. Women of color and Hispanic women receive even lower incomes than women generally. Women of color are aptly described as "doubly disadvantaged" in the labor market.[19] Until women have the economic strength available to men, they will not be secure in their freedoms.

Some of the difficulties that women face, such as harassment in the workplace, are sometimes approached as separate problems to be addressed apart from consideration of economic factors. We will make more progress in solving the problems when we see their connection to the low economic standing of women. Seeing all sexual harassment as a sexual matter is almost as foolish as seeing rape as aggressive lust. Much harassment is an exercise of power. It will continue to be a problem until women have more power, and the most important power is economic power. I believe some offensive behavior, as when an older man calls the women in his workforce "girls," is an expression of his feeling of social superiority, a matter of class distinction more than sex. Women in high official roles are not included with the girls, and file clerks, bookkeepers, and secretaries will no longer be girls when they are the economic equals of the men. Men were called "boys," perhaps still are at times, when they were members of unskilled and poorly paid work crews. We can surely address sexual harassment more effectively when we can distinguish sexual harassment from the exercise of social and economic privilege.

Affirmative Action

Affirmative action programs have been an important part of the effort to secure economic equality for women and members of minority groups. Even though almost everyone claims to be in favor of equal opportunity for everyone, people mean different things by it. Onora O'Neill made an important distinction between formal and substantial interpretations of equal opportunity.[20] Formal equality is equal freedom to use talents, with no legal or quasi-legal obstacles. It is the concept of everyone's playing by the same rules. Equality in this sense would certainly be better than the unfair treatment of women and minorities prevailing in the past, and some philosophers and others think equality in this sense should be the goal of society. Lisa Newton, who gives a stronger philosophical basis to her view than do most supporters of formal equality, thinks that the ideal of the rule of law, "equal access to the public realm," upheld by Aristotle as political justice, would be undermined by affirmative action. She says it "destroys justice, law, equality, and citizenship itself, and replaces them with power struggles."[21]

O'Neill and others find weaknesses in the formal approach. Because of different educational backgrounds and other conditions that make it difficult for some groups to compete on an equal footing with people of other groups, formal equality results in disproportionate success for some groups and failure for others. The fair rules discriminate against those who are less ready to compete. O'Neill supports programs to provide substantial equality, by which the success rates of all social groups are equal.[22]

The effort to achieve substantive equality is usually called affirmative action. It involves attempts to increase the number of women and members of minority groups in employment through announcing job openings in publications that are read by members of the targeted groups, searching in other ways for applicants from these groups, and preferential hiring. Preferential hiring refers to selecting members of targeted groups from a pool of qualified candidates. It is the preferential hiring that encounters most opposition.

One of the grounds for affirmative action is recompense for past wrongs. Most public discussion of affirmative action seems to assume that this is the basis for preferential hiring. There are a number of commonly used arguments against affirmative action that are based on problems with trying to make recompense for past social injustice, along with counterarguments.

Outside of academic circles, little is heard of a less problematic justification for affirmative action. This is to take the steps necessary to create a just society in the future. Richard A. Wasserstrom sees affirmative action as an instrumentality used to break a vicious cycle of discrimination by giving power to weak groups, providing role models, and promoting objectivity in hiring and school admission, which is a relevant social ideal. The justification of affirmative action lies in its being a way "to alter the social reality in order to bring about a greater congruence between it and the relevant social ideal."[23]

Irving Thalberg also supports a future-oriented approach to affirmative action. He sees it as action to counteract the subtle effects of previous discrimination on the attitudes of hiring officers, judicial officials, school personnel, and other people who can have a significant effect on people's lives. Thalberg used the term *visceral racism* for an unrecognized feeling of avowed liberals toward people of color. Even though these people do not think of themselves as harboring racial prejudice, they might tend to expect less of people of certain races or have other expectations of them that could influence decisions regarding hiring, awarding of fellowships, or other matters important to a young person's future. Affirmative action can help counteract this visceral racism. Some people think there is a visceral sexism that can be overcome through affirmative action.[24]

I believe that most people carry pictures around in their minds, pictures of what a professor is like, what a police officer is like, what a lawyer or a physician is like. It is not surprising that most of these pictures are of a white male. People in positions of authority or prestige have been white males in most of our experience. The problem with these pictures is that they establish our "visceral" expectations. They can give us a biased view of qualifications for the jobs and the positions that can enable women and members of minority groups to get ahead socially and economically and eventually change people's mental pictures. If nothing is done to counteract these pictures, decisions that critically affect people's lives will be made on the basis of prejudice, even on the part of well-meaning people. Wasserstrom says that the presence of women and nonwhite people in positions of prestige and importance will help change the conception of the kinds of people who are appropriate holders of such positions.[25]

Affirmative action has already started changing our society, but we need to effect more change before we can claim to be a just society. In the university where I teach, women and African-Americans, as well as people of various ethnic groups, are represented in departments and administrative positions that had only white males before affirmative action programs were put into effect. As a member of a number of search committees, I have seen how affirmative action works to contribute to the diversity of the faculty and staff of the university. There is still room to increase opportunities for women and for racial minorities.

If our affirmative action efforts are future-oriented, we will avoid some of the arguments raised against affirmative action when it is seen as paying a debt for injustices in the past. It does not matter that the victims who suffered most from injustice, and those who were the prime perpetuators, are now dead. We are trying to create a more just society for people living today and their children and grandchildren. The question of how long we need to continue the program to make up for the past wrong need not arise. We must continue the program until we have justice between groups. To determine which groups need help, we do not need to look to their history, but to the present situation.

There is one objection to affirmative action that we must face even with an approach based on building a more just future. Some people claim that preferential hiring is "reverse discrimination," an injustice to young white males. Such a charge is serious and must be taken seriously, but that does not mean that the charge is justified. We do not need to justify asking white males to make a sacrifice for the good of the country in the future, even though we could make such a case morally. Mary Anne Warren points out that affirmative action places white males in the same position they would have in a just society.[26] This may overstate the case, but it is true that white males in a just society would face competition from women and members of minority groups that white males did not face before the adoption of affirmative action programs. White males came to have certain expectations, but these expectations are based on the operation of a society that kept large parts of the society in positions that did not offer them much reward or much promise of a good future. It is difficult, of course, to find that one's expectations are not in accord with the goals of society. It seems unfair to many young men that they are the ones who face disappointment, especially when they do not see the necessity of changing the rules for the good of society.

The charge that preferential hiring is reverse discrimination fails to consider some important points. It is not like previous racist and sexist discrimination. Wasserstrom points out that the purpose of affirmative action is different from that of the discrimination against women and people of color. The old social pattern was designed to concentrate power in the hands of white males. Preferential hiring is designed to rectify this. Unlike the discriminatory practices, with preferential hiring race and sex do not automatically exclude people from consideration. There is no way programs of preferential treatment can be seen as placing white men in the same oppressed condition in which the old system put women and nonwhite people.[27]

Thalberg points out that affirmative action is not like the original discrimination in the way it operates. No one is utterly barred from jobs, good schools, or scholarships the way people were once barred because of race or sex. Another important difference is that no one is denied protection from violence, insults, or other abusive treatment under affirmative action programs. Thalberg thinks this applies to race more than to sex.[28]

One charge against affirmative action is that it stigmatizes women and members of minority groups who have achieved success through their own talent and effort. Some beneficiaries of affirmative action have claimed that it denies them the recognition or the self-satisfaction to which they are entitled.[29] There probably are people who think that successful women and minorities have not achieved what they have on their own merits. It is undoubtedly easier to think this if one has minimal or no contact with these achievers. When affirmative action works as it is supposed to, it gives members of groups that were previously denied opportunity a chance to strive for success; it does not of itself give them success. It is interesting that white males in segregated societies did not feel stigmatized because of the advantage they enjoyed.

It would be too much to hope that a program such as affirmative action would be free of all faults and problems. It does not seem right, for example, that a woman who grew up in an affluent home and had the best of educational opportunities should be favored in professional employment over a man who succeeded academically in spite of poverty and an unpromising family background. Even with its faults, however, a program such as affirmative action might be the only way for the nation to make significant strides toward justice for all sectors of the society.

A meaningful equality for men and women will require the continuation of social changes made possible by affirmative action and the legal changes that began with women's gaining the right to vote in 1920. Matters of property rights and equity in marriage and child custody followed. Catherine A. MacKinnon says that more changes in legal codes will be a necessary part of securing gender equality, and the issue of differences between males and females as well as commonality of males and females will have to be faced both in legal terms and in economic terms.[30]

It is important to understand that those who see affirmative action as a means to reaching the goal of a just society do not see affirmative action as the goal itself. It is a means to reaching a goal that has been the ideal upheld by humanistic thinkers throughout the centuries. When the goal is reached, the means will no longer be needed. A just society can be "color-blind," and it can operate on the basis of formal equality before the law and formal concepts of justice. It is a great and beautiful goal, but it cannot be reached without the painful work of clearing the debris of many centuries of injustice.

As we move beyond gender roles, new behavior patterns will evolve. We can see ahead of time that some features must be a part of the new patterns. Equality must be built on freedom and economic justice. Other aspects of a less gendered society will have to be worked out. Some people seem to fear that we may lose as much as we gain. I see no reason for this fear. I expect a society in which life will be more interesting, people will be more attractive, and freedom will be used responsibly. It cannot come too soon.

～ 12 ～

Sex Talk

The way we talk about sexual activities and relationships says a lot about us. The ordinary words of informal speech reveal our attitudes toward sex and toward members of the two sexes. In addition to reflecting our attitudes, our words for sex talk can encourage or give a kind of legitimacy to attitudes we might do well to discourage.

Several aspects of sex talk can be seen as forms of linguistic discrimination against women. In our less polite and formal talk, women are referred to in ways that degrade them. Sexual intercourse is spoken of in terms that suggest female passivity, degradation, and even injury. The English language has a built-in denigration of women in its use of male terms to refer to humans generally. In our culture women have been taught to use language in ways that identify them with passivity, irresolution, and weakness.

Robert Baker claims that the way we identify something reflects our conception of it. The conception of women in our culture is male chauvinistic. Baker says the terms used to refer to woman are similar to the terminology used by whites to refer to blacks and the related white conceptualization of blacks.[1]

Baker distinguishes several types of terms used to designate women. They are spoken of as playthings, as domesticated or pet animals or birds, in terms of typical female dress, in crude terms for sex organs, and in "neutral" terms such as *lady, gal, and broad.* Only males typically use non-neutral terms for women, use of which indicate a denigrating concept of women. These terms suggest something weak that can be controlled and used. Note that bird terms refer to small birds,

159

and even when the bird is attractive, its domesticity seems to be the relevant aspect. With the exception of *vixen* and *fox,* the animal terms refer to passive creatures like cows and chickens. Names of large and dangerous animals are not used.[2]

Robin Lakoff holds that even the neutral terms, which women might use, show sex discrimination. *Lady* as a euphemism for *woman* gives a frivolous tone to the sentence; in job terminology, *lady* is used for demeaning jobs, such as *cleaning lady. Lady doctor* and *lady lawyer* are crude expressions and never used in polite speech. In titles of organizations, *ladies* indicates lack of importance. *Girl* suggests immaturity or lack of responsibility.[3]

Lakoff's view on words such as *lady* and *girl* has been questioned. Jacqueline Fortunata thinks *cleaning lady* might be used to euphemize the profession of cleaning rather than the sex of the person. Only in situations in which the person recognizes that she is being demeaned would use of *lady* degrade women. She has found that women, who frequently refer to coworkers as "the girls," have no thought of demeaning. She says the term refers to "girl-gals," which I take to mean the women with whom a woman works or plays.[4] When the employer calls women in unsalaried positions "girls," it might well be an expression of feelings of social superiority, as I suggested in chapter 11.

It is probably inadvisable to generalize about the use of neutral expressions in the United States. Usage is affected by regions. People from the deep South and the Midwest do not seem to find in the term *lady* the same implications that might be seen elsewhere. Sundry practices, including language use, are not the same everywhere. When Lakoff talks about how girls and boys are taught to think and behave, she is on risky ground. Such things are not the same everywhere, for all ethnic groups, for all religious groups, or for people of all ages.

Lakoff gives examples of "inoffensive" but not harmless ways of referring to women, such as referring to them in terms of a man, not as an autonomous person (for example, "Mrs. Henry Smith" or "Henry's wife"). Women are described in terms of male reaction to them, with references to figure, beauty, and hair color in situations in which this would not be done with a man. Reference to the husband when it is not relevant indicates a lack of independent status of the woman. Use of "Mrs." instead of "Dr." or "Judge" seems to diminish the significance of the woman. Lakoff is not alone in objecting to "Miss" and "Mrs." when the one male title does not indicate marital status.[5]

Baker calls attention to our conception of sexual intercourse as indicated in the terms used to talk about it. The common (as contrasted with the polite) ways of talking about intercourse indicate that the male is active and the female passive. He says this is not determined by physiological differences but is the result of custom. The passive construction can indicate that the person (female) is being harmed, while the active person (male) is harming. Baker notes that the nonsexual use of these sexual terms is to show hostility or threaten harm. The different views of sex from the male perspective and from the female are indicated by the two-room illustration. A woman is lying on her back on a bed while a line of men is waiting in the hall to visit her. She is assumed to be the one being used by the men. A man in the same situation is assumed to be a lucky fellow with many women at his disposal.[6]

Barbara Lawrence holds that objection to the common words for sexual intercourse is not just a middle-class hang-up. Such words cause harm. She is concerned about words for coitus that carry notions of hurting. This is indicated by the origin of some words and by the imagery of others. There are several explanations of the etymology of the word *fuck,* but little agreement about which is correct. The term may have come from corruption of obsolete words for beat or for a club. The imagery of the term *screw* is clearly unpleasant, and *nail* is only a little less so. Lawrence also notes that some words for coitus reduce human orgasm and other functions to their most mechanical, least organic, description. Words that are taboo in polite society, but common elsewhere, suggest male self-involvement and contempt for the female partner. One of the crudest words suggests that there is no difference between vulva and anus, which she says denies women their biological identity and their humanness.[7]

So few people know or care about the etymologies of common words that the origin of words used to talk about sex may have little effect upon people's attitudes, but the imagery of some words may affect attitudes toward sexual acts and toward people of the other or one's own sex. The indication that people think of males as active and dominant in coitus and women as passive and possibly being hurt should be a matter of concern.

Stephanie Ross holds that etymologies have little influence. She thinks that certain words hurt because they have become dead metaphors. Once actual metaphors, they are not recognized as metaphors but are treated as ordinary nouns. They continue to express attitudes.[8]

Although several writers are concerned about the common terms and gutter words for talking about sex, Janice Moulton sees problems with the polite expressions for coitus. The expressions themselves, such as *intercourse,* are symmetrical, in that they suggest that the male and female activities are reciprocal. The actual dictionary definitions, however, suggest that the male action characterizes the act and is the aim of it. Thomas Aquinas held that seminal discharge defines the essence of sexual intercourse, and centuries later dictionaries define coitus in terms of insertion and ejaculation. She refers to the definition in *Webster's Third New International Dictionary.*[9] (The smaller dictionaries avoid the issue by defining *coitus* as intercourse and *intercourse* as coitus.) Moulton makes us see that we do not avoid pitfalls in our talk about sex by avoiding coarse language. She finds much of our talk dishonest. She calls talk about simultaneous orgasm and vaginal orgasm "diplomatic" misrepresentation. She denies that coitus as usually practiced is symmetrical, a mutual activity, but holds that it should involve the arousal and satisfaction of both partners.[10]

Robin Lakoff raises another aspect of language and sex. She claims that women are subjected to "linguistic discrimination" not only in the way they are talked about but in the way they are taught to use language. What she calls "women's language" is a special style of speech used by women. It becomes an excuse to keep women in a demeaning position. Little girls, she says, are taught not to talk like boys. Talking like a lady involves the choice of words used, syntactic rules, and intonational patterns.[11]

The special words of women's language include color terms that men do not ordinarily use, such as *mauve.* There is also excessive use of weak particles such as *Oh, dear!* and *My, my!* Men's stronger expletives make them appear stronger. Women's use of adjectives such as *adorable, sweet,* and *divine* suggests that women are frivolous and make trivial judgments.[12]

The syntax of women's language includes such locutions as the tag questions "isn't it?" and "don't you think so?" These are used by women to avoid making a strong assertion, which makes them seem unsure of themselves. Lakoff argues that linguistic imbalances reflect real-world inequities. She believes the situation needs changing but holds that we should not try to attack the disease by attacking all of its symptoms. We should focus on the really demeaning terms and usages. Unlike most feminists, she thinks that "pronominal neutralization" is misdirected.[13]

Is Lakoff correct about women's language? Many of my younger students do not think that girls are taught any longer to use women's language, whereas others say they were taught to talk like a lady. This shows one of the problems with generalization about cultural matters. There seem to be some significant differences by generation, region of the country, social class, ethnicity, urban or rural environment, and religion, not to mention differences in families. Students' reactions to what Lakoff says about terms like *lady* vary widely. I am amused to remember that my father used particles such as *Oh my!* and *Dear me!* and I learned them from him. Maybe he, as a clergyman, was trying to avoid profanity; I do not remember other men using the expressions.

Lakoff's dismissing of the effort to avoid using male pronouns generically seems to be a minority opinion. There is a broad consensus that this usage and use of *man* to refer to humanity should be avoided. Since words affect attitudes as well as reflect them, it seems to many people that pronouns are important and the generic use of *man* is detrimental. A number of learned societies have considered this important and have published guidelines to nonsexist language. A number of publishers avoid usage that is considered sexist. The National Council of Teachers of English, the American Psychological Association, and the American Philosophical Association have published guides. I give my students the accompanying short guide (pp. 164–65), which is based largely on the American Philosophical Association guide.[14]

Some time ago, a radical proposal was made for avoiding use of the masculine pronoun generically. This proposal was based on the fact that only the singular pronouns in English indicate gender. The suggestion was that the singular pronouns for generic use be patterned after the plural pronouns, *they, their,* and *them.* This would give us the following forms:

tey—for *he or she* (nominative case)
ter—for *his or her* (possessive case)
tem—for *him or her* (objective case)

This might look difficult, but it is very easy. I read a paper written this way[15] and found it very easy to get comfortable with the usage. I

Some Guidelines to Nonsexist Language

(Nonsexist wording is in **boldface** in the examples below.) Nonsexist language need not sound awkward. It should not be ungrammatical. Avoid disagreement between pronoun and antecedent:

"Each new student must complete their own registration form" is incorrect.
"All new students must complete their own registration form" is correct.

1. Avoid the generic use of *he* by
    a. deleting un-necessary pronouns:
        "One student may be assertive in his personal relations while another lets others dominate him."
        "One student may be assertive in personal relations while another lets others dominate."
        "Sometimes a client kills himself."
        "Sometimes a client commits suicide."
    b. pluralizing nouns:
        "The philosopher uses reason to guide him."
        "Philosophers use reason to guide them."
    c. substituting articles for pronouns:
        "The introspective student may drift into his private world."
        "The introspective student may drift into a private world."
        "The drunk driver is likely to wreck his car."
        "The drunk driver is likely to wreck the car."
    d. using *who* to avoid *he:*
        "If a shopper plans ahead, he (she) can save money."
        "The shopper who plans ahead can save money."
    e. substituting *one* (or *we* or *you*) for *he:*
        "A student can buy a diet drink if he prefers."
        "One can buy a diet drink if one prefers."
    f. using the passive voice:
        "The philosopher uses his reason to guide him."
        "The philosopher is guided by reason."
    g. using a participle to avoid a pronoun:
        "The careful driver looks both ways when he turns."
        "The careful driver looks both ways when turning."
    h. using nouns instead of pronouns:
        "The dean is the chief officer of the college; he must have academic standing and administrative skills."
        "The dean is the chief officer of the college; a dean must have academic standing and administrative skills."
        "When treated rudely by a clerk, ignore her."
        "Ignore rude clerks."
2. Eliminate the generic use of *man* by
    a. using *humanity, human beings,* and so forth
    b. rewording, referring to *we, everyone,* and so forth

(continued)

3. Avoid sexual stereotyping in roles by
   a. using titles for women such as would be used for men
      Ms., Dr., Prof.
   b. using the same titles for women and men:
      "She is chairperson of the Art Department, and he is chairman of the English Department."
      "She is chair of the Art Department, and he is chair of the English Department."
   c. using gender-free terms
      chairman/chair, chairperson
      newsman/reporter, writer
   d. avoiding first names for women when men are not being addressed by their first name
   e. avoiding irrelevant references to gender:
      woman lawyer, male nurse, authoress, waitress
   f. avoiding stereotyping in choice of examples. Include activities and interests traditionally associated with females, but do not always refer to girls' playing with dolls and boys' climbing trees.
      Note: Do not use the generic "she" with activities traditionally associated with females.
4. Direct quotations must be given verbatim, but offensive passages can be paraphrased and presented as indirect quotations.

was sorry not to see more use made of it. If any brave soul wishes to try to resurrect this sensible way to avoid unnecessary genderization of the language, I will be glad to join the crusade.

What we need to do does not require any radical changes in the language itself, but it does require some attention to what we say and how we say it. Avoiding linguistic discrimination against women is not asking very much of us. It will not be difficult, and it is only fair.

～ 13 ～

Romantic Love

Love is held in high regard in our popular culture. It is what everyone needs and wants, and it is supposed to be the answer to almost every problem. It must come as a surprise to many people to find that love is not highly acclaimed by everyone. A negative attitude toward the boy-meets-girl kind of romance has been expressed in a number of ways, some of which we see in other chapters. In the chapter on pornography, we see that some feminists seem to interpret ordinary heterosexual relationships as a kind of violence against women.[1] In explaining the awfulness of sexual assault, Pamela Foa holds that ordinary sexual intercourse is rapelike.[2]

Shulamith Firestone says that love is the pivot of women's oppression. Men, she says, live for work, whereas women live for love. Men are unable to love; they need love but cannot love. Women, as the ones who love, are vulnerable unless there is a mutual exchange in the relationship. Love can enrich and enlarge the lovers, but bliss between lovers is seldom the case. Love becomes "complicated, corrupted or obstructed by an unequal balance of power."[3]

Firestone calls the usual unequal distribution of power in the family "the sex class system." This is reminiscent of the Marxist view of the family stated by Friedrich Engels, who saw the relationship of husband and wife in terms of the class struggle; in fact, he called it the first class struggle.[4] Firestone says, however, that Marx and Engels do not give an adequate explanation; sex class does not all come from economics.[5]

Firestone traces the sex class system to psychological and sexual elements. She says that the man must romantically idealize the women in order to fall in love with her. This is necessary because he, as the person of power, must justify "his descent into a lower caste" in marriage. The woman, Firestone says, knows that this is false but demands this falling in love. What makes falling in love bad is the political context of unequal power. It would not be harmful apart from this context, and idealization of a loved one could be a case of seeing overlooked qualities. In the present context, however, certain things need to be recognized. Men cannot love, and the "clinging" behavior of women is necessary because of their social situation. The situation, she says, has not changed significantly in recent years.[6]

The love that Firestone finds harmful to women is romance, which she describes as a diseased form of love that reinforces the sex class system. She explains the components of romance by which it works as a tool to promote that system. First is eroticism, a concentration on sexuality, displacing social and affectional needs onto sex. This reinforces male dominance and the marriage structure. Second is the sex privatization of women. Men, she says, believe that all women are alike, but they do not want women to think of themselves as a class. Men keep women from recognizing their class membership by individualizing them through making the woman's sexuality synonymous with her individuality; what she has in common with all women is held to be what makes her special. Firestone says that men are conscious of this technique for duping women. The third component of romance is the beauty ideal. Women struggle to approximate a rare ideal of beauty, which tends to make them look alike, which, in turn, makes women more easily stereotyped. There is a powerful cultural apparatus to reinforce the beauty ideal, with advertising promoting image-consciousness. This is so powerful that men even become objects to themselves.[7]

What are we to think of such attacks on romantic love? We should not dismiss them out of hand just because they are radical. Although it strikes me as absurd to claim that men deliberately carry out a plot to keep women from realizing that they are members of an oppressed class, since I have a hard time believing that men are organized or clever enough to pull off such a scheme, there are good reasons to be critical of romance. Even if it does not happen from clever design, part of what Firestone says about sex privatization is realistic. Men, as well as women, fall into this attitude, the worst aspect of which, it seems to me, is that people fail to appreciate the real personhood of the people with whom they are most intimate. Hair, breasts, legs, and genital equipment, as important as they are, are not what make men or women persons. They are necessary but not sufficient conditions of being a human person. The beauty ideal has caused much un-necessary heart-ache and inexcusable expenditure of money and effort.

What are we to do about this? Firestone does not want to attack beauty or erotic relationships between people. The problem, as I see it, is that all too often romance does not develop the depth of understanding and commitment, caring and sharing, that are the marks of love. It is hard to see romance as a bad thing in a relationship that deepens and matures. In our culture, most sexual love relationships begin as romance. Even Plato, who urged a love directed toward intellectual growth, acknowledged that love begins with attraction to a body. We do not need to think of romance as being opposed to love. Romance need not be banished when love arrives.

Romance that remains on an immature level can be harmful. It is a source of heartache and sweetness that turns to hatred, the material of many country and folk ballads. Even recognizing this, we might not agree entirely with Firestone's belief that romance is the tool with which men maintain a sex class system. We might not agree that romance is always a debased form of love that lacks the realism, understanding, and commitment to a person on which love thrives, although it can become this.

Virginia Held is aware of the problems that an inequality of power can cause in a relationship, but she is much more optimistic about sexual love than is Firestone. She points out that Karl Marx, in his 1844 manuscripts, supported the ideal of mutuality in relations between men and women. Mutuality would involve several aspects. The association would not be a relation of power. Neither person would use the other self-interestedly. Each person would recognize the other's pleasure as a good in itself. Held believes that such relationships sometimes exist in purely sexual relations, but they are less frequent when other aspects of life are included.[8] If Held is correct, sexual love need not be the focus of inequality between a man and a woman. It can be the aspect of a relationship in which equality can first be practiced. As Held sees this, sex might not involve the complicating aspects of a relationship in which economic or social power would matter. Held says that mutuality in a relationship requires avoidance of paternalism or maternalism wherein one partner decides what is good for the other and attempts to coerce the other. It might be the case that sexual relations involve less ground for such efforts to coerce the partner as appear in other aspects of the relationship.

Held does not minimize the damage that an imbalance of power can do in a relationship. Disparity of power leads to the woman's hiding her feelings, since she is usually the less powerful person. This allows the man easily to avoid knowing of the woman's dissatisfaction. With equality of power, men would have to consider women's feelings. Held believes that women must have economic, social, political, and psychological independence to enable mutual relations. She thinks, however, that there can be experiments with renunciation of power.[9]

Might it be possible for a couple to ignore the power differential between them and live as equals? Held thinks of this starting in the bedroom, which is probably the most likely place for it to succeed. When the couple attempts mutuality in money matters, in their social life, in rearing the children, and in other areas of life that involve interactions in the broader society, that do not impinge upon their lovemaking, can the experiment succeed?

To be realistic about this, we need to see how men and women usually differ in power. Usually, the man makes more money than the woman; sometimes he is the only wage earner. He often has power over other people, either as their employer or supervisor or even as a customer who can withhold business. Men can, and often do, have major control over the family money. Men usually have an ability to get help and attention from police, city officials, service personnel, businesspeople, and professional people, including physicians, that the woman lacks. Women are often ignored or not taken seriously, so that the wife has to get the husband to make phone calls on her behalf. Many incidents stand out in my memory, such as the time I went shopping with a woman who wanted to leave her car with a mechanic while we were in the mall. She tried to tell him what she wanted done, and the mechanic kept talking to me, even after I told him it was not my car and I knew nothing about it. It seems that some men are not able to talk to women, and some men do not want to be helpful to women, or they do not know how. Women soon learn that they have less security—social, economic, and physical—than men take for granted. There is almost always a significant differential in power between the man and the woman. What kind of equality, mutuality, can they have, in the bedroom or in other areas of their shared lives?

Perhaps they can have much more equality than many couples realize. If there is a will to do it, they can share control of the family money. Some couples have two checking accounts, on which they can both sign (as a matter of security), but with his name first on one account and balancing the checkbook his responsibility, while her name is first on the other account and she balances the checkbook. What is in each account should be known to both. Many women have learned the importance of having credit in their name. The woman should have credit and bank cards that she can use without the man's knowledge or permission. This is an important aspect of power, because money is the most common area of disagreement between spouses.

In social matters, the woman can have more independence than many wives now have. The woman should have friends who did not come with the marriage. I think my marriage is stronger because my wife has her avocations, acting and scuba diving, neither of which I can do. Because of these activities, we go to parties to which I would not be invited if it were not for her. It is a simple matter for the woman to have her own telephone listing. In some marriages, the woman keeps her birth name, which is much easier now than it was a few years ago. Do these things help a marriage? I believe they do.

Sharing the household chores certainly helps. It makes talk of a partnership much less abstract, and a partnership approach to marriage indicates a commitment to equality.

The history of marriage and the previous experience of the man and woman in a family need not define marriage for them. It is possible for them to make of love something better than they have seen before.

Some philosophers who write about love are far more optimistic than others. Feminism incorporates different perspectives on love, all of which acknowledge that much that is said about love is unrealistic, but not all feminist perspectives on love are negative. Robert C. Solomon calls the claim that "love" is a male invention for the subjection of women and is unfair to women "an extremely persuasive polemic . . . with a tragic double bind." Put most simply, it is that "love is a lie but nevertheless one cannot live without it."[10] Solomon thinks this double bind comes from both accepting and rejecting an absurd ideal of love. We need, he says, to reject this absurd concept of love for a more reasonable notion of romantic love, one that is not in opposition to feminism but that presupposes a feminist approach.[11]

Solomon says that the "dump love" argument starts with the realization that what has been promised women, by men, is a fraud with a political purpose, that of convincing women that love is more important than power and politics. This fraud gives women an image of the feminine that is at odds with success in the world. It leaves women disappointed. Certain aspects of this "dump love" argument are not deniable or even controversial. Much that we believe about love is false or obscure. Love is not "everything"—not "the answer." It is not always desirable. At times, for some people, love is wrong. One of the things love does is provide "private compensation for public impotence or anonymity." It allows the playing of a game of being special when we are not but are "overburdened or underappreciated in our jobs and in our social roles." Romantic love, which is unknown in many parts of the world, is "a cultural creation," largely a "literary creation" from sources ranging from the Bible to the Brownings. As a cultural product of a society dominated by men, it would be in some sense created by men. Love calls for personal roles that often put women in a role that is more submissive than that of men. The promise of love is that it will compensate women for their political weakness.[12]

What does Solomon think follows from this? It is not love itself that is exploitive and stands in the way of equality between the sexes. It is illusions about love and the retention of old notions about male and female sex roles that work to the disadvantage of women. Romantic love does not require distinctive roles but can be "sex-neutral," with a significant degree of equality.[13]

Solomon does not think that the fact of love's originating in a male dominated society shows that its purpose was the domination of women. The early Greek notion of *eros* was not a weapon to use against women but an aspect of relations between men. The later concept of courtly love actually freed the concept of women from identification with their family, marital, and household roles. The belief that romantic love is a product of industrial society and capitalism is not historically sound.[14]

Solomon acknowledges that romantic roles, if they involve gender roles, are oppressive, requiring the female to be passive. Such roles are not as essential to romantic love as some novels indicate. There are, he says, three ways to overcome gender stereotypes. The first two are the two types of androgynism identified by Joyce Trebilcot, monoandrogynism and polyandrogynism, described in chapter 11.[15] Solomon does not think that either of these types of androgyny or androgynism is adequate. They both tend to identify character traits with gender. A third approach dismisses femininity and masculinity as roles in romantic love. He says that masculine and feminine roles are public roles, not private roles, and romantic love requires overcoming these roles. Gender roles are oppressive, calling for subservience on the woman's part, but romantic love requires equality. The equality romantic love requires "consists in the demand that social differences do not matter, that both lovers are mutually willing to take up the various personal and private roles that make up intimacy."[16]

Where Firestone and others see the private and personal aspects of romantic love as men's way to keep women impotent in the public arena, Solomon argues that the equality required by love fosters public equality. Also, public equality makes private and personal equality much easier to achieve. He believes romantic love has been a vehicle of personal and social equality.[17]

I believe Solomon is right in thinking that love is more compatible with equality than with subservience on the part of the woman. The man who believes that he must be superior to the woman he is to love seems to me to have little notion of what love is. From my early teen years, I remember a few words of a song: "The girl that I marry a girl I can carry must be." It is good that song was not adopted as a classic. The man who can love only a slight, frail person cannot love. To see that this is so is not to fall into sentimentality but to be realistic and clear of eye. What has often been called love is obviously just lustful desire to use another person for personal pleasure. Nothing is gained, and much is lost, in considering a desire to possess to be love. Even the need to be "mothered" by a woman or protected by a man falls far short of being love. Real love welcomes equality and fosters it.

Is Solomon correct in thinking that achieving equality in the personal and private experience of love will strengthen the possibility of achieving equality socially? Some people fear that love does compensate privately for what is unavailable socially. I doubt if this happens with the person who has felt truly equal in the personal relationship. The person who has appreciated the significance of being equal is unlikely to acquiesce in unfair inequalities in society. The person who tolerates inequality in business, political, and social matters might be comforted by feeling loved by another person, but I doubt that the love that comforts in this case is one of equality, even in private. Individual persons live in the nexus of social and personal influences, responsibilities, and sources of meaning and satisfaction. The love that rewards and refreshes us, the joy of coming home to warmth and pleasure, need not make us satisfied to fail in the social dimension of our lives. It can give us the strength, the good feeling about ourselves, that will help us succeed socially.

A number of theories about love make it hard to understand why a sensible adult would want a love relationship. Sharon Bishop notes several of these theories, such as the claims that love seek exclusive possession, that love is narcissistic, that love encourages dependency, or that love is a political ploy. These views of love may seem insightful, she says, but they seem to apply mostly to unhappy and failed relationships.[18]

Without ignoring the difficulties a couple might face in a love relationship, Bishop rejects the pessimism expressed by some writers on love. Bishop sketches the feelings and attitudes a couple might have on the good days. The account will be somewhat idealized because feelings shift with circumstances, and not all couples experience their relationship in this way. This picture applies to those who value the relationship, want it, and make room for it in their lives. The sentiment of love is a "natural" one, in contrast to moral and institutional attitudes. The love does not consist of conforming to a social role or a moral ideal. It is directed to a particular loved person. It is not directed toward attractive features of the person, but directed toward the person. Love involves liking a person, finding the person attractive, and caring about the person. Caring for the person's good is subject to much misunderstanding. It should not be understood in terms of intrinsic goods that the person should enjoy. It should not be a matter of enabling the person to perform or function well. These notions are problematical to start with, and they invite playing a role rather than loving naturally.[19]

Another feature of love can cause problems. A lover will want feelings to be reciprocated; love creates a "liability to jealousy." Also, there is some connection between love and dependency. Dependency is usually spoken of pejoratively, but Bishop holds that there are two senses of dependency, one of which is healthy, the other unhealthy. In a neutral sense of dependency, "one person is dependent on another if her desires cannot be satisfied unless the other person is present, has certain attitudes or acts in certain ways." The interests or desires that can be satisfied only by the loved one are not destructive or unhealthy, but quite healthy. Dependency can be unhealthy. This happens when a person's dependent desire is "to avoid developing her own interests, standards, and plans." Other forms of dependency develop out of social factors such as a woman's financial insecurity, but this is not a result of love.[20] I think that Bishop's contrasting of different kinds of dependency is insightful. There is a significant difference between the dependency of a weak person who depends on another person to get by day by day and a strong person who cannot attain certain levels of happiness and achievement alone. When another person becomes one's lifeline, the chance of growth in strength and independence is not promising. When two people can reach together heights of pleasure, happiness, or achievement that would not be possible for one alone, both people can be stronger because of the relationship.

From those who harshly condemn love and from those who defend romantic love while acknowledging its possible aberrations, we see that much of what is said about love in popular culture is silly, unrealistic, and even harmful to some people. Certain forms of romance, in certain contexts, can be unfair to women, contributing to their oppression. I believe that some of the criticisms of love are highly exaggerated, in that they blame love in general for the harm done by specific types of relationships, most of which have been criticized by proponents of love. This does not mean that we should ignore what is said in the "dump love" arguments. We need to see that people have been hurt by the love they have seen. We do not need, however, to accept these anguished cries as the final word on love. Also, we do not need to credit the whole male gender with the insight and ability to use love as a way of manipulating women. Both the men and the women involved in this sad affair were probably equally duped by the myths and fables, the illusions and misconceptions, about love and sexuality that have been current in our society.

We would do well to stop teaching our children about love with tales of beautiful princesses and knightly princes who fall in love and live happily ever after. I suspect that most young people already know too much about the rawness of life to respect dreamy visions of love and romance. Those who have been so protected that they can be thrilled by pretty tales will have to face the realities eventually, and they can face them better with fewer silly notions. I still think that for most people there is the possibility of love that contributes to their growth and well-being. For many people, marriage is constructive and rewarding. For many people, a family with children is the best way for them to live a part of their lives. It does not help, however, for people to expect too much or too little of love. Love brings its rewards, and it has its dangers. We need to be realistic about both the rewards and the pitfalls. I do not think there are any secrets about what makes for good love. The same values that make other aspects of life better work for love. Honesty, respect, fairness, sensitivity to the needs of others, and acceptance of responsibility are not secrets, but they are keys to constructive relationships, and people can get better at them as they go along. This is what people can do to make love contribute to life.

The social matters that affect love are just as important as the personal commitments. It is not realistic to think that personal goodness can conquer all obstacles. There are stories of people who had a good love relationship and raised a good family in adverse circumstances, and I believe many of these stories are true. Some people are exceptional, but most people do not have the exceptional strength of mind and body that success against all odds requires. Love works better in a just society that promotes the general welfare. Lack of education, unemployment, laws and customs that discriminate against any group, lack of affordable housing, health care that is not available to all people, and other social ills impinge upon the individual people and their families.

Fostering love in our society calls for educational and political programs. There is much myth and misunderstanding to overcome and some stubborn social ills to erase. Those who sincerely believe in the family and who take seriously the rearing of children cannot dump love. Love is central to aspects of life that are very important to many people. We really do need love, but we need the healthy love that requires equality between men and women and facilitates personal growth.

～ 14 ～

Marriage

Monogamous marriage is taken for granted by most people in our society. They may take liberties with the monogamous aspect of it, but they do not question the rightness of the institution. Marriage has its serious critics, however, who see it as psychologically damaging to spouses or to children. Other critics think marriage is unfair to women or to men. Some critics view marriage as a product of and a means of maintaining an unjust system of capitalism.

Friedrich Engels's criticism of the bourgeois family underlies much of the current condemnation of marriage. He traced the history of the family in the context of a Marxist view of society and class struggle. He said that male supremacy and the patriarchal family developed during early Greek history and continued in Roman history with the addition of slaves to the family. Undisputed paternity was important for the inheritance of property, an aspect of marriage that continued to be significant. Monogamy was for the woman only; hetaerism was coexistent with monogamous marriage. Bawdy tales reveal two new characters: the wife's lover and the cuckold husband. Being caught in adultery was a serious matter, however, because the husband wanted to know that his wife's children were his. The wife in Greek and Roman marriages was like a servant; her role was that of chief manager of the house and the female slaves. Antagonism between man and wife was the first class struggle; marriage was a miniature of society.[1]

Engels was critical of the bourgeois family in modern Europe. He said of the notion of marriage as a free contract that marriage was voluntary only on paper. He compared it to the workers' supposed free sale of their labor. Even with legal equality between husband and wife, there was no real equality, no economic equality. Engels looked upon marriage of convenience as a type of prostitution. "Sex-love" exists only within the oppressed classes who have no property to protect. In the proletarian family, there was no ground for male dominance, except for male brutality to women. Involvement of the wife as an industrial worker removes the basis of male dominance. When women can initiate divorce, hetaerism and adultery play a smaller role than in the bourgeois family.[2]

The revolution and the victory of the proletariat, thought Engels, would bring an end to bourgeois monogamy. Social revolution would take away private, inheritable property, thereby undercutting the form of marriage needed under capitalism. What comes after monogamy? The liberation of women would be accomplished by bringing the whole female sex into industry. Rather than disappearing, monogamy would be changed, so that it is realized completely. Engels thought the family would cease to be the economic unit of society. Housekeeping and child care would be socialized. Anxiety about pregnancy (and its economic effects) would end, resulting in more sexual freedom and freer sexual attitudes. Individual sex-love would play a greater role. In the history of sexual relations, sex-love had a limited role, but with the end of capitalism, Engels expected it to emerge as a personal right and to be recognized as ethical. Those features of monogamy that are associated with property relations would cease, bringing an end to prostitution and adultery, to male dominance, and to indissolubility of marriage. A new generation would determine the positive features of sex relations.[3]

The changes in marriage that Engels expected did not occur in the largely rural countries in which there was a communist revolution, and the industrialized countries, where the revolution was expected, did not have the sort of revolutions Marx and Engels anticipated. The criticism of marriage goes on. John McMurtry rejected the claims for monogamous marriage that it was the best way to promote affection and provided the best context for rearing children. McMurtry thinks that rather than promoting affection, monogamous marriage limits the expression of affection and stimulates sexual frustration, lack of spontaneity, fantasizing, jealousy, use of pornography, and deception.[4]

McMurtry is making psychological claims, the truth or falsehood of which must be determined through psychological research. It is unlikely that many generalizations about marriage can be supported. Marriages are not all alike, with some people very dissatisfied with marriage and other people finding it a source of joy and strength.

David Palmer holds that McMurtry's psychological views are not supported by data. The psychological effects cited by McMurtry might not be the result of monogamy, and changes to correct the problems might be possible within monogamous marriage. Alternatives to marriage might bring even greater problems.[5]

McMurtry says there is no evidence that monogamous marriage is better than other institutions for child rearing. He seems to think monogamy is bad for the parents and for the children. He says that monogamy may inhibit affection by restricting sources of affection for the young.[6] Palmer argues, against McMurtry, that there are numerous ways of giving affection and support to children within the institution of monogamous marriage, such as extended families.[7] Extended families are difficult to keep together under present conditions of urban life and the economic necessity of mobility, but there are many ways to give a child access to affection. There can be visits with grandparents, aunts and uncles, and other relatives. Friends of the parents can enrich a child's life. Nursery schools can provide valuable social contacts.

McMurtry's concept of monogamous marriage may throw some light on his negative beliefs about matrimony. He holds that the essential ground of monogamy is the right to exclusive sexual possession of the partner. He sees marriage as a form of private property. He bases this view of marriage on certain aspects of the history of the institution, such as dowries, daughter sales, property allowances, bride exchanges, the role of illegitimacy, and the imperative of premarital chastity. He also mentions that adultery was, until recently, the only ground for divorce. He refers to "alienation of affections" lawsuits, with money awards. He does not see that these are largely relics of a bygone age, evidence of profound changes in the nature of marriage. He interprets the incest taboo as protection of "sexual property" from access to parents and siblings. He appeals to language used in marriage ceremonies and in common speech.[8] He does not take note of changes in current marriage ceremonies, with many weddings abandoning the traditional words. Words once commonly used to speak of marriage are used less often today because many married people do not find meaningful the notion of owning or being owned. I agree with Palmer's opinion that McMurtry's analysis of marriage as ownership is implausible.

McMurtry looks at the economic aspects of marriage from a Marxist perspective. Marriage, he says, is indispensable to the persistence of capitalism and ownership of private property. Our capitalistic society is based on the ability to exclude others from what one needs, and monogamy is a primary case of such possession. Monogamy also supports capitalism, he claims, by limiting the expression of sexual love. How does this strengthen capitalism? It favors social ambition, channels sexual energies into social and economic competition, and makes self-interest less vulnerable to altruism. Disciplining and repressing of natural impulses make people accept repetitive and arduous work. Not only does this make people better capitalistic workers, it makes them better customers. It develops a complex of sexual repressions to which advertising can appeal, creating markets for goods. Monogamy creates high demand for homes and other commodities and services.[9] McMurtry's belief that marriage fails to facilitate the expression of affection supports his belief that capitalism makes use of marriage, which must have the services of unhappy and sexually unfulfilled people. It is hard to believe that work, under capitalism or any other system, needs a large group of sexually frustrated people. The role of families as consumers is obvious. Marriage creates a demand for services and houses and other goods, but it is hard to see marriage as simply a way to maintain capitalist markets. Marriage, as a crucial feature of society, is bound to be affected by the economic structures and ideologies of contemporary American society. In the next chapter, we will look at Juliet Mitchell's examination of the nature of the family in relation to American capitalism.

Lyla O'Driscoll clarifies some of the issues we have been discussing. She points out that there are several concepts of marriage, and some criticisms of marriage apply just to the legal, monogamous concept of marriage.[10] A similar point is made by Palmer, who points out that the definition of marriage is difficult; of the common features of marriage, none is a necessary condition. The critiques of monogamy seem not to be directed to monogamy itself but to some particular feature of marriage in a specific social context. Palmer says that the target of McMurtry's attack is unclear. It may be marriage itself or social problems and practices of a particular group of people and a particular economic system.[11]

Palmer and O'Driscoll strongly disagree with McMurtry's understanding of marriage in terms of ownership. O'Driscoll holds that the legal aspect of marriage should be seen as a civil contract, as in the views of John Locke and David Hume. She describes marriage as a witnessed, formal contract between two persons (male and female) who are of legal age and otherwise competent. It is freely consented to. It can be voided only by a competent official. It conveys certain rights and duties, such as support, fidelity, sexual congress, protection from third parties. O'Driscoll recognizes, however, that there are aspects of marriage other than the legal. One aspect of marriage is social. Marriage is a social institution that typically regulates some aspects of sex and reproduction. There is some question about what makes an institution marriage.[12]

Palmer says marriage is more like a contract than like ownership, but it is not reducible to any other kind of relationship or institution.[13]

Sara Ann Ketchum points out some problems with the notion of marriage as a contracted relationship. There are formal problems with the concept of marriage as a contract. In ordinary cases, what the bride and groom agree to is not like legal contracts. A written contract is not available for reading, and its provisions are not specifically stated before the wedding. Roles in the arrangement are set by birth, male or female. There is no choice of contracts. All of these problematic aspects violate the usual concept of contracts and civil liberties. There are also problems of the substance of a contract by which a person gives up civil liberties. According to liberal and natural law theory, there are some contracts the state ought not enforce. One cannot sell oneself into slavery or give up the right to legal protection against violence and injury. By marrying, a woman has to a great extent, especially in the past, given up certain protections. The law tends to exclude spouses from certain legal protections. There is a general principle of noninterference in marriage.[14]

The effort to understand marriage as a contract does not help us see the nature of marriage adequately. David Palmer is right in seeing that marriage is unlike any other institution. We do not learn very much through comparing it with other aspects of society.

Strong opposition to marriage comes from some radical feminists who object to marriage because of the feature that attracts many people to it, its basis in romantic love. In chapter 13, we saw some radical feminist criticisms of romantic love and some defenses of romantic love. In that chapter, we saw that the effects of a difference in the economic and social power of wife and husband are a significant concern about marriage. What is the effect of power upon a marriage? Can power outside the home be kept out of the bedroom?

An important question in understanding marriage is what one should expect of marriage. What is a realistic expectation? What are the rewards to be sought in marriage? Lyla O'Driscoll writes about the value of marriage. She holds that marriage may be valuable in itself, not just as a means to some end(s). She sees this value in terms of friendship and love.[15]

The depth of friendship found in many marriages transcends most other friendships. The marital relationship can affect a person's self-identity in ways seldom found in other friendships. There really is a merging of personal identities that firmly establishes the monogamous feature of marriage. Some people find this prospect frightening, but others see it as a priceless benefit of marriage. That one's self-identity is shaped by the marriage does not solve all problems or make everything easy. Perhaps we can understand this unity of two people better if we can talk about it without visions of hearts and flowers.

We should be careful not to describe the benefits of marriage in flowery terms. Joseph and Mary Ann Barnhart are concerned with the problem of unrealistic expectations of marriage. Sermons, popular songs, books of advice, and other sources put forward the idea that people can find completeness in marriage. The myth of finding one's completeness in marriage may induce people to marry when they should not or when they are not ready. This myth can also cause discontent when the exaggerated notion of complete happiness overshadows the ideal of a reasonably happy marriage.[16] Probably we all know people who married unwisely, expecting to solve through marriage problems that marriage has no means of solving. The person who is dissatisfied with a very good marriage because of unrealistic expectations may destroy a relationship that could contribute greatly to a good life.

Just as people can expect too much of marriage, they can expect too much of divorce. People have been disappointed when divorce did not give them the freedom or the inner peace they wanted. Divorce does not make the middle-aged young again or make plain people glamorous. There are times when divorce can end an unsatisfactory marriage and give an opportunity for a better life, but we need to be as realistic about divorce as we must be about marriage.[17]

The growing rate of divorce should not be seen as a threat to the institution of marriage. It does not indicate that people are giving up on marriage. It might indicate that people are expecting more of marriage and are willing to try again when a marriage fails. Ironically, divorce is in some cases a tribute to marriage. There may be some people who are unsuited for marriage, and for some people marriage seems to be difficult. The majority of people seem to find some form of wedded satisfaction, if not wedded bliss. We now live in a time when most people are willing to let people shape their marriages to meet their needs. Marriage has changed in significant ways in the past, and now marriages can be of different sorts, right on the same street. The rigid customs that held marriage to certain patterns in the past no longer bind us, and many of the problems of marriage that were products of particular styles and forms of matrimony no longer need to trouble us.

The increased autonomy that women now enjoy, the mobility of urban people, the lack of restrictions from members of an extended family, and other aspects of modern life have placed a strain on marriage, but they have also liberated marriage from the strains of too much restricting custom and too much pressure from the expectations of people outside the marriage. Perhaps marriage can become an even stronger and more rewarding institution than it has been in the past.

～ 15 ～

Family and Parenthood

The institution of the family has come under attack from several perspectives. We have already seen Friedrich Engels's criticism of marriage in the bourgeois family. Even though the social and economic situation in the United States is very different from conditions in Europe during Engels's life, some of Engels's criticism may still be relevant to an understanding of contemporary family life. Marxist feminists certainly take it seriously. They see the oppression of women as part of a larger class struggle. Socialist feminists do not think the Marxist account adequate, but they accept some of its insights.[1]

The family is unavoidably affected by various aspects of the economic system of the society of which it is a part. Juliet Mitchell looks at the relationship between family life and capitalistic production and changes that capitalism has made in the family. It has created a contradiction between the concept of the family in our society and the reality of the family. She says that the family has changed, but it still remains "a crucial ideological and economic unit." Under capitalistic industrialism, the family lost its role in economic production, but ideologically the family is now the focal point of "the idea of individual private property." What the family actually does is provide a labor force and support massive consumption. "The family thus embodies the most conservative concepts available; it rigidifies the past ideals and presents them as the present pleasures."[2]

Mitchell sees a contradiction between the ideology of the family and capitalist production, a contradiction between the view of the family as a unity and the forces dividing the family. The social means of production divide the family and produce extreme individuality, and the family becomes a society of individuals, separated by their jobs and other forces. The burden of trying to preserve the unity of the family falls upon the woman.[3]

Mitchell shows that the role of the family has undergone some significant changes since the rise of capitalism. She does not claim that the family is a creature of capitalism or that capitalism defines the nature of the marriage relationship. She does not call for abolition of the family as a means of liberating women. There are, however, critics of the contemporary family who advocate replacing the family with other relationships that they believe are more favorable to women.

Radical feminists see the family, especially motherhood, as the main element in the oppression of women. Shulamith Firestone notes that in spite of erosive forces, the family has held together with the aid of artificial cultural reinforcements. The family is praised and upheld in sermons, guidance manuals, and newspaper columns. It has had the support of various clubs and institutions. Marriage, she says, has not been seen as an economic contract but is seen romantically. It is the romance underlying the institution of marriage that Firestone sees as harmful, especially to women. Even though sex roles have been relaxed, contemporary family life has not been liberating for the working wife.[4]

Firestone says that people fail to recognize the problems and the faults of marriage and family life, propping up marriage, in effect, with an attitude that she calls "the privatization of the marriage experience." The couple in love think their marriage will be unique; they know that families come apart, but they will be different. With this attitude, people blame themselves, not the institution, if marriage fails.[5] Firestone sees problems for women in the institution of the family itself. Things are better than they were in olden times, but the advantages enjoyed by the modern wife do not eliminate the disadvantages. Even with help in family planning, gynecology, day care, and so forth, Firestone sees childbearing as a tyranny. The wife and mother has more physical security, but she lacks financial independence. The family is the only place where some women are socially integrated, where there is interplay between age groups and sexes. Even though sex is available steadily in a long-term relationship, there is still sexual repression.[6]

The heart of Firestone's objection to the family is motherhood. She says, "[M]arriage in its very definition will never be able to fulfill the needs of its participants, for it was organized around, and reinforces, a fundamentally oppressive biological condition that we only now have the skill to correct."[7]

Jeffner Allen argues even more bluntly that motherhood is "dangerous to women." It does not allow them to develop a subjectivity in an open and free world.[8] It is also physically dangerous, with deaths from illegal abortions, loss of life in childbirth, and infanticide of female children.[9] Allen writes of motherhood as the condition of all women. "If woman, in patriarchy, is she who exists as the womb and wife of man, every woman is by definition a mother: she who produces for the sake of man." She says women produce children, material goods, and ideas for patriarchal culture. "A mother is she whose body is used as a resource to produce men and the world of men."[10]

Allen refers to Simone de Beauvoir, Shulamith Firestone, Ti-Grace Adkinson, and Monique Wittig as women who see fertility as the ground of the oppression of women. She calls for women to vacate the role of mother, what she calls "evacuation from motherhood," which means far more than not having children but calls for abandoning "the ideology and institution of motherhood." This requires living a nonpatriarchal life and not letting their bodies be a source for patriarchal culture.[11]

Are the radical calls for the end of family life made seriously? They certainly seem to be serious proposals, and alternatives to the family are suggested. Firestone makes several suggestions for better lives for women than family life provides. One possibility is the single life organized around a chosen profession. Many women are already living this way, and surely many of them prefer this way of life. Another proposal is that women who do not need children live together, with group marriages possible eventually. For women who have or desire children, there could be group arrangements that include children, what Firestone calls "households."[12]

Most people probably think that these attacks on the family are extreme and tend to dismiss them completely. The criticisms and the proposed alternatives are extreme, which is why we call them radical, but we would do well to realize that they express feelings that would not be if all were well with family life. Such radical views of the family show that some people have been hurt, are frustrated, or are unfulfilled by family life. If there are reasons for this that point to problems that any family could face, we need to give the matter serious study.

Finding problems in the institution of the family need not lead to abandoning the family. The problems might be solved. Also, we should keep in mind that alternatives to family life might lose something of value and might bring other problems far worse than those of the contemporary family.

Some feminist writers see the problem of the family not in motherhood but in the lack of a significant role of the father in child care. Dorothy Dinnerstein described the current sexual arrangements as a malaise. The arrangements she was criticizing were "the division of responsibility, opportunity and privilege" between men and women and "the patterns of psychological interdependence that are implicit in this division." This is the traditional separation of male and female roles, with the woman rocking the cradle and the man ruling the world, child care on the one hand and business and politics on the other.[13] Part of the malaise of which Dinnerstein writes is the bad effects upon children of being left almost entirely in the care of the mother.[14]

Nancy Chodorow's psychoanalytic study of mothering and the development of gender identity deals repeatedly with the effects of the father's not having a significant role in child rearing. She describes problems for girls and boys related to the father's absence.[15] Chodorow's study is frequently quoted or cited. Virginia Held says that both parents should be equally responsible for care of a child. Each child rearing task need not be divided equally, but such equal division should be the starting presumption. Departure from this should be justified by agreement between the parents on the basis of relevant criteria.[16] Sara Ruddick looks forward to shared parenting, when men "share equally and actively" in child care. "On that day there will be no more 'fathers,' no more people of either sex who have power over their children's lives and moral authority in their children's world, though they do not do the work of attentive love."[17]

A strong affirmation of the possibility of motherhood that is life-affirming and healing appears in some of the French feminist writers, especially Luce Irigaray, who sees the mother-child relationship as a model of a feminist ethic of nurturance. Eleanor H. Kuykendall, who has translated some of Irigaray's work, says that some feminists see the capacity to nurture "as a gift, or rather as a special power at once corporeal and psychic."[18]

The disagreements among feminist writers over the nature and effects of motherhood leave us with an issue to be faced. Are there

problems in family life that impinge upon the wife and mother especially? We can become idealistic and sentimental about the role of
mother, seeing her as noble, good, tender, generous, and self-sacrific-
ing. This has been our romantic picture of mother, and it certainly has
its charm, as many poems, songs, and Mother's Day cards attest. What,
however, does this role do to the woman who tries to live up to the
ideal? There are two lines of thinking in contemporary feminism. The
positive view is that altruism is good and women should continue to be
altruistic and supportive of the husband and children. The negative
view is that altruism leads to unhealthy self-denial and oppression.
Larry Blum and his colleagues find weakness in both of these approaches.

> This weakness of the positive view is connected to a failure to see
> the "altruistic" qualities as part of the person as a whole. The positive
> view does not see that although the qualities can be associated with
> other positive qualities such as autonomy and independence, they may
> also be associated with negative qualities such as dependence, sense of
> inferiority, and self-denial. Conversely, the negative view does not
> admit the real possibility of the compatibility of altruism with auton-
> omy.[19]

Blum does not see altruism as a problem in itself. It becomes a
problem in a relationship that is not based on caring and autonomy. It
is the nature of the relationship that makes the woman's role problematical. Economic dependence on the husband, a lack of reciprocal emotional support, and lack of avenues for developing a sense of selfhood
apart from the role of wife are factors that distort altruism.[20]

Autonomy is distorted, Blum says, when one person, usually the
wife, becomes the only person responsible for maintaining the relationship. It requires great energy to be the emotional maintainer without
the benefit of reciprocation from the spouse. Lacking opportunities for
self-development, a mother may try to live through the children. There
can be several ill effects of the woman's having full responsibility for
maintaining the marriage. The man does not become capable of giving
emotional support to others, since his work seldom promotes this ability. The wife's use of time and energy is not noticed and appreciated.
The relationship becomes emotionally deficient for the wife. Eventually, the wife comes to lack confidence that she is loved; she becomes
reluctant to assert herself.[21]

The faults of the traditional partnership between father and mother, which required the father to provide for the family economically and the mother to be the primary giver of child care and to maintain the marriage, are all too obvious. The need for a real partnership in which child care is the responsibility of both parents and both husband and wife are expected to make an emotional investment in the marriage is now widely recognized.

A real partnership in marriage will be difficult for some people, especially those who have not experienced any such community of sharing. Some people have life-goals and values that are not conducive to family life. Shulamith Firestone may be correct in thinking that some people need to build their lives around careers. Many men have done this in most periods of time, along with a smaller number of women. For the women, it usually meant eschewing marriage. For both sexes, it may have led to marriages that would not be considered successful by contemporary standards. Perhaps people with a very strong career orientation should consider not marrying, or at least not becoming parents.

Another group of people who seem to have no need for marriage are the radical feminists. Not only do these women not find traditional motherhood appealing, they are scornful of what they consider halfway measures to make motherhood easier. They do not seem to want solitary lives, but they seem to need groupings of adults only.

As a society, we seem to have the task of recognizing the needs of people who can live better lives outside families of husband, wife, and children. We have a responsibility to accept living arrangements that are not traditional. In our concern for the family and with our efforts to promote good family life, we must not make life more difficult for people who do not fit the family pattern. Perhaps we need to make life better for them by reasonable changes in our laws and in our customs. It is hard to see how doing this can weaken family life.

For those people who do want families, we need to help people who grew up in families without autonomy and sharing of responsibility. We need to teach students about family life in a realistic way, and we need to support efforts to make work schedules more flexible. Family leaves for critical times in family life are now receiving the support of law, but a society that really values families will find ways to support family life on a day-by-day basis.

It will be a tragedy if support for values degenerates into a political

ploy, consisting primarily of attacks on people who cannot live a traditional family life. It will be a real loss if our society rejects new
approaches to family life and tries to maintain aspects of the old traditions that have clearly failed husbands and wives and created psychological problems for children. Life is not a Norman Rockwell painting
or a 1950s situation comedy. A sentimental attachment to the past will
not serve us well.

Is it possible to build family life around autonomy and sharing? It
seems unnecessary to ask whether something is possible while it is
being done. There are such families. Some of us even had the benefit
of growing up with fathers who regularly took a significant part in our
upbringing. Some of us were fortunate in having mothers who were
fulfilled and enjoyed the self-esteem that came of success in activities
besides mothering us.

Those who did not have the benefit of such families will need to
learn some new skills, but there are people who want the best kind of
families and are willing to try, even if it is awkward at first. There are
many sources of help for people learning to live as families. The creation of autonomous and sharing family life will be harder for those
with limited financial resources and uncooperative employers. Living
at a distance from parents will make things more difficult for some
young couples, but I am enough of a curmudgeon to acknowledge that
for some it is a distinct advantage.

In spite of obstacles, a couple can do some important things. One of
the most important is handling financial matters openly and coopera-
tively. The wife should have credit in her own name; not only is this a
boost to her self-esteem, it can be critically important in case something happens to the marriage. The man or the woman may be more
experienced or more talented at keeping the books, but the books
should be open to both and decisions made mutually. The families in
which the wife knew nothing of money matters, along with the families in which the husband brought home a pay envelope and turned it
over to the wife who managed everything, should be history.

Significant help can be found in women's groups or men's groups.
Chapter 4 explored more thoroughly the issue of separatism in various
forms, but I am a strong advocate of one-sex groups that meet regularly. Women seem to have gotten help with personal problems and
family problems from other women more easily than men could get
help from men. The reasons for this have been amply discussed, such

as competitiveness between men, the need of men to impress other men, and the need felt by men to maintain an image. Both men and women need, at least at certain times, people of the same sex with whom ideas and even feelings can be explored. This is not to say that mixed groups for learning and discussion are not also valuable. The particular format and the size of such groups are not critical, except that for some purposes small groups are better, and much can be learned by participation in a nonauthoritarian group in which leadership is shared.

There is a danger that young couples will find themselves very busy, and this can tempt them to spend too little time with other people. If there are children, it is important to let them experience other adults. One criticism made of marriage and family life is that it limits the sources of affection available to children.[22] This need not be a problem. I remember from my childhood the joy of visiting relatives, but also the visits of adult friends of my parents. Happily for me, I was allowed to be a part of the dinners, games, even to some extent the conversations, of those visits. The strongest families I have known were those most involved in community activities. Good family life is possible.

Is family life possible for everyone? Family life may well be of no advantage to some people. Let me return to an important idea. Our society will not strengthen its families by making life more difficult for those who live outside of family life. In a culturally rich society there will be different kinds of families, and there will be people not living in families. This nation voices a commitment to liberty and justice for all, and there can be no more important aspect of this than the way families and individual people are treated.

~ *Notes* ~

Notes to Chapter 1. Philosophers on Sexuality

1. Plato, *Laws,* VIII. 839a.
2. Ibid., VI. 784.
3. Plato, *Phaedo,* 64c–64a, *Phaedrus,* 237d–238b. 253c–256b.
4. Plato, *Republic,* V. 456, 458.
5. Plato, *Laws,* VII. 805, 806, 813; VIII. 833.
6. Plato, *Republic, Laws,* V. 455d. VI. 781b.
7. Plato, *Republic, Laws,* V. 449, 457. V. 739.
8. Aristotle, *Politics, Nicomachean Ethics,* I.v, xii/VIII. 10–12.
9. Epictetus, *Enchiridion* XXIII, XXXI, XXXVIII, XLI.
10. Plotinus, *Enneads,* IV. 2.
11. Plotinus, *Enneads,* I. 1; V. 1.
12. Augustine, *City of God,* 14:7, 18, 21–26. Augustine, *Confessions,* 3:1; 4:12; 6:15.
13. Thomas Aquinas, *On the Truth of the Catholic Faith.*
14. Locke, *Second Treatise on Government,* 30–32, 42–44.
15. Kant, *Lectures on Ethics,* 163–67.
16. Fichte, *Science of Right,* chap. 1, sec. 1.
17. Schopenhauer, "Metaphysics of the Love of the Sexes," 341–43, 346–48, 350.
18. De Sade, *Complete Justine,* 318.
19. Schopenhauer, *Parega and Paralipomena,* 614–15, 619, 620, 622, 623, 626.
20. Nietzsche, "Beyond Good and Evil," sec. 4, "Apothegms and Interludes," nos. 144, 145, pp. 465–66.
21. Nietzsche, "Beyond Good and Evil," sec. 7, "Our Virtues," nos. 232, 233, 237A, 238, 239, pp. 540–45.
22. Nietzsche, "Thus Spake Zarathustra," 68–69.
23. Mill, "Subjection of Women," 125, 130, 148, 149–50.

Notes to Chapter 2. What Is Sexuality?

1. Keller, *Reflections on Gender and Science.*
2. Schopenhauer, "The Metaphysics of the Love of the Sexes," 341–43, 346–48, 350.
3. Solomon, "Sex and Perversion," 272–73.
4. Baumrin, "Sexual Morality Delineated," 300–301.
5. Ibid., 302–6.
6. Sartre, *Being and Nothingness,* 477–78.
7. Firestone, *The Dialectics of Sex;* Held, "Marx, Sex, and the Transformation of Society," 175–77; and Solomon, *Love: Emotion, Myth, and Metaphor,* 300–315.
8. Merleau-Ponty, *Phenomenology of Perception,* 167.
9. Ibid., 157.
10. Sartre, *Being and Nothingness,* 508.
11. Nagel, "Sexual Perversion," 10–12, 14–15; Ruddick, "Better Sex," 284–87.
12. Solomon, "Sex and Perversion," 279–82; see also Solomon, *Love: Emotion, Myth, and Metaphor,* 253–60.
13. Pineau, "Date Rape," 233–37.
14. Goldman, "Plain Sex," 275–77.
15. Stewart and Michunas, *Exploring Phenomenology,* 96–98.
16. Merleau-Ponty, *Phenomenology of Perception,* 82, 198–99, 203–6; quotation, 82.
17. Solomon, "Sex and Perversion," 271.

Notes to Chapter 3. Does Sex Have a Purpose?

1. Schopenhauer, "The Metaphysics of the Love of the Sexes," 341–43, 346–48, 350.
2. Paul VI, *Humanae Vitae.*
3. Ibid.
4. Cohen, "Sex, Birth Control, and Human Life," 253.
5. Ibid., 254.
6. Augustine, *City of God,* book 14, sec. 18, 23–26, 466–67, 470–75.
7. Cohen, "Sex, Birth Control, and Human Life," 257–58.
8. Ibid., 255.

Notes to Chapter 4. Feminism

1. Flax, "Women Do Theory," 3–4.
2. Ibid., 3–5.
3. Jaggar, "Political Philosophies of Women's Liberation," 5, 6.
4. Ibid., 6–9.
5. Ibid., 9–12.
6. Ibid., 12–15.
7. See the section on feminist separatism, below.

8. Jaggar, "Political Philosophies of Women's Liberation," 15–18.

9. Hartsock, "Feminist Theory and the Development of Revolutionary Strategy," 59, 64–66, 71–73.

10. Frazer and Bartky, *Hypatia.*

11. Bartky, "Toward a Phenomenology of Feminist Consciousness," 425, 426, 427–29. See Mitchell, *Women's Estate,* 152–55, 156–58, for a description of how social changes have affected the family.

12. Bartky, "Toward a Phenomenology of Feminist Consciousness," 429–32, 434–38.

13. See, for example, Held, "Marx, Sex, and the Transformation of Society," 179–80.

14. Frye, "Some Reflections on Separatism and Power," 97, 99–101, 103.

15. Trebilcot, "Taking Responsibility for Sexuality," 421–28.

16. Ibid., 425–28.

17. Ketchum and Pierce, "Separatism and Sexual Relationships," 164.

18. Ibid., 165–66.

19. Raymond, *Passion for Friends,* 3, 7–8, 13.

20. Ibid., 14–18, 153, 164–66.

21. Ibid., 166–73.

22. Card, "Female Friendship," 124, 126–29; Friedman, "Individuality without Individualism," 136.

23. Friedman, *What Are Friends For?* 35–40, 64–88, 94–116, 134–41, 188–206, 247–55.

24. Jaggar, "How Can Philosophy Be Feminist?" 4–6.

25. Ibid., 6–8.

26. Sells, "Feminist Epistemology."

27. Keller, *Reflections on Gender and Science.*

28. See Harding and O'Barr, eds., *Sex and Scientific Inquiry,* for a number of feminist critiques of science.

29. Ruddick, "New Feminist Work on Knowledge, Reason, and Objectivity," *Hypatia* 8, no. 4 (Fall 1993): 140–49.

30. Alcoff and Potter, *Feminist Epistemologies.*

31. Antony and Witt, *Mind of One's Own.*

32. Tuanna, "Radical Future of Feminist Empiricism."

33. Nelson, *Who Knows.*

34. Jaggar, "How Can Philosophy Be Feminist?" 6.

35. Seigfried, *Hypatia.*

36. Code, *What Can She Know?*

37. Dixon, review of Code's, *What Can She Know?*

38. Korsmeyer, "Gender Bias in Aesthetics." In the same edition of the *Newsletter on Feminism and Philosophy* see Shrage, "Bibliography on Feminist Aesthetics."

39. *Hypatia* 5, no. 2 (Spring 1990).

40. See, for example, Rubinstein, *American Woman Artists.*

41. John Berger et al., *Ways of Seeing,* 45–64.

42. Gilligan, *In a Different Voice.* Also see Gilligan's *Mapping the Moral Domain.*

43. Kohlberg, *Psychology of Moral Development.*

44. Piaget, *Moral Judgment of the Child,* 76–84.

45. Gilligan, "Moral Orientation and Moral Development," 21–22.

46. Ibid., 22–23, 25, 30–31.

47. Baier, "Hume, the Woman's Moral Theorist?"

48. Jaggar, "Feminist Ethics," 91, 92, 93–104.

49. Aldo Leopold, *A Sand County Almanac* (London, Oxford, New York: Oxford University Press, 1949).

50. d'Eubonne, *Le Feminisme ou la Mort,* 213–52. Warren, "Power and the Promise," 125–26.

51. Warren, "Power and the Promise"; see also Warren, "Feminism and Ecology."

52. See note 46 above.

53. Cheney, "Postmodern Environmental Ethics."

54. Ruether, *New Woman/New Earth.*

55. Michael E. Zimmerman, "Feminism, Deep Ecology, and Environmental Ethics," *Environmental Ethics* 9, no .1 (spring 1987): 37.

56. Warren, "Feminism and Ecology," 3–4; see also Warren "Power and the Promise," 126–34, 138–45.

57. Mies and Shiva, *Ecofeminism.*

Notes to Chapter 5. Sexual Morality

1. Baier, *The Moral Point of View,* 200–204, 308–10.

2. Kant, *Fundamental Principles of the Metaphysic of Ethics,* sec. 2, 47.

3. Ibid., 65–69.

4. Belliotti, *Good Sex,* 93–96.

5. Bishop, "Self-determination and Autonomy," 65–67.

6. See chapters 13 and 14. Raymond Belliotti explores some feminist critiques of society that are relevant to an understanding of autonomy. See *Good Sex,* 126–71.

7. Pineau, "Date Rape," 233–37.

8. Ruddick, "Better Sex," 281–82.

9. Punzo, *Reflective Naturalism;* Hunter, *Thinking about Sex and Love;* and Scrunton, *Sexual Desire.*

10. Belliotti, *Good Sex,* 3, 56–57, 76–77.

11. Goldman, "Plain Sex," 273.

12. Belliotti, *Good Sex,* 74–77. Belliotti has a constructive chapter on ethical method, which points out common mistakes in moral reasoning about sex and develops his approach, which he calls "sexual morality in five tiers." See pp. 175–227.

13. Ruddick, "Better Sex," 284–85.

14. Ibid., 293.

15. From my work in environmental ethics, I have become aware of the importance of humans' realizing what they are and finding a suitable way of living within the natural environment. We need to accept the fact that we are animals. We are remarkable animals, and both our unique nature as humans and our biological nature as part of the natural system are morally significant, as I explain in *For People and the Planet: Holism and Humanism in Environmental Ethics.*

16. Elliston, "In Defense of Promiscuity," 223–25.

17. Ibid., 224, 231, 232.

18. For a more detailed explanation of using multiple values and several principles in making moral judgments, see Marietta, *For People and the Planet*, chapters 8 and 9.

19. Midgley, "Trying Out One's New Sword"; Ladd, "The Issue of Relativism"; Taylor, "Social Science and Ethical Relativism."

Notes to Chapter 6. Adultery and Fidelity

1. Fletcher, *Situation Ethics*, 142–43, 164–65; Wasserstrom, "Is Adultery Immoral?" 208–19; Taylor, *Having Love Affairs*, 161–84.

2. *Interpreter's Bible*, 987.

3. Gonsalves, *Fagothey's Right and Reason*, 219.

4. Wasserstrom, "Is Adultery Immoral?" 208–10.

5. Ibid., 210–12

6. Ibid., 213–14.

7. Ibid., 219.

8. Ibid.

9. Taylor, *Having Love Affairs*, 49–50, 52.

10. Fletcher, *Situation Ethics*, 142–45, 164–65.

11. Taylor, *Having Love Affairs*, 58–61.

12. Ibid., 49, 141–46.

13. Ibid., 125–38.

14. Ibid., 136–37.

15. Ibid., 133–35, 145–46.

16. Ibid., 161–81.

Notes to Chapter 7. Homosexuality

1. Leiser, *Liberty, Justice, and Morals*, 114.

2. Ibid., 47–50. See also Gould, "The 'Natural' and Homosexuality," 51–53, for other arguments against the concept of un-natural behaviors.

3. Levin, "Why Homosexuality Is Abnormal," 253–55, 361–65.

4. Leiser, *Liberty, Justice, and Morals*, 50–52.

5. Sartorelli, "Professor Dalcourt on the 'Natural,' " 49–52, cites the scientific work of Tyler, "Homosexual Behavior in Animals," 52, and Jolly, *Evolution of Primate Behavior*, 135–37. See also Ruse, "Morality of Homosexuality," 379–81.

6. Nagel, "Sexual Perversion," 9–11; Ruddick, "Better Sex," 284–89, 291–92.

7. Ketchum, "The Good, the Bad, and the Perverted," 139–47.

8. Scrunton, *Sexual Desire*, 305–7.

9. Ibid., 307–9.

10. Solomon, "Love and Feminism," 56.

11. Goldman, "Plain Sex," 280–81, 284–85.

12. Ruse, "Morality of Homosexuality," 383–84.

13. Bentham, an essay on "Paederasty," 355–66.

14. Ruse, "Morality of Homosexuality," 370–72, 374, 379–82, 386.

15. Mohr, "Gay Basics."

16. Trebilcot, "Taking Responsibility for Sexuality," 421–28.

17. Margolis, "Question of Homosexuality," 288; see also Ronald Bayer, *Homosexuality and American Psychiatry* (Princeton, NJ: Princeton University Press, 1987), 176–77.

18. Suppe, "Curing Homosexuality," 391–94.

19. Ibid., 393–95, 398–99.

20. Elliston, "Gay Marriage," 148–50.

21. Ibid., 151–55.

Notes to Chapter 8. The Morality of Abortion

1. Noonan, *Morality of Abortion,* 57.

2. Ibid., 7–46, 58.

3. Paul VI, *Humanae Vitae.*

4. Noonan, *Morality of Abortion,* 7–46, 58, traces the history of this debate.

5. Marquis, "Why Abortion Is Immoral," 189–92, 194.

6. Warren, "On the Moral and Legal Status of Abortion," 54–56.

7. English, "Abortion and the Concept of a Person," 235.

8. Ibid., 237–39.

9. Brody, "Thomson on Abortion," 339–40.

10. Thomson, "Defense of Abortion," 48–49, 55, 59, 61, 65.

11. Warren, "On the Moral and Legal Status of Abortion," 49–50.

12. Ibid., 53.

13. Ibid., 43–44. Even though these arguments are not sound as arguments for the moral rightness of abortion, they are reasonable arguments for the legalization of abortion. Legalization of abortion would make "back-alley" and "coat hanger" abortions less common. Poorer women would have fairer access to safe abortions. Legalizing abortion does not require demonstration that it is morally right.

14. Warren, "On the Moral and Legal Status of Abortion," 43–44.

15. Lichtenberg, "Is There a Middle Ground?"

16. English, "Abortion and the Concept of a Person," 240–43.

17. Callahan, *Abortion,* 493–501.

18. Schweitzer, *Philosophy of Civilization,* 318.

19. Ehrenreich, "Is Abortion Really a 'Moral' Dilemma?"

20. Jaggar, "Abortion and a Woman's Right to Decide," 348, 356, 358.

21. Ibid., 351–52, 354–55.

22. Ibid., 352–53, 356.

23. Ibid., 353–55, 357, 359.

24. Ibid., 359.

25. English, "Abortion and the Concept of a Person," 239.

26. Callahan, *Abortion,* 15.

Notes to Chapter 9. Pornography

1. Garry, "Pornography and Censorship," 395, 396; Longino, "Pornography, Oppression, and Freedom," 43, 44.

2. Garry, "Pornography and Censorship," 396, 413–16.

3. Brownmiller, *Against Our Wills,* 394.

4. Steinem, "Erotica and Pornography," 53–55.

5. Longino, "Pornography, Oppression, and Freedom," 42–43. See also Lord, "Uses of the Erotic," 296, 297; and Kittay, "Pornography and the Erotics of Domination," 148–50.

6. Tong, "Feminism, Pornography and Censorship," 2–3.

7. Willis, "Feminism, Moralism, and Pornography," 463.

8. Sobel, "Pornography," 62.

9. Several writers call attention to the feminist alliance with conservative, antisex, procensorship forces in the society. See, for example, Duggan, Hunter, and Vance, "False Promises," 131.

10. Willis, "Feminism, Moralism, and Pornography," 462.

11. Donnerstein and Linz, "Question of Pornography."

12. Berger, "Pornography, Sex, and Censorship," 188, 196–99.

13. Longino, "Pornography, Oppression, and Freedom," 48; also see Brownmiller, "Let's Put Pornography Back in the Closet," 254. Berger, "Pornography, Sex, and Censorship," 184–85; Duggan, Hunter, and Vance, "False Promises," 142; and Tong, "Feminism, Pornography and Censorship," 5–6, examine this claim critically.

14. Donnerstein and Linz, "Question of Pornography."

15. Ibid., 59.

16. Berger, "Pornography, Feminism, and Censorship," 335–36.

17. Donnerstein and Linz, "Question of Pornography," 56–57.

18. Brownmiller, *Against Our Wills,* 92–96; Dworkin, *Pornography,* 137, and "Pornography and Grief," 290. Bat-Ami Bar On surveys philosophical literature on violence against women, treating pornography as one form of violence. She also presents an extensive bibliography. See "Violence against Women: Philosophical Literature Overview" and "Violence against Women: A Bibliography."

19. D'Amico, "Meaning of Pornography," 97.

20. Willis, "Feminism, Moralism, and Pornography," 462–64.

21. Duggan, Hunter, and Vance, "False Promises," 142.

22. Willis, "Feminism, Moralism, and Pornography," 464–65. See also Duggan, Hunter, and Vance, "False Promises," 131, 139, 143.

23. Carolyn M. Shafer and Marilyn Frye, "Rape and Respect," in *Feminism and Philosophy,* ed. Mary Vetterling-Braggin, Frederick A. Elliston, and Jane English (Totowa, NJ: Rowman and Allenheld, 1977), 334, 336–37, 341, 342.

24. Foa, "What's Wrong with Rape," 347–52, 354, 355.

25. Shafer and Frye, "Rape and Respect," 333.

26. Berger, "Pornography, Sex, and Censorship," 189–90.

27. Willis, "Feminism, Moralism, and Pornography," 462.

28. Ibid., 464–65.

29. Duggan, Hunter, and Vance, "False Promises," 142–43.

30. Ibid., 145.

31. Brod, "Eros Thanatized," 47–52.

32. Ibid., 51–52, 58–59.

33. Ibid., 60–63.

34. Sartre, *Being and Nothingness,* 519 ff.
35. Foa, "What's Wrong with Rape," 354.
36. Garry, "Pornography and Censorship," 410–12.
37. Kittay, "Pornography and the Erotics of Domination," 145–46, 150, 159, 160.
38. Sobel, "Pornography," 62–73.
39. Ibid., 73–81.
40. Gould, "Why Pornography Is Valuable," Simons, *Pornography without Prejudice,* 85–90, 97–99.
41. Kristol, "Pornography, Obscenity, and the Case for Censorship," 112.
42. Gould, "Why Pornography Is Valuable," 54. See also Simons, *Pornography without Prejudice,* 91–96.
43. See note 17, above.
44. Kristol, "Pornography, Obscenity, and the Case for Censorship," 112, 113.
45. Ibid., 114.
46. Dworkin, "Lord Devlin and the Enforcement of Morals," 70.
47. Kristol, "Pornography, Obscenity, and the Case for Censorship," 114 n.
48. Brownmiller, "Let's Put Pornography Back in the Closet."
49. Berger, "Pornography, Feminism, and Censorship," 330–33; Duggan, Hunter, and Vance, "False Promises," 146.
50. Stark, "Pornography and Freedom of Speech."
51. Duggan, Hunter, and Vance, "False Promises," 131.
52. Longino, "Pornography, Oppression, and Freedom," 50–51.
53. Berger, "Pornography, Feminism, and Censorship," 330, 338–39; see also Tong, "Feminism, Pornography and Censorship," 10–11.
54. Berger, "Pornography, Feminism, and Censorship," 341.
55. Tong, "Feminism, Pornography and Censorship," 1, 13–15.
56. Berger, "Pornography, Feminism, and Censorship," 346–47.
57. Gould, "Why Pornography Is Valuable," 54–55.
58. Wicclair, "Feminism, Pornography, and Censorship," 316, 317, 319.

Notes to Chapter 10. Sex Differences

1. Mill, "Subjection of Women," 148, 149–50.
2. Ibid., 125, 130.
3. Ibid., 129.
4. Gelman et al., "Just How the Sexes Differ," 73, 83.
5. Trebilcot, "Sex Roles," 121–22.
6. Copi and Cohen, *Introduction to Logic,* 459–63.
7. Lucas, "Because You Are a Woman," 116, 118, 119.
8. Holstrom, "Do Women Have a Distinct Nature?" 51, 56.
9. Goldberg, *Inevitability of Patrimony,* 31–47.
10. Ibid., 74–91.
11. Gelman et al., "Just How the Sexes Differ," 83.
12. Weisstein, "Psychology Constructs the Female," 206. Whitbeck, "Theories of Sex Difference," 40–49, offers criticisms of psychological claims that are similar to those of Naomi Weisstein.

13. Weisstein, "Psychology Constructs the Female," 208–9.

14. Ibid., 206, 209.

15. Midgley, "On Not Being Afraid of Natural Sex Differences," 29, 31.

16. Ibid., 32–34, 37, 40.

17. Littleton, "Reconstructing Sexual Equality," 1291–92.

18. Jaggar, "Sexual Difference and Sexual Equality," 240, 242, 249.

19. Littleton, "Reconstructing Sexual Equality," 1295–1300.

20. Jaggar, "Sexual Difference and Sexual Equality," 242–45, 249, 250.

Notes on Chapter 11. Gender Equality

1. Benn, "Egalitarianism and the Equal Consideration of Interests," 62–64.

2. Frankena, *Ethics,* 51.

3. Benn, "Egalitarianism and the Equal Consideration of Interests," 62, 67–71, 76.

4. Williams, "Idea of Equality," 112–20.

5. Pierce, "Natural Law Language and Women"; Trebilcot, "Sex Roles."

6. Mill, "Subjection of Women," 141, 154.

7. Pierce, "Natural Law Language," 138.

8. Trebilcot, 128.

9. Ibid., 126–27.

10. Pierce, "Natural Law Language," 139.

11. Ibid., 137.

12. Ferguson, "Androgyny as an Ideal for Human Development," 45–46, 57–66; also, Jaggar, "On Sexual Equality," 105.

13. Trebilcot, "Two Forms of Androgynism."

14. Daly, *Beyond God the Father,* 50, 105–6; Daly, "Qualitative Leap beyond Patriarchal Religion."

15. Bishop, "Self-determination and Autonomy," 60–61. She now publishes as Sharon Bishop.

16. Ibid., 65–70.

17. Littleton, "Restructuring Sexual Equality," 1336–37.

18. Jaggar, "Sexual Difference and Sexual Equality," 252, 253.

19. Malveaux, "Gender Difference and Beyond," 233.

20. O'Neill, "How Do We Know When Opportunities Are Equal?" 145–50.

21. Newton, "Reverse Discrimination as Unjustified," 308–10, 312.

22. O'Neill, "How Do We Know When Opportunities Are Equal?" 147–54.

23. Wasserstrom, *Philosophy and Social Issues,* 52–53, 55–56.

24. Thalberg, "Visceral Racism," 43–48, 59–63. Also Thalberg, "Reverse Discrimination and the Future," 298–301.

25. Wasserstrom, *Philosophy and Social Issues,* 56.

26. Warren, "Secondary Sexism and Quota Hiring," 256.

27. Wasserstrom, *Philosophy and Social Issues,* 64–66.

28. Thalberg, "Reverse Discrimination and the Future," 301–2.

29. See, for example, Steele, "Affirmative Action," 116–18.

30. MacKinnon, "Legal Perspectives on Sexual Difference," 214–18, 222–24.

Notes to Chapter 12. Sex Talk

1. " 'Pricks' and 'Chicks,' " 249, 250.
2. Ibid., 252, 255–56.
3. Lakoff, *Language and Woman's Place,* 22–26.
4. Fortunata, "Lakoff on Language and Women," 84–88.
5. Lakoff, *Language and Woman's Place,* 27–28, 31–39.
6. Baker, " 'Pricks' and 'Chicks,' " 260, 262–65.
7. Lawrence, "———— Isn't a Dirty Word," 31.
8. Ross, "How Words Hurt," 196–208.
9. *Webster's Third New International Dictionary,* 441.
10. Moulton, "Sex and Reference," 35–36, 39–40, 42.
11. Lakoff, *Language and Woman's Place,* 5–6, 8–19.
12. Ibid., 9–14.
13. Ibid., 14–19, 43–45, 49.
14. American Philosophical Association, *Proceedings and Addresses.*
15. I regret having forgotten who made the proposal and who wrote the article. Perhaps someone who remembers will let me know who should be given credit for this.

Notes to Chapter 13. Romantic Love

1. Willis, "Feminism, Moralism, and Pornography," 464–65.
2. Foa, "What's Wrong with Rape," 354.
3. Firestone, *Dialectics of Sex,* 121–24, 129–31.
4. Engels, *Origin of the Family, Private Property, and the State,* 58.
5. Firestone, *Dialectics of Sex,* 15.
6. Ibid., 15, 123–24, 129, 131, 135.
7. Ibid., 139–44.
8. Held, "Marx, Sex, and the Transformation of Society," 171–72, 176–80.
9. Ibid., 175–78.
10. Solomon, "Love and Feminism," 53–54. Adapted from Solomon, *Love.*
11. Solomon, "Love and Feminism," 54.
12. Ibid., 55.
13. Ibid., 56.
14. Ibid., 56–58.
15. Trebilcot, "Sex Roles," 121–29.
16. Solomon, "Love and Feminism," 56–58, 60, 62–64.
17. Ibid., 64–65, 66, 70.
18. Bishop, "Love and Dependency," 147.
19. Ibid., 147–50.
20. Ibid., 152–54.

Notes to Chapter 14. Marriage

1. Engels, *Origin of the Family, Private Property, and the State,* 55–56, 58–60.

   2. Ibid., 63–64.
   3. Ibid., 66–68, 73.
   4. McMurtry, "Monogamy," 591–92, 594.
   5. Palmer, "Consolation of the Wedded," 125–26.
   6. McMurtry, "Monogamy," 592, 594.
   7. Palmer, "Consolation of the Wedded," 124–25.
   8. McMurtry, "Monogamy," 594–96.
   9. Ibid., 596–99.
  10. O'Driscoll, "On the Nature and Value of Marriage," 250, 253.
  11. Palmer, "Consolation of the Wedded," 119, 120, 123–24.
  12. O'Driscoll, "On the Nature and Value of Marriage," 250–51, 253–54.
  13. Palmer, "Consolation of the Wedded," 126–27.
  14. Ketchum, "Liberalism and Marriage Law," 266–70.
  15. O'Driscoll, "On the Nature and Value of Marriage," 256–61.
  16. Barnhart and Barnhart, "Myth of the Complete Person," 277–79.
  17. Ibid., 281–283.

Notes to Chapter 15. Family and Parenthood

   1. Jaggar, "Political Philosophies of Women's Liberation," 16–18.
   2. Mitchell, *Woman's Estate,* 152–55.
   3. Ibid., 156–58.
   4. Firestone, *Dialectics of Sex,* 206–8.
   5. Ibid., 208–9.
   6. Ibid., 201–2, 209–10.
   7. Ibid., 210.
   8. Allen, "Motherhood," 315.
   9. Ibid., 322–24.
  10. Ibid., 315–17, 320–21, 324–25.
  11. Ibid., 315–16, 320, 325–26.
  12. Firestone, *Dialectics of Sex,* 210–21.
  13. Dinnerstein, *Mermaid and the Minotaur,* 4, 28–34, 160–97.
  14. Ibid., 16 and passim.
  15. Chodorow, *Reproduction of Mothering,* 104–5, 138–39, 184–85, 187, 190, 193.
  16. Held, "Obligation of Mothers and Fathers," 7, 10–12, 18–19.
  17. Ruddick, "Maternal Thinking," 360–64.
  18. Keykendall, "Toward an Ethic of Nurturance," 263, 264, 268.
  19. Blum, et al., "Altruism and Women's Oppression," 222–23.
  20. Ibid., 229.
  21. Ibid., 232–40.
  22. McMurtry, "Monogamy," 591–93.

~ *Bibliography* ~

Anthologies

Baker, Robert, and Frederic Elliston, eds. *Philosophy and Sex*. Buffalo, NY: Prometheus Books, 1975.

————. *Philosophy and Sex*. New rev. ed. Buffalo, NY: Prometheus Books, 1984.

Bedau, Hugo A., ed. *Justice and Equality*. Englewood Cliffs, NJ: Prentice-Hall, 1971.

Bishop, Sharon, and Marjorie Weinzweig, eds. *Philosophy and Women*. Belmont, CA: Wadsworth Publishing Company, 1979.

Bowie, G. Lee, Meridith W. Michaels, and Robert C. Solomon, eds. *Twenty Questions: An Introduction to Philosophy*. San Diego: Harcourt Brace Jovanovich, 1988.

Burstyn, Varda, ed. *Women against Censorship*. Vancouver and Toronto: Douglas and McIntyre, 1985.

Dwyer, Susan, ed. *The Problem of Pornography*. Belmont, CA: Wadsworth, 1995.

Eisenstein, Zillar R., ed. *Capitalist Patriarchy and the Case for Socialist Feminism*. New York and London: Monthly Review Press, 1979.

English, Jane, ed. *Sex Equality*. Englewood Cliffs, NJ: Prentice-Hall, 1977.

Frye, Marilyn, ed. *The Politics of Reality: Essays in Feminist Theory*. Trumansburg, NY: Crossing Press, 1983.

Gould, Carol C., ed. *Beyond Domination: New Perspectives on Women and Philosophy*. Totowa, NJ: Rowman and Allenheld, 1984.

Gould, Carol C., and Marx W. Wartofsky, eds. *Women and Philosophy: Toward a Theory of Liberation*. New York: Putnam, 1976.

Griffiths, Morwenna, and Margaret Whitford, eds. *Feminist Perspectives in Philosophy*. Bloomington: University of Indiana Press, 1988.

Jagger, Alison, ed. *Living with Contradictions: Controversies in Feminist Social Ethics*. Boulder, CO: Westview Press, 1994.

Lederer, Laura, ed. *Take Back the Night*. New York: Morrow, 1980.

Mappes, Thomas A., and Jane Zembaty, eds. *Social Ethics: Morality and Social Policy.* 3d ed. New York: McGraw-Hill, 1987.

Pearsall, Marylin, ed. *Women and Values: Readings in Recent Feminist Philosophy.* Belmont, CA: Wadsworth, 1986.

Reid, Charles L., ed. *Choice and Action: An Introduction to Ethics.* New York: Macmillan, 1981.

Rhode, Deborah L., ed. *Theoretical Perspectives on Sexual Difference.* New Haven, CT: Yale University Press, 1990.

Shaw, William H., ed. *Social and Personal Ethics.* Belmont, CA: Wadsworth, 1993.

Snitow, Ann, Christine Stansell, and Sharon Thompson, eds. *Powers of Desire: The Politics of Sexuality.* New York: Monthly Review Press, 1983.

Soble, Alan, ed. *Philosophy and Sex: Contemporary Readings.* Totowa, NJ: Rowman and Littlefield, 1980.

Trebilcot, Joyce, ed. *Mothering: Essays in Feminist Theory.* Totowa, NJ: Rowman and Allanheld, 1984.

Vetterling-Braggin, Mary, Frederick A. Elliston, and Jane English, eds. *Feminism and Philosophy.* Totowa, NJ: Rowman and Allanheld, 1985.

Wasserstrom, Richard A., ed. *Today's Moral Problems.* 3d ed. New York: Macmillan, 1985.

Books and Articles

Alcoff, Linda, and Elizabeth Potter, eds. *Feminist Epistemologies.* New York: Routledge, 1992.

Allen, Jeffner. "Motherhood: The Annihilation of Women." In TREBILCOT, 315–30. See also in PEARSALL, 91–101.

American Philosophical Association. *Newsletter on Feminism and Philosophy.* April and November 1988, summer and winter 1990, fall 1991, spring 1992, fall 1993, and spring 1994.

———. *Proceedings and Addresses* 59, no. 3 (February 1986). Contains special section on feminist philosophy.

Antony, Louise, and Charlotte Witt. *A Mind of One's Own.* Boulder, CO: Westview Press, 1992.

Aristotle. *The Nicomachean Ethics.* Trans. David Ross. New York: Oxford University Press, 1980.

———. *The Politics of Aristotle.* Trans. Ernest Barker. New York: Oxford University Press, 1958.

Augustine. *The City of God.* Trans. Marcus Dods. New York: Modern Library, 1950.

———. *The Confessions of St. Augustine.* Trans. Rex Warner. New York: New American Library, 1963.

Baier, Annette. "Hume, the Woman's Moral Theorist?" In *Women and Moral Theory,* ed. Eva Feder Kittay and Diana T. Meyers, 37–55. Totowa, NJ: Rowman and Littlefield, 1987.

Names in small capital letters indicate anthologies.

Baier, Kurt. *The Moral Point of View: A Rational Basis of Ethics.* Ithaca, NY: Cornell University Press, 1958.

Baker, Robert. " 'Pricks' and 'Chicks': A Plea for Persons." In BAKER AND ELLISTON (1984), 249–67.

Barnhart, Joseph E., and Mary Ann Barnhart. "The Myth of the Complete Person." In VETTERLING-BRAGGIN, ELLISTON, AND ENGLISH, 277–90.

Bar On, Bat-Ami. "Violence against Women: A Bibliography." American Philosophical Association. *Newsletter on Feminism and Philosophy* 88, no. 1 (November 1988): 11–13.

———. "Violence against Women: Philosophical Literature Overview." American Philosophical Association. *Newsletter on Feminism and Philosophy* 88, no. 1 (November 1988): 8–11.

Bartky, Sandra Lee. "Toward a Phenomenology of Feminist Consciousness." *Social Theory and Practice* 3, no. 4 (fall 1975): 425–39. See also BISHOP AND WEINZWEIG, 252–58, and VETTERLING-BRAGGIN, ELLISTON, AND ENGLISH, 1985, 22–34.

Baumrin, Bernard H. "Sexual Morality Delineated." In BAKER AND ELLISTON (1984), 300–311.

Belliotti, Raymond A. *Good Sex: Perspectives on Sexual Ethics.* Lawrence: University Press of Kansas, 1993.

Benn, Stanley I. "Egalitarianism and the Equal Consideration of Interests." In *Nomos IX: Equality,* ed. J. Roland Pennock and John W. Chapman, 61–78. New York: Atherton Press, 1967. See also in BEDAU, 152–67.

Bentham, Jeremy. An essay on "Paederasty" (first published in 1978). In BAKER AND ELLISTON (1984), 354–69.

Berger, Fred R. "Pornography, Feminism, and Censorship." In BAKER AND ELLISTON (1984), 327–51.

———. "Pornography, Sex, and Censorship." *Social Theory and Practice* 4, no. 2 (spring 1977): 183–209.

Berger, John, Sven Blomberg, Chris Fox, Michael Dibb, and Richard Hollis. *Ways of Seeing.* New York: Penguin Books and British Broadcasting Corporation, 1972.

Bishop, Sharon. "Love and Dependency." In BISHOP AND WEINZWEIG, 147–54.

———. "Self-determination and Autonomy." In WASSERSTROM, 55–70. See also BISHOP AND WEINZWEIG, 68–77 (reprinted from the 1st edition of WASSERSTROM, 1975).

Blum, Larry, et al. "Altruism and Women's Oppression." *Philosophical Forum* 5 (1975): 222–47. See also BISHOP AND WEINZWEIG, 190–200, and GOULD AND WARTOFSKY, 222–47.

Brod, Harry. "Eros Thanatized: Pornography and Male Sexuality." *Humanities in Society* 7 (1984): 47–63.

Brody, Baruch. "Thomson on Abortion." *Philosophy and Public Affairs* 1 (1972): 335–40. See also in REID, 394–97.

Brownmiller, Susan. *Against Our Wills: Men, Women, and Rape.* New York: Simon and Schuster, 1975.

Names in small capital letters indicate anthologies.

————. "Let's Put Pornography Back in the Closet." In LEDERER, 252–55.

Callahan, Daniel. *Abortion: Law, Choice, and Morality.* New York: Macmillan, 1970. See also excerpts in MAPPES AND ZEMBATY, 22–38.

Card, Claudia. "Female Friendship: Separations and Continua." *Hypatia* 3, no. 2 (summer 1988): 123–30, 136.

Cheney, Jim. "Postmodern Environmental Ethics: Ethics as Bioregional Narrative." *Environmental Ethics* 11, no. 2 (summer 1989): 117–34.

Chodorow, Nancy. *The Reproduction of Mothering: Psychoanalysis and the Sociology of Gender.* Berkeley: University of California Press, 1978.

Code, Lorraine. *What Can She Know? Feminist Theory and the Construction of Knowledge.* Ithaca, NY: Cornell University Press, 1991.

Cohen, Carl. "Sex, Birth Control, and Human Life." *Ethics* 79, no. 4 (July 1969): 251–62. See also BAKER AND ELLISTON (1984), 185–99.

Copi, Irving, and Carl Cohen. *Introduction to Logic.* 9th ed. New York: Macmillan, 1994.

Daly, Mary. *Beyond God the Father.* Boston: Beacon Press, 1973.

————. "The Qualitative Leap beyond Patriarchal Religion." *Quest: A Feminist Quarterly* 1, no. 4 (spring 1975): 29–31.

D'Amico, Robert. "The Meaning of Pornography." *Humanities in Society* 7 (1984): 87–101.

d'Eubonne, Françoise. *Le Feminisme ou la Mort.* Paris: Pierre Horay, 1974.

Dinnerstein, Dorothy. *The Mermaid and the Minotaur: Sexual Arrangements and Human Malaise.* New York: Harper and Row, 1976.

Dixon, Beth A. Review of Code's *What Can She Know?* In American Philosophical Association, *Newsletter on Feminism and Philosophy* (fall 1993): 53–55.

Donnerstein, Edward L., and Daniel G. Linz. "The Question of Pornography." *Psychology Today* (December 1986): 56–59.

Duggan, Lisa, Nan D. Hunter, and Carole S. Vance. "False Promises: Feminist Antipornography Legislation." In *Burstyn*, 130–51. See also excerpts in JAGGAR, 165–70.

Dworkin, Andrea. "Pornography and Grief." In LEDERER, 286–91.

————. *Pornography: Men Possessing Women.* New York: Perigee Books, 1979.

Dworkin, Ronald. "Lord Devlin and the Enforcement of Morals." In *Morality and the Law,* edited by Richard A. Wasserstrom. Belmont, CA: Wadsworth, 1972, 55–72.

Ehrenreich, Barbara. "Is Abortion Really a 'Moral' Dilemma?" *New York Times,* February 7, 1985, sec. C, 2.

Elliston, Frederick. "Gay Marriage." In BAKER AND ELLISTON (1984), 148–50.

————. "In Defense of Promiscuity." In BAKER AND ELLISTON (1975), 222–43.

Engels, Friedrich. *The Origin of the Family, Private Property, and the State.* New York: International Publishers, 1942.

English, Jane. "Abortion and the Concept of a Person." *Canadian Journal of Philosophy* 5, no. 2 (1975): 233–43. See also MAPPES AND ZEMBATY, 29–38.

Epictetus. *The Enchiridion.* Trans. Thomas W. Higginson. Indianapolis and New York: Bobbs-Merrill, 1948.

Names in small capital letters indicate anthologies.

Ferguson, Ann. "Androgyny as an Ideal for Human Development." In VETTER-LING-BRAGGIN, ELLISTON, AND ENGLISH, 45–69.

Fichte, Johann Gottleib. *The Science of Right.* Philadelphia: Lippincott, 1869.

Firestone, Shulamith. *The Dialectics of Sex: The Case for Feminist Revolution.* London: Women's Press, 1970.

Flax, Jane. "Women Do Theory." *Quest* 5, no. 1 (summer 1979): 20–26. See also in PEARSALL, 2–7.

Fletcher, Joseph. *Situation Ethics: The New Morality.* Philadelphia: Westminster Press, 1966.

Foa, Pamela. "What's Wrong with Rape." In VETTERLING-BRAGGIN, ELLISTON, AND ENGLISH, 347–59. See also BISHOP AND WEINZWEIG, 140–46.

Fortunata, Jacqueline. "Lakoff on Language and Women." In *Sexist Language: A Modern Philosophical Analysis,* ed. Mary Vetterling-Braggin, 81–91. Totowa, NJ: Rowman and Littlefield, 1981.

Frankena, William. *Ethics.* 2nd ed. Englewood Cliffs, NJ: Prentice-Hall, 1973.

Frazer, Nancy, and Sandra Bartky, special eds. *Hypatia* 3, no. 3 (winter 1989). Special issue on French feminist philosophy.

Friedman, Marilyn. "Individuality without Individualism: Review of Janice Raymond's *A Passion for Friends.*" *Hypatia* 3, no. 2 (summer 1988): 131–37.

———. *What Are Friends For? Feminist Perspectives on Personal Relationships and Moral Theory.* Ithaca, NY, and London: Cornell University Press, 1993.

Frye, Marilyn. "Some Reflections on Separatism and Power." In FRYE, 95–109. See also PEARSALL, 132–38.

Gaard, Greta, ed. *Ecofeminism: Women, Animals, Nature.* Philadelphia: Temple University Press, 1993.

Garry, Ann. "Pornography and Censorship." *Social Theory and Practice* 4, no. 4 (summer 1978): 395–442. See also in BAKER AND ELLISTON (1984), 312–26.

Gelman, David, et al. "Just How the Sexes Differ." *Newsweek,* May 18, 1981, 72–83.

Gilligan, Carol. *In a Different Voice.* Cambridge, MA: Harvard University Press, 1982.

———. *Mapping the Moral Domain: A Contribution of Women's Thinking to Psychological Theory and Education.* Cambridge, MA: Harvard University Press, 1988.

———. "Moral Orientation and Moral Development." In *Women and Moral Theory,* ed. Eva Feder Kittay and Diana T. Meyers, 21–22. Totowa, NJ: Rowman and Littlefield, 1987.

Goldberg, Steven. *The Inevitability of Patrimony.* New York: Morrow, 1973.

Goldman, Alan H. "Plain Sex." *Philosophy and Public Affairs* 6 (1977): 267–88.

Gonsalves, Milton A. *Fagothey's Right and Reason: Ethics in Theory and Practice.* 9th ed. Columbus, OH: Merrill, 1989.

Gould, James A. "The 'Natural' and Homosexuality." *International Journal of Applied Philosophy* 4, no. 2 (fall 1988): 51–53.

———. "Why Pornography Is Valuable." *International Journal of Applied Philosophy* 6, no. 2 (winter 1991): 53–55.

Names in small capital letters indicate anthologies.

Harding, Sandra, and Jean F. O'Barr, eds. *Sex and Scientific Inquiry.* Chicago: University of Chicago Press, 1988.

Hartsock, Nancy. "Feminist Theory and the Development of Revolutionary Strategy." In EISENSTEIN, 56–77. See also in PEARSALL, 8–18.

Held, Virginia. "Marx, Sex, and the Transformation of Society." *Philosophical Forum* 5 (1975): 168–84.

———. "The Obligation of Mothers and Fathers." In TREBILCOT, 7–20.

Hill, Sharon Bishop. *See* Bishop, Sharon.

Holstrom, Nancy. "Do Women Have a Distinct Nature?" In PEARSALL, 51-61.

Hunter, John. *Thinking about Sex and Love.* New York: Macmillan, 1980.

The Interpreter's Bible, Vol. 1. New York, Nashville: Abingdon–Cokesbury Press, 1952.

Jaggar, Alison. "Abortion and a Woman's Right to Decide." *Philosophical Forum* 5, nos. 1–2 (fall–winter 1973–1974): 347–59. See also in BAKER AND ELLISTON (1984); 218–30.

———. "Feminist Ethics: Some Issues for the Nineties." *Journal of Social Philosophy* 20, nos. 1 and 2 (spring/fall 1989): 91–107. See also in SHAW, 78–88.

———. "How Can Philosophy Be Feminist?" American Philosophical Association, *Newsletter on Feminism and Philosophy* (April 1988): 4–8.

———. "On Sexual Equality." In ENGLISH, 93–109.

———. "Political Philosophies of Women's Liberation." In VETTERLING-BRAGGIN, ELLISTON, AND ENGLISH, 5–21. See also in BISHOP AND WEINZWEIG, 258–65 (reprinted from the 1977 edition of VETTERLING-BRAGGIN, ELLISTON, AND ENGLISH).

———. "Sexual Difference and Sexual Equality." In RHODE, 239–54, 302–3. See also in JAGGAR, 18–34.

Jolly, Alison. *The Evolution of Primate Behavior.* New York: Macmillan, 1985.

Kant, Immanuel. *The Fundamental Principles of the Metaphysic of Ethics.* Trans. Otto Manthey-Zorn. New York: Appleton-Century-Crofts, 1938.

———. *Lectures on Ethics.* Trans. Louis Infield. New York: Harper Torchbooks, 1963.

Keller, Evelyn Fox. *Reflections on Gender and Science.* New Haven, CT: Yale University Press, 1986.

Ketchum, Sara Ann. "The Good, the Bad, and the Perverted: Sexual Paradigms Revisited." In SOBLE, 139–47.

———. "Liberalism and Marriage Law." In VETTERLING-BRAGGIN, ELLISTON, AND ENGLISH, 264–76.

Ketchum, Sara Ann, and Christine Pierce. "Separatism and Sexual Relationships." In BISHOP AND WEINZWEIG, 163–71.

Keykendall, Eleanor H. "Toward an Ethic of Nurturance: Luce Irigaray on Mothering and Power." In TREBILCOT, 263–74.

Kittay, Eva Feder. "Pornography and the Erotics of Domination." In GOULD, 145–74.

Kohlberg, Lawrence. *The Psychology of Moral Development.* San Francisco: Harper and Row, 1984.

Korsmeyer, Carolyn. "Gender Bias in Aesthetics." American Philosophical Association, *Newsletter on Feminism and Philosophy* 89, no. 2 (winter 1990): 45–48.

Names in small capital letters indicate anthologies.

Kristol, Irving. "Pornography, Obscenity, and the Case for Censorship." *New York Times Magazine,* March 28, 1971, 24–25, 112–16.

Ladd, John. "The Issue of Relativism." In *Ethical Relativism,* ed. John Ladd, 107–29. Belmont, CA: Wadsworth, 1973.

Lakoff, Robin. *Language and Woman's Place.* New York: Harper and Row, 1975. See also excerpts in ENGLISH, 220–30.

Lawrence, Barbara. "——— Isn't a Dirty Word." *New York Times,* October 27, 1973, 31. Reprinted as "Four-Letter Words Can Hurt You" in BAKER AND ELLISTON (1975): 31–33.

Leiser, Burton M. *Liberty, Justice, and Morals: Contemporary Value Conflicts.* New York: Macmillan, 1973.

Levin, Michael. "Why Homosexuality Is Abnormal." *Monist* 67, no.2 (1984): 251–83. See also in SHAW, 350–57.

Lichtenberg, Judith. "Is There a Middle Ground?" *Report from the Institute for Philosophy and Public Policy* 10, no. 2 (spring 1990): 11–13.

Littleton, Christine A. "Reconstructing Sexual Equality." *California Law Review* 75, no. 4 (1987): 1279–1337. See also in JAGGAR, 34–39.

Locke, John. *Second Treatise on Government.* Ed. C.B. Macpherson. Indianapolis: Hackett, 1980.

Longino, Helen E. "Pornography, Oppression, and Freedom: A Closer Look." In LEDERER, 26–39. See also in PEARSALL, 167–76.

Lord, Audre. "Uses of the Erotic: The Erotic as Power." In LEDERER, 295–300.

Lucas, J.R. "Because You Are a Woman." In ENGLISH, 111–20.

MacKinnon, Catherine A. "Legal Perspectives on Sexual Difference." In RHODE, 213–25, 298–301.

Malveaux, Julianne. "Gender Difference and Beyond: An Economic Perspective on Diversity and Commonality among Women." In RHODE, 226–38, 301–2.

Margolis, Joseph. "The Question of Homosexuality." In BAKER AND ELLISTON (1975): 288–302.

Marietta, Don E., Jr. *For People and the Planet: Holism and Humanism in Environmental Ethics.* Philadelphia: Temple University Press, 1994.

Marquis, Don. "Why Abortion Is Immoral." *Journal of Philosophy* 86, no. 4 (April 1989): 183–202. See also in MAPPES AND ZEMBATY, 27–32, and SHAW, 140–49.

McMurtry, John. "Monogamy: A Critique." *Monist* 66, no. 4 (1972): 587–99. See also in BAKER AND ELLISTON (1984), 107–18.

Merleau-Ponty, Maurice. *Phenomenology of Perception.* Trans. Colin Smith. London: Routledge and Kegan Paul, 1962.

Midgley, Mary. "On Not Being Afraid of Natural Sex Differences." In GRIFFITHS AND WHITFORD, 29–41.

———. "Trying Out One's New Sword." In *Heart and Mind: The Varieties of Moral Experience,* ed. Mary Midgley. New York: St. Martin's Press, 1981. See also in BOWIE, MICHAELS, AND SOLOMON, 587–90.

Mies, Maria, and Vandana Shiva. *Ecofeminism.* Halifax, Nova Scotia: Fernwood Publications, 1993.

Names in small capital letters indicate anthologies.

Mill, John Stuart. "The Subjection of Women." In *Essays on Sex Equality: John Stuart Mill and Harriet Taylor Mill,* ed. Alice S. Rossi. Chicago: University of Chicago Press, 1970.

Mitchell, Juliet. *Woman's Estate.* New York: Pantheon Books, 1971.

Mohr, Richard D. "Gay Basics: Some Questions, Facts, and Values." In SHAW, 358–68.

Moulton, Janice. "Sex and Reference." In BAKER AND ELLISTON (1975), 34–44.

Nagel, Thomas. "Sexual Perversion." *Journal of Philosophy* 66, no. 1 (January 16, 1969): 5–17. See also in BAKER AND ELLISTON (1984), 268–79.

Nelson, Lynn H. *Who Knows? From Quine to a Feminist Empiricism.* Philadelphia: Temple University Press, 1990.

Newton, Lisa. "Reverse Discrimination as Unjustified." *Ethics* 83, no. 4 (July 1973): 308–12. See also in ENGLISH, 156–60.

Nietzsche, Friedrich. "Beyond Good and Evil," sec. 4,"Apothegms and Interludes," and sec. 7,"Our Virtues." In *The Philosophy of Nietzsche.* Trans. Thomas Common. New York: Modern Library, updated.

———. "Thus Spake Zarathustra." In *The Philosophy of Nietzsche,* Trans. Thomas Common. New York: Modern Library, undated.

Noonan, John T. "An Almost Absolute Value in History." In *The Morality of Abortion: Legal and Historical Perspectives,* ed. John T. Noonan, 1–59. Cambridge, MA: Harvard University Press, 1970.

O'Driscoll, Lyla H. "On the Nature and Value of Marriage." In VETTERLING-BRAGGIN, ELLISTON, AND ENGLISH, 249–63.

O'Neill, Onora. "How Do We Know When Opportunities Are Equal?" In ENGLISH, 144–54. Originally Nell, Onora. "How Do We Know When Opportunities Are Equal?" In GOULD AND WARTOFSKY, 334–46.

Palmer, David. "The Consolation of the Wedded." In BAKER AND ELLISTON, (1984), 119–29.

Paul VI. *Humanae Vitae.* Washington, DC: U.S. Catholic Conference, 1968. See also in BAKER AND ELLISTON (1984), 167–84.

Piaget, Jean. *The Moral Judgment of the Child.* New York: Free Press, 1965.

Pierce, Christine. "Natural Law Language and Women." In ENGLISH, 130–42.

Pineau, Lois. "Date Rape: A Feminist Analysis." *Law and Philosophy* 8 (1989): 217–43. See also excerpts in SHAW, 334–45.

Plato. *The Collected Dialogues of Plato,* ed. Edith Hamilton and Huntingdon Cairns. New York: Bolligen Foundation, 1961.

Plotinus. *Complete Works of Plotinus.* Trans. K.S. Guthrie. New York: Gordon Press, 1977.

———. *The Enneads.* Trans. Steven MacKenna. New York: Viking Penguin, 1991.

Punzo, Vincent. *Reflective Naturalism.* New York: Macmillan, 1969.

Raymond, Janice G. *A Passion for Friends: Toward a Philosophy of Female Affection.* Boston: Beacon Press, 1986.

Ross, Stephanie. "How Words Hurt." In *Sexist Language: A Modern Philosophical Analysis,* ed. Mary Vetterling-Braggin, 194–213. Totowa, NJ: Rowman and Littlefield, 1981.

Names in small capital letters indicate anthologies.

Rubinstein, Charlotte Streifer. *American Women Artists: From Early Indian Times to the Present.* Boston: G.K. Hall, 1982.

Ruddick, Sara. "Better Sex." In BAKER AND ELLISTON (1984), 280–99.

———. "Maternal Thinking." *Feminist Studies* 6, no. 2 (summer 1980): 342–67. See also in TREBILCOT, 213–30.

Ruether, Rosemary Radford. *New Woman/New Earth: Sexist Ideologies and Human Liberation.* New York: Seabury Press, 1975.

Ruse, Michael. "The Morality of Homosexuality." In BAKER AND ELLISTON (1984), 370–90.

Sade, Marquis de. *The Complete Justine.* New York: Grove Press, 1965.

Sartorelli, Joseph. "Professor Dalcourt on the 'Natural.' " *International Journal of Applied Philosophy* 8, no. 2 (winter–spring 1994): 49–52.

Sartre, Jean-Paul. *Being and Nothingness.* Trans. Hazel E. Barnes. New York: Washington Square Press, 1966.

Schopenhauer, Arthur. "The Metaphysics of the Love of the Sexes." In *The Philosophy of Schopenhauer,* ed. Irwin Edman. New York: Modern Library, 1956.

———. *Parega and Paralipomena: Short Philosophical Essays.* Vol. 2, Trans. E.F.J. Payne. Oxford, U.K.: Clarendon Press, 1974.

Schweitzer, Albert. *The Philosophy of Civilization.* Trans. C.T. Campion. New York: Macmillan, 1951.

Scrunton, Roger. *Sexual Desire: A Moral Theory of the Erotic.* New York: Free Press, 1986.

Seigfried, Charlene Haddock, special ed. *Hypatia* 8, no. 2 (spring 1993).

Sells, Laura. "Feminist Epistemology: Rethinking the Dualisms of Atomic Knowledge." *Hypatia* 8, no. 3 (summer 1993): 202–10.

Shrage, Laurie. "Bibliography on Feminist Aesthetics." American Philosophical Association, *Newsletter on Feminism and Philosophy* 89, no. 2 (winter 1990): 56–60.

Shrage, Laurie, special ed. American Philosophical Association, *Newsletter on Feminism and Philosophy* 89, no. 2 (winter 1990), and 89, no. 3 (winter 1990). Special issues on feminist aesthetics.

Simons, G.L. *Pornography without Prejudice.* London: Abelard-Schuman, 1972.

Sobel, Alan. "Pornography: Defamation and the Endorsement of Degradation." *Social Theory and Practice* 11, no. 1 (spring 1985): 61–87.

Solomon, Robert C. *Love: Emotion, Myth, and Metaphor.* Garden City, NY: Doubleday-Anchor, 1981.

———. "Love and Feminism." In BAKER AND ELLISTON (1984), 53–70.

———. "Sex and Perversion." In BAKER AND ELLISTON (1975), 268–87.

Stark, Cynthia. "Pornography and Freedom of Speech: A Map of the Debate." *Newsletter of the Center for Values and Social Policy* 11, no. 2 (summer 1992): 1–3.

Steele, Shelby. "Affirmative Action: The Price of Preference." In *The Content of Our Character,* 111–25. New York: St. Martin's Press, 1990.

Steinem, Gloria. "Erotica and Pornography: A Clear and Present Difference." *Ms. Magazine,* November 1978, 53–55. See also in DWYER, 29–33.

Names in small capital letters indicate anthologies.

Stewart, David, and Algis Michunas. *Exploring Phenomenology.* 2d ed. Athens: Ohio University Press, 1990.

Suppe, Frederick. "Curing Homosexuality." In BAKER AND ELLISTON (1984), 391–420.

Taylor, Paul. "Social Science and Ethical Relativism." *Journal of Philosophy* 55 (1958): 32–44. See also in REID, 63–73.

Taylor, Richard. *Having Love Affairs.* Buffalo, NY: Prometheus Books, 1982.

Thalberg, Irving. "Reverse Discrimination and the Future." In GOULD AND WARTOFSKY, 298–301. See also in ENGLISH, 161–69

———. "Visceral Racism." *Monist,* 56, no. 4 (1972): 43–63. See also in WASSERSTROM, 187–204.

Thomas Aquinas. *On the Truth of the Catholic Faith.* Book 3, pt. 1, Trans. Vernon J. Bourke. New York: Doubleday, 1956.

Thomson, Judith Jarvis. "A Defense of Abortion." *Philosophy and Public Affairs* 1, no. 1 (1971): 47–66. See also in BAKER AND ELLISTON (1984), 201–17.

Tong, Rosemary. "Feminism, Pornography and Censorship." *Social Theory and Practice* 8, no. 1 (spring 1982): 1–18.

Trebilcot, Joyce. "Sex Roles: The Argument from Nature." In ENGLISH, 121–29.

———. "Taking Responsibility for Sexuality." In BAKER AND ELLISTON (1984), 421–30.

———. "Two Forms of Androgynism." *Journal of Social Philosophy* 8, no. 1 (January 1977): 4–8. See also in VETTERLING-BRAGGIN, ELLISTON, AND ENGLISH, 70–78.

Tuanna, Nancy. "The Radical Future of Feminist Empiricism." *Hypatia* 7, no. 1 (winter 1992): 100–114.

Tyler, P. A. "Homosexual Behavior in Animals." In *The Psychology of Sexual Diversity,* ed. Kevin Howells. Oxford, U.K.: Blackwell, 1984.

Warren, Karen J. "Feminism and Ecology, Making Connections." *Environmental Ethics* 9, no: 1 (spring 1987): 3–20.

———. "The Power and the Promise of Ecological Feminism." *Environmental Ethics* 12, no. 2 (summer 1990): 125–46.

Warren, Karen J., ed. *Ecological Feminism.* London, New York: Routledge, 1994.

Warren, Karen J., special ed. *Hypatia* 6, no. 1 (spring 1991). Issue on feminism and environmentalism.

Warren, Mary Anne. "On the Moral and Legal Status of Abortion." *Monist* 57, no. 1 (January 1973): 43–61. See also in MAPPES AND ZEMBATY, 9–17.

———. "Secondary Sexism and Quota Hiring." *Philosophy and Public Affairs* 6 (spring 1977): 240–61. See also in BISHOP AND WEINZWEIG, 237–47.

Wasserstrom, Richard A. "Is Adultery Immoral?" In WASSERSTROM, 208–19. See also in BAKER AND ELLISTON (1984), 93–106 (reprinted from the 2d edition of WASSERSTROM, 1979).

———. *Philosophy and Social Issues: Five Studies.* Notre Dame, IN: University of Notre Dame Press, 1980.

———. "Racism, Sexism, and Preferential Treatment." *UCLA Law Review* (February 1977): See also in BISHOP AND WEINZWEIG, 5–20.

Names in small capital letters indicate anthologies.

Webster's Third New International Dictionary of the English Language (unabridged). Ed. in chief Philip Babcock Gove. Springfield, MA: Merriam, 1971.

Weisstein, Naomi. "Psychology Constructs the Female." In ENGLISH, 205–15.

Whitbeck, Caroline. "Theories of Sex Difference." In PEARSALL, 34–51.

Wicclair, Mark R. "Feminism, Pornography, and Censorship." In MAPPES AND ZEMBATY, 314–20.

Williams, Bernard. "The Idea of Equality." In *Philosophy, Politics, and Society.* Series 2, ed. Peter Laslett and W.G. Runciman, 110–31. Oxford, U.K.: Blackwell, 1962. See also in BEDAU, 116–37, and ENGLISH, 79–92.

Willis, Ellen. "Feminism, Moralism, and Pornography." In SNITOW, STANSELL, AND THOMPSON, 460–67. See also in DWYER, 170–76, and JAGGAR, 165–70.

Names in small capital letters indicate anthologies.

~ *Index* ~

215

Don E. Marietta, Jr., is the Adelaide R. Snyder Distinguished Professor of Ethics and Professor of Philosophy at Florida Atlantic University, where he has taught for more than thirty years. Prior to that he was a clergyman and university chaplain. He is the author of *For People and the Planet: Holism and Humanism in Environmental Ethics* (1994), co-editor (with Lester Embree) of *Environmental Philosophy and Environmental Activism* (1995), and the recipient of a number of teaching awards.